'Austerity as a policy harms the many and benefits the few. In a democracy that's supposed to be hard to sell. Yet the democracies most effected by the European financial crisis saw no such democratic revolt. Mercille tells us why. Updating and deploying the Chomsky-Herman propaganda model of the media in a systematic and empirical way, he shows us how alternative policies are sidelined and elite interests are protected'.

Mark Blyth, *Professor of International Political Economy, Brown University*

'This is one of the most important political economy books of the year. Julien Mercille's book is set to become the definitive account of the media's role in Ireland's spectacular and transformative economic boom and bust. He argues convincingly that critical political economic perspectives are a rarity in the Irish media and Mercille's devastating critique painstakingly chronicles the persistent failures of the Irish media'.

Dr. Tom McDonnell, *Macroeconomist at the Nevin Economic Research Institute (NERI)*

'The European economies remain trapped in high levels of unemployment while more austerity is promoted as the solution. Yet the media plays a key role in presenting these austerity policies as though "there is no alternative". This book, with a focus on Ireland, provides compelling evidence on the ideological role of the media in the presentation of the policies favoring the economic, financial and political elites. A highly recommended read for its analyses of the crises and of the neo-liberal interpretation from the media'.

Malcolm Sawyer, *Emeritus Professor of Economics, University of Leeds*

'The basic story of the economic crisis is simple. The world economy was being driven by housing bubbles in most major wealthy economies. When these bubbles burst, there was nothing to replace this massive source of demand, leading to a prolonged period of underemployment and stagnation. Julien Mercille tells this story well, and explains the media's role in convincing the public that it was all very complicated and that government policy can do little to improve the situation'.

Dean Baker, *Co-director of the Center for Economic and Policy Research*

'Julien Mercille has written a superb case study of the role of news media in shaping fundamental policy debates surrounding the economy, particularly during a time of crisis. It provides a model not only for examining the Irish or European press, but the news media across the world. The political implications for those concerned with having a solid and sustainable economy, and a vibrant democracy, could not be more clear'.

Robert W. McChesney, co-author of *The Endless Crisis*

'Julien Mercille has produced outstanding research on the role of the Irish media, demonstrating the importance of property relations among the media, banks, and real estate, not to mention the close connections with the state machinery and the grip of neoliberal ideology. Meticulous, balanced and clear, his work casts light on the media interests that have abetted the destruction of the Irish economy. This book is a model for similar research across the Eurozone periphery'.

Costas Lapavitsas, *Professor of Economics, School of Oriental and African Studies, University of London*

The Political Economy and Media Coverage of the European Economic Crisis

The European economic crisis has been ongoing since 2008 and while austerity has spread over the continent, it has failed to revive economies. The media have played an important ideological role in presenting the policies of economic and political elites in a favourable light, even if the latter's aim has been to shift the burden of adjustment onto citizens. This book explains how and why, using a critical political economic perspective and focusing on the case of Ireland. Throughout, Ireland is compared with contemporary and historical examples to contextualize the arguments made.

The book covers the housing bubble that led to the crash, the rescue of financial institutions by the state, the role of European institutions and the International Monetary Fund, austerity, and the possibility of leaving the eurozone for Europe's peripheral countries.

Through a systematic analysis of Ireland's main newspapers, it is argued that the media reflect elite views and interests and downplay alternative policies that could lead to more progressive responses to the crisis.

Julien Mercille is a Lecturer in the School of Geography, Planning and Environmental Policy, University College Dublin, Ireland.

Routledge Frontiers of Political Economy

The Political Economy and Media Coverage of the European Economic Crisis

The case of Ireland

Julien Mercille

Routledge
Taylor & Francis Group

LONDON AND NEW YORK

First published 2015
by Routledge
2 Park Square, Milton Park, Abingdon, Oxon OX14 4RN

and by Routledge
711 Third Avenue, New York, NY 10017

Routledge is an imprint of the Taylor & Francis Group, an informa business

British Library Cataloguing in Publication Data
A catalogue record for this book is available from the British Library

Library of Congress Cataloging in Publication Data
Mercille, Julien.
   The political economy and media coverage of the European economic crisis : the case of Ireland / Julien Mercille.
      pages cm. – (Routledge frontiers of political economy)
   Includes bibliographical references and index.
      1. Ireland–Economic conditions–21st century–Press coverage. 2. Ireland–Economic policy–21st century–Press coverage. 3. Financial crises–Ireland–Press coverage. 4. Global Financial Crisis, 2008-2009. 5. Mass media and public opinion–Ireland. 6. Press and politics–Ireland. I. Title.
   HC260.5.M47 2014
   330.94'0561–dc23
                  2014005975

ISBN: 978-0-415-72109-7 (hbk)
ISBN: 978-1-315-86357-3 (ebk)

Typeset in Times New Roman
by Taylor & Francis Books

MIX
Paper from
responsible sources
FSC
www.fsc.org   FSC® C013604

Printed and bound by CPI Group (UK) Ltd, Croydon, CR0 4YY

Contents

List of illustrations

Figures

Tables

Acknowledgements

For comments on chapters and discussions related to the book, I would like to thank Kieran Allen, Dean Baker, Alan Cibils, Constantin Gurdgiev, Tom Healy, Costas Lapavitsas, Brian Lucey, Tom McDonnell, Terry McDonough, Enda Murphy, NAMAWineLake, Nat O'Connor, Michael Taft, Mark Weisbrot and Karl Whelan. For help with the translations of German news articles, I would like to thank Jasmin Marston and Yannick Treige. The Routledge editorial team, and in particular Andy Humphries, provided outstanding support throughout the project, for which I am very grateful. Parts of the following three articles by the author have been used in the book: 'The Role of the Media in Sustaining Ireland's Housing Bubble', *New Political Economy*, 2014, vol. 19, no. 2, pp. 282–301; The Role of the Media in Fiscal Consolidation Programmes: The Case of Ireland', *Cambridge Journal of Economics*, 2014, vol. 38, no. 2, pp. 281–300; and 'European Media Coverage of Argentina's Debt Default and Recovery: Distorting the Lessons for Europe', *Third World Quarterly*, 2013, vol. 34, no. 8, pp. 1377–91. Permission to reprint figures has been granted by the Economic and Social Research Institute (ESRI), the Irish Fiscal Advisory Council, and Michael Taft.

List of abbreviations

AIB	Allied Irish Banks
CBI	Central Bank of Ireland
CDO	collateralized debt obligation
CDS	credit default swap
EBS	EBS Building Society (previously Educational Building Society)
ECB	European Central Bank
EFSF	European Financial Stability Facility
ELA	Extraordinary Lending Assistance
EMU	Economic and Monetary Union of the European Union
ESRI	Economic and Social Research Institute
EU	European Union
FDI	foreign direct investment
GDP	gross domestic product
GIPSI	Greece, Ireland, Portugal, Spain, Italy
GNP	gross national product
IBEC	Irish Business and Employers Confederation
IBRC	Irish Bank Resolution Corporation
ICTU	Irish Congress of Trade Unions
IFSC	International Financial Services Centre
IL&P	Irish Life and Permanent
IMF	International Monetary Fund
INBS	Irish Nationwide Building Society
ISIF	Ireland Strategic Investment Fund
ISME	Irish Small and Medium Enterprises Association
MBS	mortgage-backed security
MEP	Member of the European Parliament
MNC	multinational corporation
NAMA	National Asset Management Agency
NATO	North Atlantic Treaty Organization
NERI	Nevin Economic Research Institute
NPRF	National Pension Reserve Fund
OECD	Organisation for Economic Co-operation and Development

OPEC	Organization of the Petroleum Exporting Countries
OMT	Outright Monetary Transactions
REBLL	Romania, Estonia, Bulgaria, Lithuania and Latvia
RTÉ	Raidió Teilifís Éireann (Ireland's national state broadcaster)
SIPTU	Services, Industrial, Professional and Technical Union
TARP	Troubled Assets Relief Program
TASC	Think Tank for Action on Social Change
TNC	transnational corporation
VAT	value-added tax

Newspapers

DT	*Daily Telegraph*
DW	*Die Welt*
IE	*Irish Examiner*
II	*Irish Independent*
IT	*Irish Times*
FAZ	*Frankfurter Allgemeine Zeitung*
FT	*Financial Times*
LF	*Le Figaro*
LM	*Le Monde*
NYT	*New York Times*
SBP	*Sunday Business Post*
SI	*Sunday Independent*
ST	*Sunday Times*
SZ	*Süddeutsche Zeitung*
TT	*The Times* (London)
WSJ	*Wall Street Journal*

1 Introduction

'The most significant changes since World War II'

The European economic crisis started in 2008 and has received much attention from scholars, journalists and policy analysts. Yet, critical political economic perspectives remain a minority in the large amount of commentary on the subject. Also, little has been written about the role of the media in interpreting the crisis and presenting governments' responses to it. This is what this book seeks to accomplish, focusing on Ireland to make points often applicable to other European countries. Throughout the book, comparisons will be made with the experience of other 'GIPSI' countries (Greece, Ireland, Portugal, Spain, Italy), Iceland, Scandinavia, the United States, Ecuador, Argentina and Latvia, among others, to contextualize the Irish case. In the conclusion, Irish media will be compared with European and American media in relation to their coverage of the crisis. It will be seen that Irish news organizations tend to be more conservative than European ones, and are, in this respect, more similar to the US media.

The argument can be stated succinctly. As explained in detail in the following pages, the policy response to the European crisis has reflected the interests of political and economic elites. The principle is readily demonstrated by the fact that when banks faced acute difficulties in 2008, European governments immediately mobilized national resources to support them. Conversely, since then, the majority of the population have not been bailed out, but have lived under austerity programmes that have attacked work conditions and public services. Media coverage of the crisis has mostly presented the views of political and economic elites because news organizations are themselves part and parcel of the corporate sector (or government sector if they are state-owned). This was stated candidly at the outset of the crisis by the *Sunday Business Post*, which declared that the 'primary interest for the government to take into account is that of Ireland Inc'.[1] Thus, the media do not present a broad range of opinions, but rather a relatively narrow spectrum of ideas. They present elites' economic prescriptions favourably to the public and thus contribute to shape dominant political and economic ideologies. This does not mean that the population is always entirely convinced of the adequacy and fairness of the economic system and governmental policy, but it is safe to say that the media play a role in reducing popular opposition to them. Nor does it mean that critical viewpoints do not appear in the pages of newspapers. Of course, there is a diversity of opinions that appear in the media, including a number of individuals who have strongly challenged government policy, as will be seen in subsequent chapters. However, the point is that they are not representative of the general trends in media coverage.

The next chapter situates the European response to the crisis within the neoliberal economic model that has come to characterize advanced economies over the last four decades. The period has seen the financialization of the economy reach much higher levels than during the two or three decades following World War II, while credit- and debt-led growth has become more prominent. Moreover, there have been repeated assaults on the welfare state which have led to rising levels of inequality as elites have sought to reassert and maintain their position of power in society. The ongoing austerity implemented in Europe is a clear example of such dynamics.

That the crisis is used as an opportunity to dismantle the welfare state is no mere academic interpretation. It has been announced explicitly by European authorities. For example, Mario Draghi, the European Central Bank (ECB) president, declared in an interview with the *Wall Street Journal* that the European 'traditional social contract is obsolete' and that 'there is no escape from tough austerity measures'. He further said that continuing 'shocks' would 'force countries into structural changes in labor markets'. Accordingly, Europe's population faces repeated challenges from corporate and political elites, a fact noted by the *New York Times* recently when it observed that 'Americanized labor policy is spreading in Europe'. It remarked that in 2008, 1.9 million Portuguese private sector workers were covered by collective bargaining agreements, but that the number is now down to 300,000. Greece has cut its minimum wage by almost a quarter, Ireland and Spain have frozen it, and in general labour protections have been reduced in peripheral Europe, so that austerity is 'radically changing the nature of Europe's society'. The developments will transform the social fabric so deeply that the chief economist of the International Labour Organization described them as 'the most significant changes since World War II'.[2]

The book proceeds chronologically and discusses the housing bubble, the rescue of the banks in 2008–9, the role of European institutions and the International Monetary Fund (IMF) in bailing out countries in difficulty, and austerity. In Ireland, these topics have received attention from a number of authors, but their accounts have often focused on the personalities of bankers, builders and developers, and the political intrigues surrounding the economic crash, instead of interpreting the events within a critical political economic framework.[3] Alternative policies that could be, or could have been, useful in dealing with the crisis are also addressed, such as debt default, economic stimulus and the possibility of leaving the eurozone. In each case, it is shown how the media have largely sided with government policy and corporate interests while opposing fairer strategies. In general, it will be seen that under neoliberalism, profits are privatized and losses are socialized. The bailout of private banks at taxpayers' expense perhaps best illustrates this assertion. Moreover, there has been a democratic deficit in responding to the crisis, as the population has effectively not been consulted on which strategies should be implemented.

The book focuses on the print press, and in particular on the *Irish Times, Sunday Times, Irish Independent, Sunday Independent* and *Sunday Business Post*. They are appropriate for this study because in addition to being the most popular newspapers in Ireland, they are agenda setters. They shape to a great extent what other news outlets cover in print and on radio and television, and thus play an important role in determining the nature of public debate. The *Irish Times* is often referred to as 'Ireland's newspaper of record' and has a readership of 390,000, while the *Irish Independent* has 650,000 readers. The *Sunday Independent* is the most popular of the Sunday newspapers, with a readership of about 940,000. The *Sunday Times* has a readership of over 400,000 and the *Sunday Business Post* reaches nearly 150,000 people.[4] The methodology varies by chapter, depending on what is most appropriate and feasible to analyze media coverage of specific issues. Sometimes, a systematic quantitative analysis is used, for example to examine what proportion of news articles favour austerity versus those that oppose it. Elsewhere, media reporting is organized into themes that are prominent in the coverage of specific issues. Throughout, Ireland is compared to relevant cases, both contemporary and from recent history. This highlights the range of possible policy alternatives in responding to economic problems.

Ireland has often been presented as a poster child for austerity. In fact, the results have not been impressive, as will be discussed in more detail in later chapters. Economic growth is still weak or negative after a significant fall in 2008–9, GDP is still 8 per cent below its pre-crisis level, unemployment is still very high and debt has accumulated since the beginning of the crisis.

After increasing strongly during the 'Celtic Tiger' boom preceding the crisis, gross domestic product (GDP) and gross national product (GNP) dropped massively between 2008 and 2010, and economic growth has been relatively flat since then, which is not a satisfactory performance (see Figure 1.1). Irish data must be treated with caution, given the large impact of multinationals' activities in the country. Transfer pricing, profit repatriation, royalty payments and accounting peculiarities greatly affect the published data, which may thus diverge significantly from economic reality. In particular, in most countries, there is little difference between GNP and GDP, but in Ireland, GNP is lower than GDP. The difference is mainly due to the profits repatriated abroad by foreign-owned multinationals operating in Ireland. Therefore, many researchers consider the lower GNP figure a better indicator of the state of the economy. In addition, GNP figures for the last several years have been artificially inflated because of the effect of 'redomiciled companies'. These are companies that have relocated their headquarters to Ireland but do not generate any real economic activity in terms of employment or purchases of domestic inputs. Their numbers have grown very rapidly since 2008. Although they bring no benefit to the Irish economy, due to accounting rules,

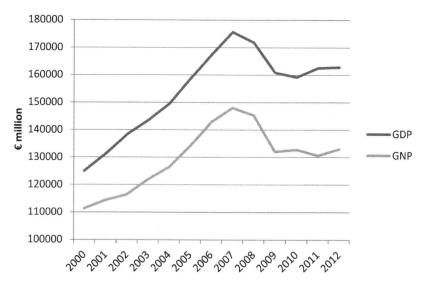

Figure 1.1 Ireland's GDP and GNP (constant market prices)
Source: Central Statistics Office database, www.cso.ie

they raise Irish GNP, giving a rosier picture of economic activity than the reality. This means that the collapse of the economy has been deeper than the official data imply (Figure 1.2). Nevertheless, this book uses official data, bearing in mind the above caveats.[5]

During the boom years, unemployment was relatively stable, at about 5 per cent. It started rising rapidly in 2008, from 4.9 per cent (January 2008), to 9.5 per cent (January 2009), to 13.1 per cent (January 2010), and peaked at around 15 per cent in early 2012. Since then, it has decreased slightly, settling at a little more than 12 per cent in late 2013. However, as some analysts have noted, if broader measures of unemployment are used and the large numbers who have emigrated during the crisis are considered, the unemployment rate could have reached nearly 30 per cent. Also, beyond the numbers employed and job creation statistics, the quality of work and remuneration are important. For example, a recent government statistical release heralded the 58,000 growth in employment – or 3.2 per cent – in the year to the third quarter of 2013. While this is positive, a not insignificant portion of the added jobs were in the hospitality sector, the lowest paid and lowest value-added sector of the market economy.[6]

Government debt has surged in relation to the size of the economy ever since austerity started to be implemented (Figure 1.3). Early in the crisis, claims were heard that when government debt reaches the threshold of 90 per cent of GDP, the economy is in danger. As debt accumulated, this limit was breached and the new announced danger zone threshold became 100 per cent. It was then pushed up to 120 per cent after it was breached again. Austerity

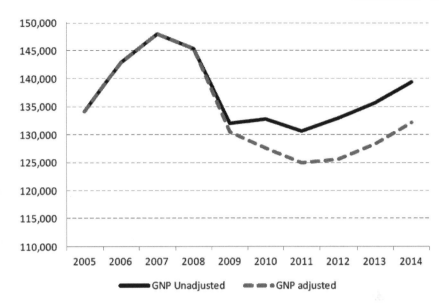

Figure 1.2 GNP adjusted for the effect of redomiciled companies (€ million, constant prices)
Source: ESRI, Quarterly Economic Commentary, Autumn 2013, www.esri.ie

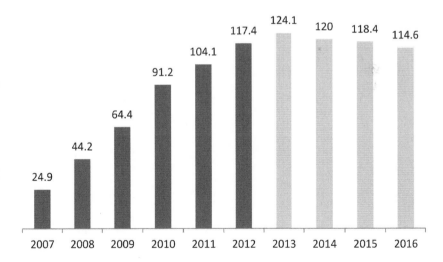

Figure 1.3 General government debt as a percentage of GDP (%) (2013–16 are estimates)
Source: National Treasury Management Agency, www.ntma.ie

has not succeeded in reducing the state's debt burden, and in fact has increased it. For example, general government debt as a percentage of GDP grew from 25 per cent in 2007 to 64 per cent in 2009 to 104 per cent in 2011 and is projected to reach 124 per cent for 2013. The situation may be even worse than those numbers indicate. If GNP is used instead of GDP, the debt ratio has increased from 29 per cent of GNP in 2007 to 78 per cent in 2009 to 130 per cent in 2011 and is projected to reach 153 per cent for 2013. Government projections, which have turned out to be over-optimistic in the past, do not even forecast a significant reduction in the debt ratio. They estimate a slow, gradual decrease in debt-to-GDP to 115 per cent by 2016, and to 150 per cent relative to GNP.[7]

The next chapter describes the neoliberal political economy which has characterized developed countries since the 1970s and this book's interpretation of news organizations. This sets the stage for the discussion of media coverage of the economic crisis in the remainder of the book.

Notes

1 R. Curran, 'Riding to the Banks' Rescue', *SBP*, 30 November 2008.
2 B. Blackstone, M. Karnitschnig and R. Thomson, 'Europe's Banker Talks Tough', *WSJ*, 24 February 2012, online.wsj.com/news/articles/SB1000142405297020396080 4577241221244896782 (accessed 11 December 2013); E. Porter, 'Americanized Labor Policy is Spreading in Europe', *NYT*, 3 December 2013, www.nytimes.com/2013/12/04/business/economy/the-americanization-of-european-labor-policy.html?ref=business&_r=1& (accessed 11 December 2013).
3 For example, see S. Carswell, *Anglo Republic: Inside the Bank that Broke Ireland*, London: Penguin, 2011; M. Cooper, *How Ireland Really Went Bust*, London: Penguin, 2011; T. Lyons and B. Carey, *The FitzPatrick Tapes: The Rise and Fall of One Man, One Bank, and One Country*, London: Penguin, 2011; F. McDonald and K. Sheridan, *The Builders: How a Small Group of Property Developers Fuelled the Building Boom and Transformed Ireland*, London: Penguin, 2008; S. Ross, *The Bankers: How the Banks Brought Ireland to its Knees*, London: Penguin, 2009; S. Ross and N. Webb, *The Untouchables: The People Who Helped Wreck Ireland – and are Still Running the Show*, Dublin: Penguin Ireland, 2012.
4 National Newspapers of Ireland, 'Joint National Readership Survey (JNRS) 2012/2013'. nni.ie/jnrs-20122013/ (accessed 20 October 2013).
5 For a discussion of GDP and GNP in Ireland, see S. Coffey, 'What's the Story with GNP?' Economic Incentives, 21 September 2012, economic-incentives.blogspot.ie/2012/09/whats-story-with-gnp.html (accessed 25 October 2013).
6 Central Statistics Office, 'Unemployment Rate (SA), %', www.cso.ie/indicators/default.aspx?id=2LRM03 (accessed 29 November 2013). For discussion, see C. Gurdgiev, 'Broader Unemployment & Underemployment in Ireland: Q3 2013', True Economics, 26 November 2013, trueeconomics.blogspot.ie/2013/11/26112013-broader-unemployment.html (accessed 2 December 2013); and Michael Taft, 'Quick Notes on the CSO's Employment Numbers – Some Commentators Should Look Harder', Unite's Notes on the Front, 27 November 2013, notesonthefront.typepad.com/politicaleconomy/2013/11/quick-notes-on-the-csos-employment-numbers-some-commentators-should-look-harder.html (accessed 3 December 2013).
7 National Treasury Management Agency, 'Debt Projections', www.ntma.ie/business-areas/funding-and-debt-management/debt-profile/debt-projections/,   and   'Debt

Figures Since 1990', www.ntma.ie/business-areas/funding-and-debt-management/debt-profile/historical-information/ (both accessed 5 December 2013); Michael Taft, 'What's at Stake', Unite's Notes on the Front, 26 November 2013, notesonthefront.typepad.com/politicaleconomy/2013/11/whats-at-stake.html (accessed 5 December 2013).

2   The crisis and the role of the media

The European and Irish crises

The European economic crisis is essentially a product of three factors. First, the impact of the US financial crisis on European financial institutions acted as a trigger for the current turbulence in Europe. However, second, the European crisis would most likely have happened anyway, due to the continent's own imbalances and asset bubbles which developed in the years prior to 2008 and in particular since the adoption of the euro in 1999. Those dynamics arose within the context of the neoliberalization and financialization of Western economies since the 1970s. Indeed, it is possible to see the European crisis as 'the culminating logic of 30 years of neoliberal policy'. However, a third factor must be added, which is the oil thrown on the fire by speculators who have attacked peripheral countries' sovereign debt and by European elites who have adopted policies that have exacerbated the problems caused by the first two factors. For example, and as will be seen in later chapters, if the ECB had followed different priorities, the original crisis may well have been resolved by now, or at least considerably alleviated.[1]

Neoliberalism is a set of ideas and practices that seek to maintain or restore the power of economic elites. It has characterized advanced economies to varying degrees since the 1970s and involves market deregulation, privatization of state enterprises, the weakening of labour's bargaining position and work conditions, and attacks on the welfare state. Importantly, it has been marked by the financialization of Western economies and the relocation of manufacturing to Asia and elsewhere to capture cheaper labour pools and cut production costs. Consequently, economic growth has come to depend to a larger extent on credit and debt accumulation (corporate, personal, governmental), given the deindustrialization of the West and the stagnation of real wages during the last several decades.[2]

Neoliberalism contrasts with the so-called 'golden age' of capitalism which lasted for nearly three decades after World War II. During that time, most advanced economies followed a Keynesian model of economic policy. Internationally, a new liberal world order was built through the Bretton Woods agreements, and institutions like the World Bank, the IMF and the United

Nations were set up to regulate the global economy under the umbrella of the United States' political, military and economic power. A system of fixed exchange rates anchored by the convertibility of the US dollar into gold at a fixed price supported the expansion of trade in goods. Governments in Western Europe, Japan and North America accepted that the state should prioritize economic growth and full employment. In order to accomplish these goals, the state intervened in parallel to, or instead of, free market processes. Keynesian fiscal and monetary policies were thus used to smooth business cycles and redistribute income to some extent. Government intervention in industrial policy was common as well as in the establishment of standards for the social wage through setting up various welfare systems, as in health care, education and other areas.

This set of political economic institutions is sometimes referred to as 'embedded liberalism' to denote how a series of political and social regulations constrained market, corporate and entrepreneurial activities. In contrast, as David Harvey notes, the 'neoliberal project is to disembed capital from these constraints'. Yet, embedded liberalism's performance was clearly superior to the neoliberal era of the last four decades. Western countries on average saw markedly higher levels of economic growth during the golden age period than during neoliberal years. A range of principles which the current orthodoxy decries as allegedly posing obstacles to growth were in fact associated with much more satisfactory economic performance. Those include redistributive politics such as (limited) political integration of trade unions and support for collective bargaining, controls and limits over the mobility of capital, expansion of government spending and welfare state expenditures, and active government intervention in the economy along with industrial planning.

Embedded liberalism broke down in the 1970s for reasons that are still debated. Profits were falling, unemployment and inflation were rising and a phase of 'stagflation' (economic stagnation combined with inflation) characterized the decade. The 1973 Organization of the Petroleum Exporting Countries (OPEC) oil embargo compounded the situation while the system of fixed exchange rates was abandoned for one in which currencies were allowed to float freely. The reaction to such disturbances ushered in the emergence and establishment of neoliberalism as the set of principles used to regulate economies, exemplified by the policies of the Reagan Administration in the United States and Margaret Thatcher in the United Kingdom. It constituted a way for corporate elites and the wealthy to restore and maintain their privileged position, which was threatened by worsening economic performance. The effects can be seen in the rising levels of inequality between rich and poor that have swept the advanced economies since the 1980s. For example, an Economic Policy Institute study concludes that 'Income inequality in the United States has grown sharply over the last few decades', which is 'evident in nearly every data measure and is universally recognized by researchers'. In the United States, from 1979 to 2007, real wages for the top 1 per cent of wage earners increased 156 per cent, compared to 17 per cent for the bottom 90 per cent. From 1983 to 2010, 38 per cent of the wealth growth went to the top 1 per cent of the population and 74 per cent to the top 5 per cent, while the bottom 60 per cent suffered a decline in wealth. Also, the ratio of CEO salaries relative to median compensation of workers surged from 30:1 in the early 1970s to 100:1 in the early 1990s to 300–400:1 in the 2000s. Even among top earners, incomes have become more concentrated, so that 'the share of the top 0.1 per cent in total pre-tax income quadrupled in the 30 years to 2008'.[3]

A similar, although less pronounced, pattern of rising inequality has emerged in other developed countries, as documented in recent Organisation for Economic Co-operation and Development (OECD) reports. It is a fact that in most advanced economies, 'the gap between rich and poor has widened over the past decades', and even in traditionally egalitarian countries like Sweden, Denmark and Germany the income gap has been expanding during the past several decades of neoliberalism. The growing disparities and larger share of income captured by top earners are explained by the 'emergence of a winner-take-all culture in many countries' and the weakening of labour protections. The West has also witnessed 'a move away from highly progressive income tax rates and the elimination of net wealth taxes' since the 1980s. The 'surge' in the share of top incomes in the 1990s and 2000s is accounted for by the fact that top rates of personal income tax, which used to be about 60–70 per cent in major developed countries, had fallen to around 40 per cent by the late 2000s, with the effective tax rate for the top percentile group even lower, in the order of 35–38 per cent.[4] In Europe, inequality has 'risen quite substantially since the mid 1980s' and in the late 2000s, income distribution on the continent 'was more unequal than in the average OECD country', although less unequal than in the United States. While European Union (EU) enlargement is one explanatory factor, it is not the only one because inequality has also increased within core European countries. 'Large income gains among the 10% top earners' are the 'main driver' behind this trend, as 'the 10% highest income recipients have seen their incomes grow much more rapidly than the rest of the population over the past 25 years' while 'the poorest 10% are losing ground'.[5] In sum, since the late 1970s, although 'economic policies predictably redistributed wages, income, and wealth upward, there was no corresponding benefit in the form of faster overall economic growth. In fact, economic growth from the 1970s onward was slower than the economic growth in the prior 30 years'.[6]

Neoliberalism is often described as privileging market forces over state intervention in the economy, but this is misleading. Neoliberal states selectively intervene in the economy to assist elites in maintaining their power over the rest of the population, by enacting legislation on financial (de)regulation, wages, unionism, tax policy, etc. Although the official neoliberal discourse calls for a small state that interferes only minimally in the economy and lets entrepreneurial spirits flourish, the reality is different. In fact, the government takes an active role in supporting business needs, while the forces of the market are reserved for workers and the marginalized. There is no better example of this process than the moves of governments across the advanced economies in 2007–9 to bail out their banks which would have collapsed without massive state support, followed by the imposition of austerity over ordinary people through spending cuts and tax hikes.

A neoliberal ideology is important to present policies and practices favourably to the public, especially when they are contrary to the popular interest. This is accomplished by governmental and corporate public relations spin, but also by a range of institutions like think tanks, universities and the media. This ideological role can be interpreted in terms of establishing what Antonio Gramsci calls 'common sense', which typically grounds popular consent to government policies. Subsequent chapters will document in detail the many ways in which news organizations have provided positive renderings of government policies addressing the crisis. Of course, there are limits to the capacity of the media to convince the audience that what elites propose is the right path to follow. Nevertheless, it would be naive to assume that such messages have no impact on popular perceptions of the state of the economy.[7]

In the United States, debt-led growth and financial deregulation manifested themselves in the late 1990s in the form of a housing bubble that grew alongside a stock bubble for a few years, before the latter collapsed. Asset bubbles lead to increased consumption through the 'wealth effect' whereby people owning the inflated assets feel richer and are more inclined to consume. It is one way to stimulate an economy when wages are held down and industrial production has moved abroad. In fact, the stock bubble induced a consumption boom which involved people spending some of their increasing stock wealth on housing. This rising demand led to higher prices because housing supply is relatively fixed in the short term. Rising prices became internalized into expectations of still higher prices, which led homebuyers to be more willing to spend on real estate, making the expectations self-fulfilling. By 2002, house prices had risen by almost 30 per cent in real terms, indicating that they were not justified by the fundamentals of the market. The fact that rents had increased by less than 10 per cent when adjusted for inflation provided more evidence that the property sector was in bubble territory. The stock bubble collapse of 2000–2 inflated the housing bubble further because millions of people, having lost faith in the stock market, turned to bricks and mortar as an apparently safer investment alternative. Moreover, the US economy was very slow to recover from its 2001 recession, which incited the Federal Reserve to keep cutting interest rates, which pushed down the interest rates on mortgages. For example, the average rate on 30-year fixed rate mortgages dropped to 5.25 per cent in 2003, a 50-year low. This supported more borrowing to purchase properties, which further fuelled the run-up in house prices. Between 2002 and 2006, real house prices rose by an additional 31.6 per cent, equivalent to an annual rate of 7.1 per cent. Increased construction and the wealth effect stimulated the economy as a whole.[8]

However, the building boom produced so much oversupply of properties that the bubble started deflating in 2007 and a downward spiral rapidly brought prices down. The collapse of a housing bubble that had expanded to more than US$8 trillion was bound to affect the economy seriously. Indeed, it led to a loss of annual demand for 2009 and 2010 of $1.3 trillion, composed of about $450 billion from the reduction in housing construction, $700 billion in reduced consumption, and $200 billion due to collapse of the bubble in the non-residential property.[9]

As the bubble collapsed, a large number of mortgages could not be repaid. The spread of defaults in the subprime market in particular led to a drastic reduction in the valuation of mortgage-backed securities (MBS) that contained important quantities of subprime mortgages. Because so many instruments and financial institutions were exposed to risk from the subprime market, a series of credit squeezes hit the markets beginning in 2007. Investors could not know with confidence the nature of a large number of assets and institutions because it was not generally possible to know with any certainty the extent of their exposure to bad mortgage debt.

Importantly, about half of the securitized products made on Wall Street were sold overseas. During the US housing bubble, foreign banks, pension funds and other institutions had purchased these securities. The table was thus set for significant ripple effects: when a subprime borrower in the United States defaulted on his mortgage, it ultimately hit everyone from investment banks in New Zealand to Norwegian pensioners. The largest portion of these securities was perhaps bought by European banks (the data are not transparent). Some of them had direct exposure to the subprime crisis due to their holdings of collateralized debt obligation (CDO) tranches and other instruments. In other cases, such as with BNP Paribas and UBS, hedge funds attached to them placed risky bets on a range of subprime securities, and when those investments went bad, the banks got hit. This led them to reduce lending to the corporate sector, which impeded economic growth.

Furthermore, many European banks also engaged in their own securitization excesses, bundling mortgages from homeowners in European countries, with most of the loans provided by Britain, Spain and the Netherlands. In 2007 alone, nearly €500 billion-worth of European loans became the basis of mortgage-backed securities, asset-backed securities and CDOs. While Europe's excesses in this respect were relatively moderate in comparison with what was taking place in the United States, standards were still lax. Also, many European banks made risky loans to emerging Europe, in particular to Latvia, Ukraine, Hungary and Bulgaria. When the crisis hit, many of those countries' currencies fell sharply, which made it more difficult to repay their borrowings, and Austrian, Italian, German, Swedish and Belgian banks that had lent to them suddenly took massive losses. This set the stage for the crisis on the continent. Therefore, as Nouriel Roubini observed, many economies, 'particularly those in Western Europe, could not avoid the crisis because they suffered from many of the same vulnerabilities: housing bubbles, an overreliance on easy money and leverage, and an enthusiastic embrace of high-risk assets and financial innovation'.[10]

The US crisis should thus be seen as a trigger for the crisis in Europe, which suffered from its own problems and imbalances. For example, in the United Kingdom, the crisis was largely the result of the British model of capitalism, centred on financial services, deregulated markets and credit-led booms, which increased the country's vulnerability.[11] Macroeconomic policy rejected the Keynesian model of the golden age period and instead prioritized low inflation, shareholder value, market deregulation and liberalization of capital flows. It is not without reason that London has been an important geographical base for the financial industry. Britain's economy thus contained the conditions that led to the financial crash, such as abundant cheap credit made available to large numbers of low- and middle-income households, a housing bubble, a lightly regulated banking sector and a boom in derivatives and futures trading among a highly paid financial elite. In September 2007, Northern Rock bank suffered a run on its retail deposits and the crisis soon began.

In the eurozone, the introduction of the euro in 1999 made investors feel safe about sending their money to countries that until then had been considered relatively risky. Interest rates in peripheral countries had historically been higher than in Germany because investors required a premium to compensate for the higher risk of devaluation or default. With the euro, such premiums collapsed and Spanish, Greek, Irish and Italian debt were treated as almost as safe as German debt. For example, whereas in the early 1990s, Greek and Irish 10-year government bond yields were at about 22 per cent and 8 per cent, respectively, by the year 2000 they had both settled at just over 5 per cent.[12] This amounted to much lower borrowing costs in the periphery, which thus witnessed credit booms. In Spain and Ireland, this manifested itself through huge housing bubbles. In Portugal and Greece, it took the shape of credit-fuelled consumption booms. Peripheral economies were thus stimulated by debt-led growth strategies. Local banks did not have enough deposits to support all their lending, and they therefore tapped the wholesale market on a massive scale, borrowing funds from European core banks, mainly in Germany and France (Irish banks also borrowed significantly from banks in the United Kingdom). There were thus huge amounts of capital flowing from the European core to the booming periphery.[13]

Such capital flows into the periphery recycled core countries' current account surpluses. As Costas Lapavitsas put it, the years following the introduction of the euro saw 'a structural current account surplus for Germany, mirrored by structural current account deficits for peripheral countries'. Consequently, 'German FDI [foreign direct investment] and bank lending to the Eurozone have increased significantly', in order to finance the trade deficits in the periphery.[14] For the latter to repay those borrowings would have required them to generate trade surpluses, but they faced instead chronic current account deficits.[15] One factor that made it difficult for the periphery to compete with Germany is that the latter held down wage costs relative to other eurozone countries. For example, in the decade after the introduction of the euro, whereas unit labour costs (wages adjusted for productivity) increased about 35 per cent in Southern Europe, they only rose by 9 per cent in Germany. Until about 20 years ago, Germany's industrial relations system, its welfare state and labour legislation resulted in economic growth whose benefits were distributed to large segments of the population. Its export-oriented model based on high value-added and high-quality manufacturing as well as a skilled workforce ensured that the country remained Europe's economic leader. However, in the wake of the reunification of East Germany followed a decade and a half of significant political and economic transformation, which 'in its radicalism far outstripped the adjustments to the neoliberal mainstream that took place in most other EU countries'.[16] Among other things, wage growth has been restrained like in no other EU country since the introduction of the euro, which contributed to Germany building up a very large export surplus vis-à-vis other eurozone countries. Deregulation of the German financial sector allowed such funds to flow more easily to the periphery, fuelling credit expansions and bubbles.

However, this does not imply that rising wages in the periphery have caused the crisis and that they therefore need to be cut. Such an argument's logical conclusion is a European race to the bottom, with each country successively reducing its wage costs to outcompete others until, presumably, workers could barely survive. There are other reasons behind the periphery's deteriorating current account balances. One is a lack of investment to increase productivity, which would in turn raise competitiveness, especially if directed toward economic sectors that could improve trade balances such as manufacturing, instead of, say, the construction sector, which led to unsustainable housing bubbles. Moreover, countries like Ireland saw significant funds leave the country in the form of profit repatriation by multinational corporations operating on Irish soil, which worsened the country's current account balance.[17]

Contrary to an often repeated story, Europe's problems have not been caused by fiscal irresponsibility or profligacy. The claim that governments were undisciplined and ran excessive budget deficits, which led to debt accumulation, may only apply to Greece, and perhaps Portugal to some extent. It is not what characterized Europe on the eve of the crisis. For example, Ireland had a budget surplus and low debt levels. George Osborne, now Britain's Chancellor of the Exchequer, called it in 2006 'a shining example of the art of the possible in long-term economic policy-making'. Spain had low debt and a budget surplus as well. Italy was bringing its debt-to-GDP ratio down. In fact, as a group, GIPSI countries' debt-to-GDP ratio was steadily and significantly on a downward path between 1999 and 2007, before it started rising rapidly from the onset of the crisis. This means that far from being fiscally irresponsible, the countries now in trouble were actually improving their fiscal position over time.[18]

Greece is a partial exception. In the 1980s and 1990s, it ran persistently expansionary policies, seeking to increase personal income and public consumption, perhaps an understandable response to the previous decades of instability. Given low productivity growth, this led to rising debt and widening deficits. The lowering of borrowing costs due to the adoption of the euro partly made this possible. Because Greece was able to borrow more easily, money became more abundant domestically and financed both consumption and investment. A weak tax collection system and a failure to raise revenues from the better off segments of the population also compounded problems.[19]

Spain and Ireland directed much of their borrowings into investment in the real estate sector, creating large housing bubbles. They saw respectively a 115 per cent and 160 per cent increase in house prices between 1997 and 2007, although the size of Spain's economy being seven times Ireland's makes it more significant for Europe as a whole. In Spain, at the height of the boom, construction accounted for 14 per cent of GDP and 16 per cent of employment and loans to developers amounted to nearly 50 per cent of GDP in 2007. When the bubble collapsed, unemployment surged from 8 per cent to 25 per cent in three years, and youth unemployment reached 52 per cent in 2012. GDP shrank by over 6 per cent in the first quarter of 2009 alone.

One of Spain's differences with Ireland is that whereas mortgage lending and subsequent solvency problems are centred on a few main banks in the latter, Spain's large banks have been somewhat hedged against domestic instability because of their internationalization. For example, the two major banks, Banco Santander and BBVA, with the aid of the euro's purchasing power, snapped up investment opportunities in Latin America where they became important actors. The main mortgage lenders were Spain's 45 *cajas de ahorros* (regional savings banks or credit unions). Regional and local councils could earn significant revenues by re-zoning sites for urban development and selling the land to a developer, who would purchase it thanks to a loan from a *caja* run by the same councillors or their friends. Given that house prices were rising at about 12 per cent annually, the scheme benefited all parties involved. The fact that 'corruption and nepotism were given full rein' did not seem to matter in the short term.[20]

As will be seen in the following pages, eurozone countries face serious constraints that limit the range of possible responses that their governments can adopt to manage the economy. Before the introduction of the euro, when they still had their own currencies, they could react to a balance of payments problem by devaluing their currency to regain competitiveness. However, the euro has left competitive adjustment dependent on reducing labour costs and/ or raising productivity, since devaluation, government deficit spending and money printing are either no longer possible or restricted. The euro is an international reserve currency that was created to meet the needs of large European, and in particular German, industrial and financial interests within a context of financialization. Individual European economies are not large enough to secure a global role for their currency, but together, the goal is possible. The Economic and Monetary Union of the European Union's (EMU) institutional mechanisms have sought to ensure the viability of the euro in its role as a global means of payment and hoarding (reserve). The ECB was created to control monetary policy and preserve the stability of the currency as a unit of account. Its task is to keep inflation below 2 per cent, contributing to making the euro acceptable as a means of payment and reserve. To the same end, the 1997 Growth and Stability Pact was designed in parallel to provide the required fiscal discipline from member states by imposing limits of 3 per cent of GDP for budget deficits and 60 per cent of GDP for public debt.[21]

The common currency and eurozone framework have provided significant advantages to European elites in the core and periphery. The growing acceptability and recognition of the euro as a leading international reserve currency has allowed European banks to acquire foreign assets more cheaply and to expand globally. The euro also provides a common market for bank lending within the eurozone and facilitates borrowing and lending on the global market by European banks, as happened in peripheral states in the years preceding the crisis. Moreover, a strong currency makes imports cheaper, which keeps inflation low, a goal of the financial industry. The euro has also supported the overseas expansion of industrial corporations while helping them to impose discipline on workers in Europe because cutting labour costs remains the principal way to gain competitiveness when devaluation is no longer possible. Moreover, industrial corporations benefit from reduced transaction costs within the common market thanks to the single currency, which assists capital allocation within the eurozone. This facilitates the outsourcing of parts of the productive chain to more advantageous regions and places. It is true that the manufacturing sector could be expected to oppose a strong currency because it hurts export competitiveness. On the other hand, it is favourable to a strong currency because it permits investments abroad at a lower cost, and makes it possible to outsource production where costs are lower, in particular for labour, such as in Asia. Companies that offshore production benefit from cheaper imports of those goods, which allows them to outcompete their domestic rivals whose production is concentrated at home. Finally, better off segments of the population also benefit from a strong euro, which makes imported luxury goods more affordable and foreign holidays and travel cheaper. Although this latter point is not the driving factor behind the establishment of the euro, it could be maintained that it contributes to preserving support for the single currency among political and economic elites.[22]

Since independence, Ireland's political system has been dominated by two right-of-centre parties – Fianna Fáil and Fine Gael – which have left little room for progressive alternatives. Indeed, the main cleavage in the political system is not between right and left, but goes back to pro-treaty and anti-treaty positions at the time of independence in the 1920s. In terms of economic policy, when Ireland became independent, industry was mostly located in the north-east of the country. Because that area became part of the United Kingdom, the Irish Republic was left with an economy heavily based on agriculture. From the 1960s, Ireland adopted a liberal and open economic model and sought to attract export-oriented manufacturing, a scheme that may be seen as a precursor to what would later be called 'neoliberal'. However, this strategy still remained dependent on foreign companies, resulting in an underdeveloped indigenous industrial base.[23]

The case of Ireland over the past several decades can be conceived as a case of neoliberalization, following a number of analysts.[24] Although Irish governments have never explicitly adopted a neoliberal ideology, political economic institutions have nevertheless been transformed along these lines. This 'neoliberalism Irish-style' has borrowed elements of US neoliberalism, such as public-private partnerships, privatization of public services, low corporate and individual taxation, low level of government expenditures on social programmes and light regulation of the financial system. It also incorporates aspects of European social welfarism, such as social partnership, EU directives and a developmental state.[25] During the pre-crisis, Celtic Tiger years, Irish economic performance was impressive. Between 1988 and 2007, real GDP grew at an annual average of 6 per cent, while unemployment fell from 16 per cent in 1994 to 4 per cent in 2000, which meant 'essentially full employment for the first time in history'.[26] Since 2008, however, the Irish economic model has been questioned as it ushered in a period of crisis and austerity.

Irish elites are well connected across economic and financial sectors through boards of directors and other channels – a network referred to as a 'golden circle' by one think tank, and which has been at the centre of the Irish development model.[27] A number of commentators have observed how in this model the state 'prioritises goals of economic competitiveness over those of social cohesion and welfare'.[28] This has included a relatively low level of government expenditures on social programmes, light regulation of the financial system, large dependence on foreign capital, and flexible labour markets.[29] Seán Ó Riain has noted the 'class bias' in government policy through 'the imposition of competitive pressures upon the weakest' in society. The state has intervened in favour of the better off, but much less so to support the disadvantaged, as 'the cold chill of competition is experienced most strongly by those with the least resources' so that 'the welfare state was in some respects strengthened for the middle classes even as it remained a minimalist support for the most excluded'.[30] Similarly, the Irish government intervenes selectively in favour of the privileged, as the state's 'capacity to win high levels of foreign direct investment in key targeted sectors contrasts with its low social spending'.[31]

As will be seen in subsequent chapters, a phase of export-based expansion in the 1990s enabled Ireland to emerge from a long period of economic stagnation. This was made possible by large investments by multinational corporations seeking access to the EU single market. However, as export growth rates fell sharply after 2000, a second phase characterized by financialization and a credit-fuelled housing boom sustained high rates of economic growth. The crisis began when the bubble collapsed. Since 2008, the Irish government has addressed the crisis by following neoliberal principles. As scholars at Ireland's National Institute for Regional and Spatial Analysis have put it, 'the solution to the crisis has employed a deepening of neoliberalised policy designed ... to protect as much as possible the interests of the developer and financial class'.[32] The government first implemented an austerity programme on its own at the outset of the crisis, and after late 2010, did so within the context of a €67.5 billion EU-IMF bailout.

The role of the media

There has been little research investigating the media's role in the current economic crisis, in Ireland or elsewhere. In the United States, one empirical study found that in the years prior to the crisis, the American media could be described as 'the watchdog that didn't bark' since 'the business press institutionally lost whatever taste it had for head-on investigations of core practices of powerful institutions'.[33] Similar conclusions apply to the performance of British journalism.[34] Other studies have examined aspects of media coverage of the crisis in Argentina, Switzerland, Germany and Spain.[35] In Ireland, some commentators have noted that news organizations failed to give proper warnings of the impending crash.[36]

This literature leaves many gaps in our understanding of the media's role during the economic crisis and in the years leading up to it. In particular, with a few exceptions, existing research does not examine news organizations within a critical political economic framework. Indeed, explanations for poor media performance have centred around journalists' 'herd mentality' and hubris and the time pressures preventing them from pursuing in-depth investigative stories, combined with reporters' lack of training in finance. Other studies have described the metaphors and language used by the media to describe the crisis but neglected to examine the political economic system of which the media are part and parcel.[37]

This book argues that news organizations convey the views of political and economic elites. It is true that there are many debates taking place in current affairs reporting, but they are confined to the relatively narrow range of opinions within the establishment. This interpretation has been adopted by a number of critical media analysts, and is associated with the work of Noam Chomsky and Edward Herman. Their 'propaganda model' identifies a number of 'filters' that shape what we see and hear on the news. What follows is an adaptation and update of the model that draws on the work of a number of theorists.[38] It is argued that four main factors account for the nature of coverage of the economic crisis: the media's links with the corporate and governmental sectors, advertising pressures, sourcing, and neoliberal ideology.

Corporate and governmental links

Both private and state-owned media organizations largely convey corporate and political establishment views, but for somewhat different reasons. Private media organizations are large corporations embedded in a capitalist economic system and are thus integral parts of the broader corporate sector. This has several consequences. First, in order to start and successfully run a media company with any substantial outreach, significant financial investments are necessary, which means that only wealthy individuals and corporations are able to do so. As will be seen below, Ireland's media landscape is dominated by a relatively small number of conglomerates, reducing the diversity of views presented to its citizens.

Second, media firms are integrated into the market and feel the pressures of bankers, shareholders and directors to generate profits. Links with the broader corporate sector and political elites are created and maintained through boards of directors as well as general business and social interactions. For example, media organizations are in close contact with bankers for lines of credit, loans, receiving service and advice on the issuance and sale of shares and bonds, in addition to mergers, acquisitions and threats of takeover by other investors. Banks themselves, along with a range of other institutional investors, are also often large owners of shares in media companies. Such investors want profits and act as a constant pressure on media corporations to prioritize the bottom line. Media diversification has also increased the integration of news organizations into the broader corporate world. Newspapers and television stations have acquired a range of other media and non-media businesses while non-media businesses have acquired interests in media organizations. In short, media firms have very similar interests to the corporate sector of which they are key entities, and thus the stories they present tend to reflect such interests and viewpoints. Indeed, it would be surprising if news organizations emphasized stories critical of key aspects of the corporate world, such as the profit motive and market control by a few entities, as this would directly undermine their own position.

Third, the media also have a close relationship with the government, which is able to some extent to pressurize them to conform to its viewpoints. This is because news corporations depend on the state for licences and franchises. Thus, the government is in a position to exert some leverage over the orientation taken by the media in their news coverage. However, it is also because the media, as any other business, depend on the state to maintain a healthy business climate favourable to private enterprise, at home and abroad if they wish to expand internationally.

In 2008, PricewaterhouseCoopers conducted a detailed study of the ownership, size and concentration of the media in Ireland which illustrates the above statements. Independent News & Media (INM) is arguably the dominant media conglomerate and is listed on the Irish and London stock exchanges. At the time of the study, it generated annual revenues of €1.67

billion (in 2012 this had dropped to €540 million), owned 200 newspapers and magazines, 130 radio stations and 100 online sites in Ireland, the United Kingdom, South Africa, India, Australia and New Zealand. In Ireland, it owns seven national and 17 local newspapers, and 27 websites. Some of those are leading titles, such as the *Irish Independent, Sunday Independent, Sunday World* and *Irish Daily Star*. Its main bankers are Bank of Ireland, AIB and Ulster Bank Ireland, which were all deeply involved in the housing bubble and which have been at the centre of the subsequent crisis.[39]

Sir Anthony O'Reilly bought the company in 1973 and controlled it until 2009, expanding and diversifying it. Over the years, O'Reilly has been involved through investment and management in numerous corporations in Ireland and globally, having been CEO of Heinz, board member of Eircom, Waterford Wedgwood, the New York Stock Exchange, Bankers Trust, General Electric and Mobil Oil among others. However, O'Reilly recently lost control of INM to two other prominent Irish businessmen, Denis O'Brien and Dermot Desmond. Financier Dermot Desmond, known as 'The Kaiser' for his distinctive moustache, has a net worth estimated at $1.8 billion, the fifth highest in Ireland. He founded NCB Stockbrokers in 1981, which later became Ireland's largest independent brokerage. He started his career at Citibank and today has investments in a range of sectors from biometrics to health care.[40] Denis O'Brien, a cell phone tycoon, has a net worth estimated at $5.2 billion, the second highest in Ireland. In addition to being INM's largest shareholder, he is also the owner of Communicorp, another major Irish media group with media assets in five countries, including Ireland. It owns a number of radio stations with listeners estimated at 20 million per week. According to its website, Communicorp's 'mission is to push the boundaries of commercial media'. It was recently revealed that O'Brien is one of the largest borrowers from Anglo Irish Bank, to which he reportedly owes €833.8 million.[41]

INM board members are deeply linked to the Irish and global political and economic establishment. At time of writing, INM board members included Leslie Buckley, vice-chairman of telecommunications company Digicel and who is also 'a Director and shareholder of a number of other Irish companies', and Terry Buckley, an executive whose 'knowledge of the advertising industry [is] of considerable benefit to the Board'. Over the years, directors have also included Brian Hillery, a Director of the Central Bank of Ireland, Commissioner of the National Pensions Reserve Fund Commission, and former Fianna Fáil member of parliament; Dermot Gleeson, the chairman of AIB during the housing bubble years; B.E. Summers, a director of AIB; J.C. Davy, a senior executive at Davy Stockbrokers (Dublin) and former director of Abbey (property and construction company); A.C. O'Reilly, former investment banker at Goldman Sachs; and A.J. O'Reilly Jr, chief executive of Providence Resources (involved in oil and gas exploration) and director of Lundin Mining Corporation.[42]

Such links show how media companies are interconnected with the broader corporate sector. An explicit example of such ties is the acquisition by the

Irish media of a direct financial interest in the sustenance of the housing bubble through the purchase of property websites. For example, in 2006, INM bought PropertyNews.com (along with the PropertyNews monthly news-paper), the 'largest internet property site on the island of Ireland' listing 'nearly 20,000 properties for sale'. Sir Anthony O'Reilly said that the 'com-bination of *PropertyNews.com* and *INM*'s online and newspaper operations will allow the group to offer estate agents and home-owners an unrivalled package'.[43]

In 2006, the *Irish Times* bought the property website MyHome.ie for €50 million, along with the website newaddress.ie, which aims to make it easier for home owners to move residences. Interestingly, MyHome.ie had until then been owned by three prominent Irish real estate agents (Sherry Fitzgerald, Douglas Newman Good and the Gunne Group) and AIB Bank, showing that many benefited from the property bubble. The *Irish Times* even had its own property website previously, but MyHome.ie was a site of a much higher profile – at the time, over 850 Irish estate agents advertised property in it and it attracted a heavy user traffic, with 29 million page views in May 2006 alone. The media's stakes in the housing bubble were clear. Indeed, Maeve Donovan, managing director of the *Irish Times*, said that the combination of MyHome.ie and her newspaper 'creates a dynamic force for growth in the Irish online property market'. The *Irish Times* seemed to have wished for higher home prices to such an extent that in October 2007, it was reported that MyHome.ie had run into a controversy because it was 'blocking access to bloggers who have been compiling lists recording the steep falls in house prices over the past year'.[44]

The *Irish Times*' board has included a number of individuals linked to the corporate and political establishment, such as David Went, CEO of Irish Life & Permanent, a bank deeply involved in the housing bubble – in 2007 Went left IL&P, just before the crash, after which he was promoted to chairman of the *Irish Times* board; Brian Caulfield, a venture capitalist; Eoin O'Driscoll, who has been on the board of a number of private software and tele-communications companies, and a member of the National Executive Council of IBEC, Ireland's largest business and employers' lobbying organization; John Fanning, chairman of McConnell's Advertising with expertise in brand-ing; and Gregory Sparks, partner in RSM Farrell Grant Sparks (a business services firm).[45]

Similarly, the *Sunday Times* is owned by Rupert Murdoch's News Cor-poration, which generates revenues of more than $33 billion annually and is one of the largest media corporations in the world. Rupert Murdoch's net worth is estimated at approximately $13.4 billion.[46] The *Sunday Business Post* was owned by Thomas Crosbie Holdings until 2013 when the paper was put into examinership. A group of investors including capital markets firm Key Capi-tal and Paul Cooke, the former chief executive of the tabloid *Irish Daily Star*, subsequently took it over. Thomas Crosbie was one of the main media groups in Ireland, owning print titles, websites and radio stations.

Government-owned media are by definition controlled by the government to a greater or lesser extent, through funding and appointments of principal officers. In theory, state-owned media could be more representative of popular concerns than private media since they are part of the democratic structure of government. However, this only goes so far as the government is democratic, and in Ireland as elsewhere, national politics are largely dominated by a few parties representing various factions of the establishment. RTÉ is Ireland's state-owned media organization and is the dominant television player in the country, although it also has significant stakes in radio and the internet. It is funded through advertising revenues, indicating an important commercial dimension, but also by the government through licence fees collected from the public. For example, in 2012, RTÉ's commercial revenues amounted to €156 million and licence revenues to €181 million. Moreover, the government appoints RTÉ's board, giving it additional influence on the organization. During the boom years, RTÉ had as chairman Patrick J. Wright, who was at the same time director of Anglo Irish Bank, which epitomized more than any other bank the excesses of the Celtic Tiger and property lending.[47] He was also vice-chairman of Aer Lingus (national airline), chairman of Aon Mac-Donagh Boland Group (insurance company) and president of the Jefferson Smurfit Group (paperboard company). In 2006, Mary Finan took over as chair, with a résumé including positions such as chief executive of Wilson Hartnell (public relations company), president of the Dublin Chamber of Commerce, director of Canada Life (insurance company) and the ICS Building Society, a Bank of Ireland subsidiary mortgage lender that offered 100 per cent mortgages from 2005 onwards and eventually covered by the 2008 government guarantee.[48]

In sum, the Irish media are intertwined with the governmental and corporate world of which they are integral parts. Therefore, it is to be expected that news organizations will convey viewpoints that largely reflect such interests, as the contrary would amount to undermining their own position and even existence as we know it.

Advertising

Advertising revenues are crucial to today's news industry. They allow newspapers to be sold for a cheaper price, thus making them more competitive. Media unable to attract ads are at a serious disadvantage in the market and run the risk of bankruptcy. This affects news content because corporate advertisers tend not to subsidize television programmes or news stories that seriously question or attack their own business or the political economic system of which they are part, which would be directly contrary to their interests. For example, oil companies are unlikely to sponsor a news outlet filled with stories about environmental degradation and climate change caused by car driving. Sometimes news organizations can lose advertising funding if they are too critical, as when Gulf + Western cut its corporate funding to public television station WNET in the United States after the station showed a documentary with material critical of multinational corporate activities in developing countries. The CEO of Gulf + Western told the station that the programme was 'virulently anti-business if not anti-American'.[49]

One particularly clear example of the significance of advertising to the Irish media is the large amount of funding from property advertising received during the housing boom years. (As seen above, the Irish media went even further than benefiting from property advertising money: they became owners of the property websites themselves, acquiring a direct stake in the growing housing bubble.) For example, most newspapers published weekly supplements for commercial and residential property, 'glamorizing the whole sector', while 'Glowing editorial pieces about a new housing estate were often miraculously accompanied by a large advertisement plugging the same estate', in the words of Shane Ross, former *Sunday Independent* business editor. Ross also shows the power of advertisers in influencing news content when he states that 'Unfavorable coverage of developers and auctioneers in other parts of the newspapers was regularly met by implied threats from property interests that advertising could go elsewhere'.[50] Moreover, a reporter working for an Irish news organization stated that journalists 'were leaned on by their organisations not to talk down the banks [and the] property market because those organisations have a heavy reliance on property advertising'.[51] As *Irish Times* columnist Fintan O'Toole remarked, 'There is no question that almost all of the Irish media for the last 10–15 years has had a crucial economic stake in a rising property market. Because property advertising is very lucrative and is a very important part of what makes the Irish media tick'.[52]

Sourcing

Journalists depend mostly on mainstream institutions for their reports. Because of limited resources, time constraints and a competitive news environment, reporters need to connect with those institutions that provide a steady flow of news, which in practice means large organizations that have themselves the resources to produce and release such a stream of material. The government and corporations are two such sources, with the result that their points of view are predominant in the media. Also, sourcing stories to those organizations confers an image of objectivity and credibility. Moreover, conveying the government's and corporations' views offers some protection to the media against potential libel suits, which would be more numerous if stories were critical and challenged mainstream thinking. One result of the sourcing relationship between journalists and powerful institutions is that close relationships develop between reporters and members of the corporate sector and government. The latter can then deny privileged information to journalists who do not adopt the expected storylines, as happened during the housing bubble in Ireland.[53]

Indeed, there are many examples illustrating the above claims in the Irish context, as revealed by a study based on interviews with Irish financial journalists. One said that because of the need for regular contact and interaction with financial sources, 'some journalists are reluctant to be critical of companies because they fear they will not get information or access in the future'. Another business journalist related how 'many developers and bankers limited access to such an extent that it became seen to be better to write soft stories about them than to lose access. Extremely soft stories would be run to gain access' to them as well. Threats of legal action limit the possibility of undertaking investigative financial reporting because banks and real estate companies can easily drag news organizations into expensive legal procedures, so that 'Very often a threat of an injunction is enough to have a story pulled', while many legal actions by powerful individuals or corporations are 'executed purely to stifle genuine inquiry'. One journalist even mentioned that reporters face much pressure from the industry to influence news content, and that it is 'well known that some PR [public relations] companies try to bully journalists by cutting off access or excluding journalists from briefings'.[54]

Neoliberal ideology

Since the 1970s, the neoliberal project has necessitated a certain level of popular consent in order to establish itself in various countries in the world, let alone to permit its proponents to win elections. Dominant ideological and cultural forces constitute a form of hegemony in Gramsci's sense, that is, such forces induce popular consent to the rule of elites in society. Civil society institutions play an important role in establishing this hegemony, including the education system, the Church and the media.[55] In this respect, some have noted the rise of 'neoliberal newspeak' in news organizations and intellectual circles, which, through 'perpetual media repetition has gradually transformed into a universal common sense' key neoliberal notions and values, such as the efficiency of the free market and individual responsibility.[56] Simply put, because the media reflect the views of the corporate world, and that the latter has been transformed along neoliberal lines in recent decades, it is no surprise that news organizations are imbued with a neoliberal ideology which permeates the stories they present.

In Ireland, it has been shown in detail how a 'Celtic Tiger discourse' has been used by policy makers at home and on the international stage in order to present a convincing programme of economic, political and social development. Although Irish governments have never explicitly adopted a neoliberal ideology, neoliberalism has nevertheless permeated much of policy making and even popular understandings of economy and society.[57] For example, Seán Ó Riain mentions 'the neo-liberal stories that Irish society and elites have told themselves of the successes of the past fifteen years', while others have argued that Ireland 'is being marketed' as a 'neoliberal "Tiger"', and that the 'hegemonic discourse of Irish modernity is driven by a neoliberal ...

imperative'.[58] Some have maintained that the Celtic Tiger years were bound up with a cultural discourse of entrepreneurship and individualism 'both as personal attributes to be cultivated by the individual (and which educational institutions are expected to play a central role in facilitating) and as dominant social values'. It has also been noted that those 'dominant meanings are constructed to legitimise power hierarchies'.[59] Peadar Kirby describes a 'new class of wealthy and powerful entrepreneurs' in Ireland, whose values 'have become the values of neo-liberal Ireland, and enterprise culture made up of attitudes, values and norms which serve the needs of the market and which are actively promoted by government agencies'.[60]

Of course, the crisis has led to a questioning of such values by a range of groups and grass-root organizations which work toward a more egalitarian and progressive society. However, Kieran Allen and Brian O'Boyle have argued that the celebration of neoliberal values during the Celtic Tiger years was so extensive in Irish society that it partly accounts for the relative lack of protest in Ireland compared to other European countries since 2008. When the crisis struck, their argument goes, Irish people had been left somewhat unaware of economic alternatives, which impeded popular resistance to troika (IMF, ECB and European Commission) prescriptions. On the other hand, elites, including the media, have sought to reassert neoliberal values in their response to the economic turbulence, using discourses which foreground the need to 'tighten our belts', increase 'civic discipline' and raise competitiveness both domestically and globally. As will be seen in the following pages, the media have played a prominent role in circulating such ideas, in particular in their defence of the austerity programme implemented by successive Irish governments since the beginning of the crisis.[61]

Criticisms

There has been sympathetic commentary about the model of the media used in this book, but it has also been subject to a number of criticisms.[62] It has been argued that it is 'conspiratorial', 'anecdotal', 'moralizing', 'totalizing', 'deterministic' and 'exaggerated'; that it does not pay enough attention to cultural studies and literary theory; that it homogenizes elites; and that it assumes that the public is a naive mass of people with little capacity for critical judgement when it is exposed to media messages.[63]

Ultimately, the validity of such criticisms is to be determined empirically, and in subsequent chapters, it will be argued that media coverage of the economic crisis conforms very closely to what would be expected from the model. However, many criticisms are simply misplaced. For example, the model makes no recourse to conspiracy theory. A conspiracy refers to decisions made by a few individuals, in secret, outside the normal institutional channels. Such decisions thus subvert the normal political process to the benefit of a few conspirators. However, the model squarely rejects the proposition that this explains mass media coverage of current events. On the contrary, the model is an institutional analysis of news organizations and their place within the corporate sector. Its conclusions depend directly on the normal workings of the corporate world, not on a conspiracy subverting it.

Joshua Cohen and Joel Rogers argue that the model 'exaggerates' the significance of the media in explaining popular consent to government policies in capitalist democracies. However, audience reception of messages is not part of the model. Of course, there is an assumption that the mass media do shape public opinion to some extent, but its precise influence is difficult to determine, and the model is not concerned with examining this proposition in detail. It focuses on explaining why news organizations produce certain messages and not others. Moreover, the same authors maintain that the model assumes that elites are always rational, but they claim that they can be irrational at times, trapped in their own ideology and propaganda: 'elite-generated ideologies' are thus not always functional for elite interests. However, the model does not assume that every single move by elites is entirely rational in the short, medium and long term. There are certainly instances of mistakes made by elites that turn out to be counterproductive even in their own self-interest. However, in general, elites act rationally, and the decisions they make reflect their own interests. Although a number of examples will be provided, it can be stated as a basic principle that the system of inequality in power and wealth that characterizes Ireland and other countries simply could not be preserved if those that dominate it and maintain it were so irrational – if this were the case, the system would collapse, which it certainly has not.[64]

Neither does the model assert that the media parrot official government policy. Rather, media coverage reflects the debates and viewpoints that are found among elite circles. There is thus a range of opinions found in the media, but it is relatively narrow. Debates are mostly of a 'tactical' nature – namely, they share common assumptions and are mostly restricted to how best to implement policy in line with fundamental principles which seek to preserve the existing political economic system. Incompetence and incapability to implement policy typically lead to much criticism in the media. For example, when government officials are unable to push through austerity measures, they are criticized for being 'weak', 'indecisive', or 'unable to deliver', but this is a tactical criticism, not one that questions the fundamental policy of austerity, let alone social and economic inequalities in general. Finally, there are, of course, a number of instances of commentary that challenge government policy in a fundamental way, but they are exceptions.[65]

Related, the model is not deterministic, because it accepts that there is a (narrow) diversity among elite viewpoints. Neither does it assume that the public will be entirely convinced or, to use a more pejorative term, 'brainwashed', or that it cannot protest or contest what the media present. There have been a number of examples of resistance to dominant ideologies in recent years, in Ireland and elsewhere, but this does not mean that media messages do not reflect, largely, elite viewpoints. It simply points to the limits of such messages to influence popular views. Nevertheless, it would be naive to assume that the mass media have only a small influence over public opinion. Even if they only sow doubt about the desirability of alternative policies over those preferred by elites, or convince only a segment of the population, those are in themselves significant achievements.[66]

One interesting issue is whether the internet and new media, including social media, blogs and podcasts, weaken the model because they give people the opportunity to access a wider variety of news and permit critical journalists to disseminate their work to a larger, indeed global, audience. However, although the internet's potential is indeed real, in practice it has not democratized the news, for a number of reasons. First, the traditional media themselves are dominant news providers on the internet, and alternative news websites reach a much smaller audience. Traditional news organizations have the resources and pre-existing audiences to provide them with a huge competitive advantage over others. Second, alternative news websites often seek advertising revenues to be able to survive, which subjects them to the same pressures as referred to above and compromises their alternative nature. Third, a lot of the online media are oriented toward networking and facilitating social connections, with news and political issues often secondary or absent. In short, although new media have the potential to democratize the news, this has so far been limited, although it may change in the future.[67]

The next chapter discusses the role of the media in sustaining the housing bubble, the deflation of which led to the economic crisis in Ireland. It will be seen that the model presented in this chapter explains well the performance of news organizations. The media largely closed their eyes on house price inflation, until after the market started to collapse.

Notes

1 N. Roubini and S. Mihm, *Crisis Economics: A Crash Course in the Future of Finance*, London: Penguin, 2011; P. Krugman, *End this Depression Now!*, New York: W.W. Norton, 2012.
2 D. Harvey, *A Brief History of Neoliberalism*, Oxford: Oxford University Press, 2005; *The Enigma of Capital and the Crises of Capitalism*, London: Profile Books, 2010; G. Duménil and J. Lévy, *The Crisis of Neoliberalism*, Cambridge, MA: Harvard University Press, 2011.
3 Economic and Policy Institute (EPI), *The State of Working America*, 12th edn, 2013, p. 6, www.stateofworkingamerica.org/subjects/overview/?reader (accessed 11 December 2013); *Divided We Stand: Why Inequality Keeps Rising*, OECD Publishing, 2011, p. 38, dx.doi.org/10.1787/9789264119536-en (accessed 12 November 2013); H.-J. Chang, *23 Things They Don't Tell You about Capitalism*, London: Allen Lane, 2010, pp. 148–56.
4 OECD, *Divided We Stand*, pp. 3, 18, 40. See also *Growing Unequal? Income Distribution and Poverty in OECD Countries*, OECD Publishing, www.keepeek.com/Digital-Asset-Management/oecd/social-issues-migration-health/growing-unequal_9789264044197-en#page1 (accessed 11 December 2013).
5 Bonesmo Fredriksen, K., 'Income Inequality in the European Union', Economics Department working papers no. 952, Paris: OECD Publishing, 2012, pp. 2, 8, 18, dx.doi.org/10.1787/5k9bdt47q5zt-en (accessed 11 December 2013).

6 EPI, *The State of Working America*, p. 7.
7 A. Gramsci, *Selections from the Prison Notebooks*, trans. Q. Hoare and G. Nowell Smith, London: Lawrence & Wishart, 1971.
8 D. Baker, 'The Housing Bubble and the Financial Crisis', *Real-World Economics Review*, 2008, no. 46, pp. 73–81, paecon.net/PAEReview/issue46/Baker46.pdf (accessed 10 December 2013).
9 D. Baker, *False Profits: Recovering from the Bubble Economy*, Sausalito, CA: PoliPointPress, 2010, p. 101.
10 Roubini and Mihm, *Crisis Economics*, ch. 5.
11 D. Grimshaw and J. Rubery, 'Reinforcing Neoliberalism: Crisis and Austerity in the UK', in S. Lehndorff (ed.) *A Triumph of Failed Ideas: European Models of Capitalism in the Crisis*, Brussels: European Trade Union Institute, 2012, pp. 41–58, www.etui.org/Publications2/Books/A-triumph-of-failed-ideas-European-models-of-capitalism-in-the-crisis (accessed 8 December 2013).
12 See the graph in M. Blyth, *Austerity: The History of a Dangerous Idea*, Oxford: Oxford University Press, 2013, p. 80.
13 Lapavitsas, C. *et al. Crisis in the Eurozone*, London: Verso, 2012.
14 Lapavitsas *et al.*, *Crisis in the Eurozone*, pp. 33–34; see also J. Bibow, 'The Euro Debt Crisis and Germany's Euro Trilemma', Working paper no. 721, Levy Economics Institute of Bard College, May 2012, www.levyinstitute.org/pubs/wp_721.pdf (accessed 11 December 2013); R. Boyer, 'The Four Fallacies of Contemporary Austerity Policies: The Lost Keynesian Legacy', *Cambridge Journal of Economics*, 2012, vol. 36, no. 1, pp. 283–312; K. Laski and L. Podkaminer, 'The Basic Paradigms of EU Economic Policy-making Need to be Changed', *Cambridge Journal of Economics*, 2012, vol. 36, no. 1, pp. 253–70.
15 M. Pettis, *The Great Rebalancing: Trade, Conflict, and the Perilous Road Ahead for the World Economy*, Princeton and Oxford: Princeton University Press, 2013.
16 S. Lehndorff, 'German Capitalism and the European Crisis: Part of the Solution or Part of the Problem?' in S. Lehndorff (ed.) *A Triumph of Failed Ideas: European Models of Capitalism in the Crisis*, Brussels: European Trade Union Institute, 2012, p. 80, www.etui.org/Publications2/Books/A-triumph-of-failed-ideas-European-models-of-capitalism-in-the-crisis (accessed 8 December 2013).
17 M. Burke, 'Ireland – The Nature of the Crisis', *Socialist Economic Bulletin*, 9 October 2009, socialisteconomicbulletin.blogspot.ie/2009/10/ireland-nature-of-crisis.html (accessed 2 January 2013).
18 Krugman, *End this Depression Now!*, p. 178.
19 Blyth, *Austerity*, p. 62–63.
20 Blyth, *Austerity*, pp. 64–68; I. López and E. Rodríguez, 'The Spanish Model', *New Left Review*, 2011, vol. 69, May/June, p. 17.
21 This discussion of the euro draws principally from C. Lapavitsas, 'Default and Exit from the Eurozone: A Radical Left Strategy', *Socialist Register*, 2012, vol. 48, pp. 288–97; 'The Eurozone Crisis through the Prism of World Money', in Martin H. Wolfson and Gerald A. Epstein (eds) *The Handbook of the Political Economy of Financial Crises*, Oxford: Oxford University Press, 2013, pp. 378–94; Lapavitsas *et al.*, *Crisis in the Eurozone*.
22 See an analogous argument for the United States in D. Baker, *The End of Loser Liberalism: Making Markets Progressive*, Washington, DC: CEPR, 2011, pp. 80–81.
23 C. McCabe, *Sins of the Father: Tracing the Decisions that Shaped the Irish Economy*, Dublin: The History Press, 2011.
24 N. Brenner *et al.*, 'Variegated Neoliberalization: Geographies, Modalities, Pathways', *Global Networks*, 2010, vol. 10, pp. 182–222; K. Allen, *Ireland's Economic Crash: A Radical Agenda for Change*, Dublin: Liffey Press, 2009; A. Fraser *et al.*, 'Deepening Neoliberalism via Austerity and "Reform": The Case of Ireland', *Human Geography*, 2013, vol. 6, no. 2, pp. 38–53; P. Kirby, *Celtic Tiger in*

Collapse: Explaining the Weaknesses of the Irish Model, Basingstoke: Palgrave Macmillan, 2010; R. Kitchin *et al.*, 'Placing Neoliberalism: The Rise and Fall of Ireland's Celtic Tiger', *Environment and Planning A*, 2012, vol. 44, pp. 1302–26.

25 Kirby, *Celtic Tiger in Collapse*, p. 147; D. O'Hearn, *Inside the Celtic Tiger: The Irish Economy and the Asian Model*, London: Pluto, 1998; R. Kitchin and B. Bartley, 'Ireland in the Twenty First Century', in B. Bartley and R. Kitchin (eds) *Understanding Contemporary Ireland*, London: Pluto Press, 2007, pp. 1–26; Kitchin *et al.*, 'Placing Neoliberalism'.

26 P. Honohan, 'The Irish Banking Crisis: Regulatory and Financial Stability Policy 2003–8. A Report to the Minister for Finance by the Governor of the Central Bank', 2010, p. 21, www.bankinginquiry.gov.ie/ (accessed 27 December 2012); P. Clinch *et al.*, *After the Celtic Tiger: Challenges Ahead*, Dublin: O'Brien Press, 2002; T. Friedman, 'Follow the Leapin' Leprechaun', *NYT*, 1 July 2005.

27 P. Clancy *et al.*, 'Mapping the Golden Circle', Dublin: TASC, 2010, www.tascnet. ie/upload/file/MtGC%20ISSU.pdf (accessed 2 July 2013).

28 P. Kirby and M. Murphy, 'Globalisation and Models of State: Debates and Evidence from Ireland', *New Political Economy*, 2011, vol. 16, no. 1, p. 26.

29 P. Kirby, *The Celtic Tiger in Distress: Growth with Inequality in Ireland*, Basingstoke: Palgrave, 2002; O'Hearn, *Inside the Celtic Tiger*.

30 S. Ó Riain, 'Competing State Projects in the Contemporary Irish Political Economy', in M. Adshead, P. Kirby and M. Millar (eds) *Contesting the State: Lessons from the Irish Case*, Manchester: Manchester University Press, 2008, pp. 169, 179, 175.

31 Kirby and Murphy, 'Globalisation and Models of State', p. 125.

32 Kitchin *et al.*, 'Placing Neoliberalism', p. 1317; K. Allen and B. O'Boyle, *Austerity Ireland: The Failure of Irish Capitalism*, London: Pluto, 2013; Fraser *et al.*, 'Deepening Neoliberalism via Austerity and "Reform"'.

33 D. Starkman, 'Power Problem', *Columbia Journalism Review*, 2009, May/June, p. 30; A. Harber, 'When a Watchdog Doesn't Bark', *Rhodes Journalism Review*, 2009, September, pp. 20–21.

34 M. Fraser, 'Five Reasons for Crash Blindness', *British Journalism Review*, 2009, vol. 20, pp. 78–83; D. Schechter, 'Credit Crisis. How Did We Miss it?' *British Journalism Review*, 2009, vol. 20, pp. 19–26.

35 M.A. Becerra and G. Mastrini, 'Crisis. What Crisis? Argentine Media in View of the 2008 International Financial Crisis', *International Journal of Communication*, 2010, vol. 4, pp. 611–29; M. Schranz and M. Eisenegger, 'The Media Construction of the Financial Crisis in a Comparative Perspective – An Analysis of Newspapers in the UK, USA and Switzerland between 2007 and 2009', *Swiss Journal of Sociology*, 2011, vol. 37, no. 2, pp. 241–58; O. Quiring and M. Weber, 'Between Usefulness and Legitimacy: Media Coverage of Governmental Intervention during the Financial Crisis and Selected Effects', *The International Journal of Press/Politics*, 2012, vol. 17, pp. 294–315; A.M.R. López and M.A.O. Llopis, 'Metaphorical Pattern Analysis in Financial Texts: Framing the Crisis in Positive or Negative Metaphorical Terms', *Journal of Pragmatics*, 2010, vol. 42, pp. 3300–13.

36 G. Kerrigan, *The Big Lie: Who Profits from Ireland's Austerity?* London: Transworld Ireland, 2012; C. Brady, 'Did the Media Fail to Sound the Alarm Bells before the Financial Crisis?' *IT*, 6 March 2010; M.B. Marron, 'British/Irish Media Excel in Episodic Coverage, Fail in Probing', *Journalism Studies*, 2010, vol. 11, no. 2, pp. 270–74.

37 Marron, 'British/Irish Media Excel in Episodic Coverage, Fail in Probing'; Fraser, 'Five Reasons for Crash Blindness'; Schechter, 'Credit Crisis. How Did We Miss it?'; López and Llopis, 'Metaphorical Pattern Analysis in Financial Texts'; K.J. McCarthy and W. Dolfsma, 'What's in a Name? Understanding the Language of the Credit Crunch', *Journal of Economic Issues*, 2009, vol. XLIII, no. 2, pp. 531–48; G.L. Clark

et al., 'Performing Finance: The Industry, the Media and its Image', *Review of International Political Economy*, 2004, vol. 11, no. 2, pp. 289–310.

38 E. Herman, 'The Propaganda Model: A Retrospective', *Journalism Studies*, 2000, vol. 1, no. 1, pp. 101–12; B. Bagdikian, *The New Media Monopoly*, Boston: Beacon Press, 2004; E. Herman and N. Chomsky, *Manufacturing Consent: The Political Economy of the Mass Media*, New York: Pantheon, 2002; D. Kellner, *Media Culture: Cultural Studies, Identity and Politics between the Modern and the Postmodern*, London: Routledge, 1995; R. McChesney, *Rich Media, Poor Democracy: Communication Politics in Dubious Times*, New York: New Press, 2000; R. McChesney, *The Problem of the Media: U.S. Communication Politics in the 21st Century*, New York: Monthly Review, 2004; *The Political Economy of Media: Enduring Issues, Emerging Dilemmas*, New York: Monthly Review, 2008.

39 PwC, 'Media Research Required by the Advisory Group on Media Mergers', in Advisory Group on Media Mergers, *Report to the Tánaiste and Minister for Enterprise, Trade and Employment, Mary Coughlan TD*, June 2008, p. 149, www.djei.ie/publications/commerce/2008/advisorygrouponmediamergersreport2008.pdf (accessed 10 September 2013); INM, *Annual Report 2007*, www.inmplc.com/investor-relations/reports-andpresentations/archive (accessed 20 August 2012).

40 *Forbes*, 'Dermot Desmond Profile', www.forbes.com/profile/dermot-desmond/ (accessed 12 November 2013).

41 *Forbes*, 'Denis O'Brien Profile', www.forbes.com/profile/denis-obrien/ (accessed 12 November 2013); Communicorp website, www.communicorp.ie/ (accessed 12 November 2013); PwC, 'Media Research Required by the Advisory Group on Media Mergers'; T. Lyons, 'Revealed: Top 13 Borrowers Who Owe Anglo', *II*, 15 April 2012.

42 INM, 'Annual Report', various years, www.inmplc.com/investor-relations/reports-and-presentations/archive (accessed 10 March 2013).

43 INM, 'Independent Acquires PropertyNews.Com', press release, 27 March 2006, www.investegate.co.uk/articlePrint.aspx?id=200603271144344282A (accessed 10 March 2013).

44 D. Buckley, 'Agents to Benefit from Sale of Irish Property Website', EGi Web News, 31 July 2006, available from *Nexis* database; 'Paper's Website Deal is Looking Shaky', *SI*, 21 October 2007.

45 *Irish Times* website, www.irishtimes.com/about-us/the-irish-times-trust#group (accessed 8 December 2013); *Irish Times*, 'Directors' Report and Consolidated Financial Statements', www.irishtimes.com/about-us/the-irish-times-trust#financial (accessed 8 December 2013).

46 *Forbes*, 'Rupert Murdoch Profile', www.forbes.com/profile/rupert-murdoch/ (accessed 1 December 2013).

47 S. Carswell, *Anglo Republic: Inside the Bank that Broke Ireland*, London: Penguin, 2011.

48 RTÉ, 'Annual Report', various years, www.rte.ie/about/en/policies-and-reports/annual-reports/ (accessed 10 December 2013).

49 Herman and Chomsky, *Manufacturing Consent*, p. 17.

50 S. Ross, *The Bankers: How the Banks brought Ireland to its Knees*, London: Penguin, 2009, pp. 157–58.

51 D. Fahy *et al.*, 'Combative Critics or Captured Collaborators? Irish Financial Journalism and the End of the Celtic Tiger', *Irish Communications Review*, 2010, vol. 12, p. 15.

52 'The Media and the Banking Bailout', MediaBite, 2009, www.mediabite.org/article_The-Media-and-the-Banking-Bailout_679566551.html (accessed 10 July 2013).

53 Starkman, 'Power Problem'; P. Chakravarty and D. Schiller, 'Neoliberal Newspeak and Digital Capitalism in Crisis', *International Journal of Communication*, 2010, vol. 4, pp. 670–92; McChesney, *The Problem of the Media*.

54 Fahy *et al.*, 'Combative Critics or Captured Collaborators?' pp. 13–14.
55 Harvey, *A Brief History of Neoliberalism*; Gramsci, *Selections from the Prison Notebooks*; M. Durham and D. Kellner, *Media and Cultural Studies: Keyworks*, 2nd edn, Hoboken, NJ: Wiley-Blackwell, 2012.
56 P. Bourdieu and L. Wacquant, 'NewLiberalSpeak. Notes on the New Planetary Vulgate', *Radical Philosophy*, 2001, vol. 105, January/February, p. 3; Chakravarty and Schiller, 'Neoliberal Newspeak and Digital Capitalism in Crisis'.
57 N.J. Smith, *Showcasing Globalisation: The Political Economy of the Irish Republic*, Manchester: Manchester University Press, 2005; Kirby, *Celtic Tiger in Collapse*.
58 Ó Riain, 'Competing State Projects in the Contemporary Irish Political Economy', p. 184; C. Kuhling and K. Keohane, *Cosmopolitan Ireland: Globalisation and Quality of Life*, London: Pluto, 2007, pp. 7, 18.
59 P. Kirby *et al.*, 'Introduction: The Reinvention of Ireland: A Critical Perspective', in P. Kirby *et al.* (eds) *Reinventing Ireland: Culture, Society and the Global Economy*, London: Pluto, 2002, p. 13.
60 P. Kirby, 'Contested Pedigrees of the Celtic Tiger', in Kirby *et al.* (eds) *Reinventing Ireland*, p. 34.
61 Allen and O'Boyle, *Austerity Ireland*, ch. 9.
62 E. Herring and P. Robinson, 'Too Polemical or too Critical? Chomsky on the Study of the News Media and US Foreign Policy', *Review of International Studies*, 2003, vol. 29, pp. 553–68; A. Mullen and J. Klaehn, 'The Herman-Chomsky Propaganda Model: A Critical Approach to Analysing Mass Media Behaviour', *Sociology Compass*, 2010, vol. 4, no. 4, pp. 215–29; O. Boyd-Barrett, 'Judith Miller, the *New York Times*, and the Propaganda Model', *Journalism Studies*, 2004, vol. 5, no. 4, pp. 435–49; C. Sparks, 'Extending and Refining the Propaganda Model', *Westminster Papers in Communication and Culture*, 2007, vol. 4, no. 2, pp. 68–84. For a review of reactions to the model, see J. Pedro, 'The Propaganda Model in the Early 21st Century, Part I and Part II', *International Journal of Communication*, 2011, vol. 5, pp. 1865–905, 1906–26.
63 For example, see G.N. Brahm, Jr, 'Understanding Noam Chomsky: A Reconsideration', *Critical Studies in Media Communication*, 2006, vol. 23, no. 5, pp. 453–61; J. Cohen and J. Rogers, 'Knowledge, Morality and Hope: The Social thought of Noam Chomsky', *New Left Review*, 1992, vol. 187, pp. 5–27; J. Corner, 'The Model in Question: A Response to Klaehn on Herman and Chomsky', *European Journal of Communication*, 2003, vol. 18, no. 3, pp. 367–75; Kurt Lang and Gladys Engel Lang, 'Noam Chomsky and the Manufacture of Consent for American Foreign Policy', *Political Communication*, 2004, vol. 21, no. 1, pp. 93–101.
64 Cohen and Rogers, 'Knowledge, Morality and Hope', pp. 22–23.
65 J. Klaehn, 'A Critical Review and Assessment of Herman and Chomsky's "Propaganda Model"', *European Journal of Communication*, 2002, vol. 17, no. 2, pp. 147–82.
66 J. Klaehn, 'Behind the Invisible Curtain of Scholarly Criticism: Revisiting the Propaganda Model', *Journalism Studies*, 2003, vol. 4, no. 3, pp. 359–69.
67 A. Mullen, 'The Propaganda Model after 20 Years: Interview with Edward S. Herman and Noam Chomsky', *Westminster Papers in Communication and Culture*, 2009, vol. 6, no. 2, pp. 12–22; Pedro, 'The Propaganda Model in the Early 21st century, Part II'.

3 The housing bubble

Property, longer term, is a better bet than any other form of investment, short of discovering oil in your back garden.
(Kevin O'Connor, *Irish Times*, 22 November 2007[1])

Far from collapsing, our economy and property prices will do more than hold up.
(Marc Coleman, *Sunday Independent*, 23 September 2007[2])

The Celtic Tiger period was composed of two distinct and successive booms. First, an export-based expansion in the 1990s enabled Ireland to emerge from a lengthy period of economic stagnation. The government favoured deregulation, entrepreneurialism and free market principles and sought to attract export-oriented FDI. The success of this phase was made possible by large investments from transnational corporations into the country, made attractive due to its status as a 'tax haven' for US and other multinationals seeking access to the EU single market. A corporation tax rate of only 10 per cent in the 1980s, raised to 12.5 per cent in 2003, led many financial and manufacturing companies to flock to the country, while a host of related tax and transfer pricing arrangements allowed them to maximize profits further. A pool of IT experts resulting from Ireland's educational policies was also attractive, as were moderate wage inflation and labour flexibility. A booming US economy during those years led to large investments abroad, a unique circumstance that contributed significantly to Irish growth.[3]

In the second phase, from the late 1990s to 2007, as export growth rates fell sharply after 2000, a credit-fuelled construction boom took over and sustained high rates of economic growth. Real residential property prices rose threefold between 1994 and 2006, 'the highest [increase] in any advanced economy in recent times'. A number of factors explain the emergence of this second phase, mostly related to the financialization and liberalization of the economy. Credit was made more freely available due to the significant fall in interest rates (including for mortgages) brought about by Ireland's entry into the EMU. As domestic lending increased so substantially, bank deposits came short of providing sufficient funding. Therefore, financial institutions filled this funding gap by borrowing abroad and then directing the funds toward the domestic property market. The interbank market in the United Kingdom was the main source of funding for Irish banks. The Irish financial sector was also liberalized starting in the 1980s, further increasing credit availability. For example, there was an easing in banks' reserve ratio with the Irish Central Bank from 10 per cent in 1980 to 2 per cent in 1999, freeing up funds for lending to households. Further, a number of taxation incentives for the construction sector were enacted. Stamp duty rates were lowered multiple times in the years up to 2007 and significant income tax concessions were made for many categories of construction investment, leading to over-building and high vacancy rates.[4]

Another factor stimulating the expansion of credit was the opening of the domestic market to foreign banks, which increased competition. These banks offered better terms to customers and new products such as high or 100 per cent loan-to-value mortgages, tracker mortgages, and interest only mortgages, leading to increased pressures to grow market share and lending. However, competitive pressure also came from within Ireland, especially from Anglo Irish Bank, whose market share rose from 3 per cent to 18 per cent in ten years while its loan portfolio grew at an average rate of 36 per cent annually. This motivated other banks to increase lending more aggressively. Moreover, mortgage brokers who paid little attention to the ability of borrowers to pay back their loans became more prominent in the market, and there was an overall 'distinct decline in loan appraisal quality for residential mortgages'. Of course, loans to property developers and builders also increased and many were of very low quality and turned out to be the banks' major weakness.[5]

As a result, bank lending rose from the late 1990s until 2007 and fuelled the housing bubble. Lending by Irish banks increased from a stock of €120 billion in loans and advances to customers in 2000 (or 1.1 times GDP) to nearly €400 billion by 2007 (2.2 times GDP). Property-related lending grew significantly more rapidly than lending to other sectors, rising by almost €200 billion between 2002 and 2008 and accounting for 80 per cent of all credit growth over the period. At the peak of the housing bubble, construction accounted for over 20 percent of national income (the average level for a developed country is about 5 percent). Between 1996 and 2005, over half a million housing units were built and, by 2007, Ireland, along with Spain, was producing over twice as many units per capita than elsewhere in Europe. Over that time, the proportion of the Irish workforce engaged in construction increased from 7 per cent to 13 per cent. As a result, numerous 'ghost estates' and poorly designed urban developments lacking basic amenities emerged on the Irish landscape.[6]

Because the boom was beneficial to key sectors of the Irish corporate and political establishment, it was never seriously challenged. Rising property prices directly benefited builders and developers, banks, the government and property firms, and indirectly, the broader economy, thanks to high growth levels. The government, led by the Fianna Fáil party, was able to collect large tax revenues from the property boom through stamp duty, capital-related taxes and income taxes on construction workers, and VAT on construction materials. While total property-related taxes accounted for 4 per cent of government revenue in 1996, they accounted for over 17 per cent by 2006. Bankers could increase the size of their loan books and profits, just like builders and developers, as long as house prices kept rising. Those converging interests in sustaining the real estate bubble led to a thick web of corruption, bribery and unethical relationships between key officials in the public and private sectors, as the Tribunal of Inquiry Into Certain Planning Matters and Payments (Mahon Tribunal) has revealed.[7]

Real estate prices reached a peak at various months in 2007 depending on the type of property and location. Borrowers stopped taking on increasingly large amounts of debt and a reverse self-reinforcing spiral of falling prices and borrowing ensued as investors tried to exit the market and shed assets before prices fell further. As of this writing, the national residential price index is about 50 per cent lower than its 2007 peak. With the property bubble bursting, Irish banks' share prices also fell and in September 2008 a run in wholesale markets on Anglo Irish Bank brought the crisis to a head.[8]

The media analysis that follows depends to some extent on whether or not the bubble could have been identified before it burst, and if the size of the crash could have been reasonably estimated beforehand. The answer is yes on both counts, although the precision of the analysis is obviously greater in hindsight. (If it was not possible to identify a property bubble before it burst, it would be difficult to criticize the media for failing to warn about it.) There are two main measures to determine whether property prices are in bubble territory: the price-to-earnings ratio and the price-to-income ratio. The price-to-earnings ratio compares average house prices to average rental prices. Its rise – that is, when house prices significantly outpace rents – is evidence of a bubble. Indeed, if a rise in house prices was accounted for by 'fundamentals' such as a growing population or housing supply shortages, both property prices and rents would be expected to increase. Thus, prices taking off relative to rents is evidence that property is 'being bought in the expectation of capital appreciation rather than underlying fundamentals' – the definition of a bubble. The price-to-income ratio compares average house prices to average personal disposable income. A significant rise in the ratio means that house prices levels do not reflect income levels anymore, which would be expected in a normal market.[9]

The Economist magazine used those indicators to warn about property bubbles around the world early on. In 2002, it stated that the Irish housing market had been 'displaying bubble-like symptoms in recent years' and in 2003 it calculated that Ireland's property market was over-valued by 42 per cent relative to the average of the previous three decades. Many other countries also experienced their own housing bubble at that time, such as the United States, Dubai, Australia, New Zealand, Spain, Iceland, Estonia, China, Latvia and South Africa. In 2005, the total value of residential properties in developed countries had doubled since 2000 – a gain of $40 trillion – in what could be 'the biggest bubble in history'.[10]

In Ireland, economist David McWilliams warned about the unsustainability of the boom as early as January 1998, when he wrote that 'fundamentals count for nothing if your house is built on a bubble' and pointed to the fact that mortgage lending in Ireland 'has been growing at 15 per cent per annum for the past four years. This cash has been funnelled with the help of significant fiscal incentives, into bricks and mortar, pushing, as we all know, prices through the roof. On top of this, general credit in the economy is up more than 20 per cent in 1997 alone. A quick glance at property prices suggests that we are definitely entering asset-price bubble territory'. Until the crash, McWilliams was one of the few analysts in Ireland to warn publicly and unambiguously about the growing bubble and its eventual collapse.[11]

One other Irish analyst to have done so is economist Morgan Kelly. He looked at nearly 40 property booms and busts in OECD economies since 1970 and showed that there is a strong relationship between the size of the boom and ensuing bust: typically, 'real house prices give up 70 per cent of what they gained in a boom during the bust that follows'. This 'iron law' can be stated by reference to the ratios mentioned above, as the 'more house prices rise relative to income and rents, the more they subsequently fall'. Kelly observed that between 2000 and 2006, house prices in Ireland had doubled relative to rents, while the price-to-income ratio had also significantly outpaced its historical level. This showed that Irish property prices were no longer sustained by fundamentals such as rising employment, immigration, or rising income. He predicted a fall in real house prices of '40 to 60 per cent over a period of 8 to 9 years', which seems relatively accurate as of this writing.[12]

However, overwhelmingly, Irish analysts and institutions, including the media, maintained that there was no bubble and that the boom would eventually end in a 'soft landing'. The Nyberg Commission on the crisis interviewed a number of finance industry officials who said that if they had pursued contrarian policies going against the euphoria, 'they may ultimately have lost their jobs, positions, or reputations'. In short, there was a large amount of 'herd behaviour' among financial institutions and 'groupthink' within them – both pointing to an uncritical acceptance and following of the dominant trends and decisions that sustained the boom and led to the bust.[13] The remainder of the chapter shows that media performance also fits this description.

Media coverage

The first point to emphasize is the clear discrepancy between coverage of the housing bubble before and after it burst. Before 2008, the media tended to largely ignore it and it is only months after it had started deflating that discussion of the subject became more prevalent. Once the housing market collapsed, the media simply could not ignore its downward trajectory, hence the increased coverage. This reflected the views of political and economic elites, who eventually had to face reality, let alone because Ireland's creditors would soon force them to do so.

Figures 3.1 and 3.2 show the number of articles on the housing bubble that appeared in newspapers by year.[14] The keywords used for the news database search were 'housing bubble', 'property bubble' and 'real estate bubble'. Other terms, such as 'housing boom' or 'housing affordability', would have returned articles on related subjects, but would not necessarily have denoted coverage of a housing bubble, which by definition refers to abnormally inflated housing prices. For example, the phrase 'housing boom' has positive connotations and was often used in the media before the crash to give overly optimistic assessments of the property market. Similarly, there have been news stories about corruption in the planning and political systems as related to housing, but those rarely considered the fact that, at the macro level, the property market was in bubble territory.[15]

On average, the *Irish Times* had 5.5 times more articles on the bubble per year in 2008–11 than in 1996–2007. Similarly, the *Irish Independent/Sunday Independent* had on average 12.5 times more such articles in 2008–11 than in 1999–2007.[16] Moreover, the few articles published during the earlier period often denied that there was a bubble. For example, *Irish Times* articles' titles included: 'Irish property market has strong foundations', 'Study refutes any house price "bubble"', 'Bricks and mortar unlikely to lose their value', 'Prices to rise as equilibrium is miles away', 'House prices "set for soft landing"', 'Property market unlikely to collapse, says Danske chief' and 'House prices rising at triple last year's rate'.[17]

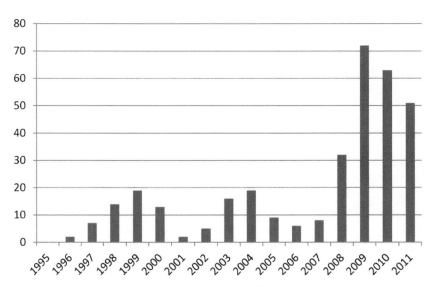

Figure 3.1 Number of articles on the housing bubble, *Irish Times*
Source: Mercille (2014a)

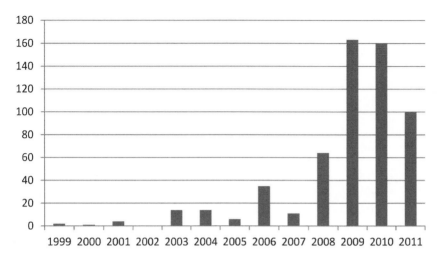

Figure 3.2 Number of articles on the housing bubble, *Irish Independent/Sunday Independent*
Source: Mercille (2014a)

The *Irish Independent/Sunday Independent* reveal the same pattern, with headlines such as: 'NCB [Stockbrokers] rejects house value threat from burst bubble', 'Property "bubble" is not yet ready to burst', 'The property bubble never looked like bursting in County Roscommon', 'House prices not about to fall soon, insist auctioneers', 'Dire predictions of collapse in value of homes dismissed', 'Price of houses "not over-valued" says new report', 'There is no property bubble to burst, despite doomsayers', 'Influx of workers gives big boost to property' and 'Property "bubble" could continue expanding'.[18]

The residential and commercial property sections and supplements presented articles and glossy pictures encouraging readers to invest in the real estate market. Such stories described various properties on sale and were virtually indistinguishable from advertisements. For example, one entitled 'There's a billion reasons to buy' introduced new luxury 'extra spacious' apartments by noting that they 'feature quality designer kitchens with integrated AEG appliances and stone worktops; top notch bathrooms with ceramic tiles, heated towel rails and chrome fittings; recessed lighting and centralised heating'. It continued by assuring the reader that such a 'high spec naturally positions this development at the upper end of Dublin's residential market and it is set to become a benchmark for the capital'. Potential buyers should waste no time: 'However you don't have to be a millionaire to buy into such billion euro territory – 355,000 is all it takes to stake your claim. But numbers are strictly limited – you'd want to stake it fast'.[19]

Articles celebrated Ireland's newly found pride in entrepreneurialism at home and abroad. One profiled the 'ever-bullish Irish property buyer … looking for the hot new property market' wherever it is in the world. As such, in 'Victorian times, it was fashionable for the British to suggest that "the sun never sets on our Empire". Now the sun never sets on Ireland's burgeoning property empire'. Indeed, thanks to their 'ever-expanding horizons and an insatiable thirst for buying, Irish investors are laying claim to holiday homes and office blocks around the world'. After 'having scoured Eastern Europe and the Iberian Peninsula for bargains ... buyers are continuing their splurge in "old Europe" (countries such as France, Germany, and Belgium) and venturing much further afield'. For example, Irish investors were leading a 'Berlin invasion' and 'those with a gambling instinct are turning to Thailand, Dubai, Brazil, Africa and even New Zealand in the hope of making easy money'.[20]

Of course, there were a few articles warning about the bubble, such as those by David McWilliams and Morgan Kelly. However, such warnings were outnumbered by articles either denying there was a bubble, remaining vague about it or simply talking about something else. For instance, between 2000 and 2007, the *Irish Times* published more than 40,000 articles about the economy – but only 78 were about the property bubble, or 0.2 per cent.[21] This is small coverage for what was the most important economic story in those years. Articles that cautioned against the possible negative repercussions of a real estate bubble were often met with stories throwing doubts on such claims or arguing that things would be fine. For example, in 2003, an *Irish Times* article dampened possible worries of an overvalued property market with a story entitled 'IMF points to "significant risk" of overvaluation on house prices: the Irish property market may be in "bubble territory". Or then again maybe it's not. Even the IMF can't make up its mind'.[22]

The media relied on so-called 'experts' from the financial or real estate industry to describe the market, which thus received almost invariably upbeat analysis.[23] For example, as late as November 2007, the *Irish Times* conducted a survey among 'property experts' to predict how the market would evolve in 2008. The six experts selected all held high-level positions with property firms:

- Pat Gunne, Managing Director, CBRE (global commercial real estate services firm)
- Ann Hargaden, Investments Director, Lisney (leading Irish real estate agency)
- Angus Potterton, Managing Director, Savills HOK (global real estate services provider)
- Fintan Tierney, Managing Director, Sherry FitzGerald (leading Irish real estate agency)
- Sean Mulryan, Managing Director, Ballymore (Irish property company)
- Niall Gaffney, Chief Executive, IPUT (largest property trust in Ireland)
- Nicholas Corson, Director, Finnegan Menton (Irish property consultancy firm)

Not surprisingly, their forecast was enthusiastic. Their responses included statements such as: 'We have an underlying economy which by any standards is good'; 'The good times are not over'; 'There is a lot of cash out there looking for safe homes in an economy that is continuing to grow'; with 'capital values likely to bounce back during the course of the year, the timing is right to buy development land to catch the upswing for residential development'; 'The broad macro economic fundamentals of the Irish economy are sound'; 'we are in a cooling off period and not a collapse'; and 'the commercial investment market will provide solid positive performance'.[24]

Similar individuals had given their predictions in the *Irish Times*' property outlook the previous year. The article started thus: 'Anxious? Worried? Relax – next year's property market will be steady rather than heady say the experts',[25] and contained the following assertions by experts:

- Mark FitzGerald, CEO, Sherry FitzGerald Group: 'The market in Dublin will be fine. With more moderate prices, yields will get more attractive … You will have high profile private treaty sales and higher valued houses sold privately'.
- Sean FitzPatrick, chairman, Anglo Irish Bank: 'the equity in the housing market is still very strong, which is a positive. The commercial market is very bullish. There is a wall of money out there chasing investment so the outlook is very positive. The immigration impact will have a softening effect on the market. Banks need to be mature, and not overreact to exacerbate the problem – 5 per cent of non-performing loans is no big deal'.
- Ray Grehan, property developer, Glenkerrin Homes: 'I am confident that demand will remain strong for 2007 as continued growth in total employment and a net increase in population of 100,000 will continue to underpin demand'.
- Dan McLaughlin, chief economist, Bank of Ireland: 'The year 2007 will be another strong one in terms of transactions. We are likely to see something of the order of 85,000 to 90,000 houses built again'.
- Ken MacDonald, managing director, Hooke & MacDonald: 'I feel that the spring market will be good. There is a pent-up demand out there'.
- Jim Miley, chief executive, MyHome.ie: 'Contrary to popular myth, the property market has not "stagnated" or "ground to a halt" as some commentators would have you believe. In the month of November alone, more than 2,000 properties that had been advertised on MyHome.ie were sold or sale agreed. While this was down somewhat on the rate of sale in the first half of the year, it represents an active market'.
- John O'Sullivan, residential director, Lisney: 'A lot is about to happen. We are starting to see offers and people making decisions'.

The views of experts were also used directly to discredit suggestions that the market was overheating. For example, an article entitled 'Study refutes any house price "bubble"' started with the following sentences: 'There is no house price bubble, according to Mr Jim O'Leary, chief economist at Davy

Stockbrokers. In the latest report on the housing market, Solid Foundations, Mr O'Leary said the market has been driven by fundamental factors and these would need to reverse for the market to collapse'.[26]

Elsewhere, Ken MacDonald, managing director at Hooke and MacDonald, a firm specializing in the sale of new homes, wrote a piece in March 2007 entitled 'Property market's no house of cards', in which he told readers that 'Property holds a fascination for Irish people' and that there is a 'deep-rooted desire by most Irish people to own their own home'.[27] He attacked those who cautioned against rising home prices in an alleged 'hysterical negativity' about the market's prospects, and asserted that 'Price moderation is mistaken for weakness, when in fact it represents maturity and long-term sustainability'. His conclusion is worth quoting at length:

> As one who has been involved in the Irish property market for 40 years and has experienced every type of market scenario, I am totally convinced that the market is currently in good shape and that anyone buying now will do extremely well in the years ahead. There is no better investment than Irish property at present, and I believe that I will be proved right in this conviction.
>
> Why do we allow scaremongers and doomsayers with unfounded pessimism and unbridled negativity dictate our thinking and blunt consumer confidence? The Irish economy is the envy of the world. Job creation is phenomenal with more than 7,000 new jobs being created each month – despite the gloomy attention given to periodic job losses in some sectors ... We should be celebrating our success on a daily basis. In any event, the Irish love affair with property will continue undaunted despite the knockers.

Other figures often quoted included Marian Finnegan, chief economist at Sherry FitzGerald, who said in early 2008 that she expected a 'gradual improvement' in the property market in 2008, which should be 'somewhat brighter' than in 2007. Paul Murgatroyd, economist at Douglas Newman Good, a real estate company, said in early 2008 that there had been a 'significant pick up' in buyer activity since Christmas in a piece entitled 'Buyers reclaim the market'. A number of journalists simply acted as 'cheerleaders' for the property sector, as Morgan Kelly described them on the television show *Prime Time*. Brendan O'Connor of the *Irish Independent* wrote an article in July 2007 entitled 'The smart, ballsy guys are buying up property right now', urging readers to buy property, saying himself: 'Tell you what, I think I know what I'd be doing if I had money, and if I wasn't already massively over-exposed to the property market by virtue of owning a reasonable home. I'd be buying property. In fact, I might do it anyway ... anyone who is out there in the jungle will tell you that it is a buyer's market bigtime'. Kevin O'Connor argued in the *Irish Times* in November 2007 that 'Property, longer term, is a better bet than any other form of investment, short of discovering oil in your back garden'. This is because of an alleged baby boom and a constant inflow of immigrants: 'What do you get when you cross 150,000 baby buggies with 150,000 impending immigrants? A leap in property values starting around 2009'.[28]

Journalists persisted in rejecting the view that the Irish property market had been in a bubble months after it started collapsing. A few examples have already been given above of articles published in mid- to late 2007 still claiming that the housing sector would either continue to go up in value or that a soft landing was the worst that could be expected. Other similar stories appeared in 2008, such as the following: 'The faint-hearted agonise over buying, hoping that prices will fall further. But don't wait. Buy now, don't listen to the doomsayers'; and 'We all got such a fright last year, that we huddled up in the far corner of the field waiting for the sheepdog to herd us towards the gate. Well the property gate is open again. Not quite as wide open as it had been before, but open nevertheless. So let's get moving. You can never buy at the wrong time'. In April 2008, the *Sunday Independent* conveyed the thoughts of estate agent Peter Wyse, 'one of Dublin's leading and most established agents', who believed that 'the time to buy is now. There is certainly great value in the market at the minute but it doesn't mean people can dilly dally'.[29]

One of the most revealing example of a journalist who acted to prop up the housing market is Marc Coleman, the former *Irish Times* economics editor, who now hosts his own show on the radio station *Newstalk* and writes a weekly column for the *Sunday Independent*. What follows examines all his newspaper articles on the property market published since 2004 as well as his book *The Best is Yet to Come*, written in 2007.[30] Perhaps the clearest examples of how wrong he has been come from pieces such as one penned in September 2007, in which he labelled those who warned of a housing collapse as 'careless talkers' who make meaningless 'simplifications and generalisations' and threaten to 'run down our economy'. Coleman claimed that 'Far from an economic storm – or a property shock – Ireland's economy is set to rock and roll into the century'. He thought the economy was so strong that he wrote that 'Ireland enters the 21st Century in a position of awesome power', which 'promises a future more flourishing than ever before; a future that will turn economic prosperity from a statistical fact to a reality'. The country was doing well enough that worldwide, 'hundreds of millions of people are on the move, looking for a country like Ireland to make their home'. After all, 'Far from collapsing, our economy and property prices will do more than hold up'. All that was required to protect Ireland against a crisis was not to talk about it, because 'unless we talk ourselves into one, an economic storm is not going to happen'. The country needed to proceed as if there was no problem at all: 'If we keep our eyes fixed forward and our heads cool, then the best is yet to come'.[31]

In March 2007, just as the housing bubble reached its peak, he asserted confidently that 'Nothing exciting is in prospect for the market over the next two or three years, but nothing dangerous is in prospect either'.[32] Later that month, he wrote that 'some commentators on the property market ... are predicting the downfall of the market, the collapse of the economy and the sky falling on our heads', but those people are 'talking nonsense', and 'dangerous nonsense at that': 'Doom merchants and indulgent parents are bad for the market'. He didn't like those 'irrational predictions of doom' because 'the market is correcting, not collapsing' and in any case we should not worry because there is only a 'modest amount of overvaluation in the market' and 'the safety nets for house price levels in 2008 are effectively already in place'.[33]

A number of his articles over the years reinforced the notion that house prices were set to climb higher or, at worst, would gently stabilize in a 'soft landing', such as those entitled 'Housing demand set to stay strong', 'Risk from collapse in house prices "has receded"', and 'House prices "set for soft landing"'. Another piece, entitled '"Ryanair" effect adds to confidence in housing market', stated that the 'Irish housing market will experience another strong year, due in part to Ryanair [an Irish airline] making Ireland a more accessible place to work, according to Irish Intercontinental Bank (IIB) chief economist Austin Hughes'. Another entertaining thesis was presented in an article entitled 'Legalisation of contraception a "major factor" in house price rise', reporting on a study entitled 'Condoms and house prices' by Alan Ahearne of NUI Galway and Robert Martin of the US Federal Reserve Board. Another piece, entitled 'Economists forecast 15 more years of strong growth', stated that as a result of population growth, 'the number of houses is expected to continue growing by around 65,000 units a year until at least 2020'. Later, a story entitled 'Housing market set for "soft landing"' reassured readers that 'Negative equity is here – but only for a tiny percentage of the market'. In October 2008, he attacked those who suffer from 'illiterate panic-mongering' and talk down the property market and who 'with no quantitative discipline to back their statements, tell us that house prices are going to fall by another 40 per cent'.[34]

Coleman's book was published in November 2007. It presents a very optimistic picture of the Irish economy, which he saw as merely 'pausing for breath', in other words: 'Ireland's economic miracle is far from over. As anxiety mounts about the end of Ireland's boom, *The Best is Yet to Come* argues that Ireland is not experiencing the beginning of the end, but rather the end of the beginning', as stated on the book's back cover.[35]

Television is not the focus of this book, but it is interesting to see that it followed the same pattern as the print press. During the boom, RTÉ sustained the national obsession with houses by presenting programmes like *House Hunters in the Sun*, *Showhouse*, *About the House* and *I'm an Adult, Get Me Out of Here*. Leading current affairs programmes like *Prime Time* also sustained the housing bubble. Between 2000 and 2007, there have been a total of 717 shows aired, according to RTÉ's website.[36] Of those, only ten, or about 1 per cent of the total, had a segment concerned with the housing boom. These presented a total of 26 guests or interviewees: 11 came from the property or financial sectors (banking, insurance or stockbrokers); four were politicians from Ireland's main political parties (Fianna Fáil, Fine Gael and Labour); four were journalists; four were academics or researchers; and three were economic consultants. With respect to their views on the housing boom, only two (David McWilliams and Morgan Kelly) stated clearly that there was indeed a bubble and that it would burst. The 24 others remained either vague or argued explicitly that the housing market was and would remain strong in the years to come, or that a soft landing was to be expected if the boom decelerated at some point.

For example, economic consultant Peter Bacon said that the 'housing market is well underpinned by demographics' (27 August 2003). Fianna Fáil politician Seán Fleming declared that 'definitely, the house market is going to be very strong in Ireland for the years to come' because of 'growing population' and because 'incomes are strong' (12 April 2006). On the same show, Shane Daly (of real estate company Gunne New Homes) said that 'people exaggerate often the level of debt that people are getting into'. A few months later, on 18 October 2006, Marian Finnegan (of real estate company Sherry Fitzgerald) said that 'we are looking at a soft landing'. As late as 6 June 2007, Eunan King (of NCB Stockbrokers) stated that there would not be a crash. When asked whether Ireland was over-dependent on property and construction, he said: 'We're not, because we're a very young population, we're growing employment at a tremendous rate. We need a lot of office space for that. We need a lot of accommodation for our young population, and that's an influence that's going to continue for most of the next ten years ... There isn't a crisis'. It was only in April 2008 that *Prime Time* seemed to acknowledge as fact the sharp drop in house prices.[37]

In April 2007, RTÉ aired a one-hour programme entitled *Future Shock: Property Crash*, which outlined some of the possible dangers of a drop in house prices. Even though it came several years after *The Economist* had clearly presented the fact that Ireland was in a housing bubble, it still generated vigorous counterattacks in the Irish media. Prime Minister Bertie Ahearn denounced its maker, Richard Curran, as 'irresponsible' on the radio. The Construction Industry Federation, representing Ireland's builders, said that the programme was politically motivated.[38] Clíodhna O'Donoghue, the *Irish Independent*'s property editor, wrote that 'Future Shock was very much a shock tactics programme and many within the property and construction industry have already labelled it irresponsible, partly inaccurate and wholly sensationalist ... the programme still did much damage to market confidence'. Marc Coleman asked, 'why does RTÉ want to run down our economy?' by presenting the programme by Curran, who is a 'careless talker'. It is true that the programme offered a more critical perspective than much of the previous news coverage. However, when one considers that it aired just as the housing bubble started deflating, it cannot be considered to be a demonstration that the media offered clear warnings of a bubble that had been growing for over a decade.[39]

In sum, the media strongly supported the housing bubble, even after it started deflating. A similar pattern of acquiescence toward government policy will be illustrated in the following chapters, which discuss the policy response to the crisis.

Notes

1 K. O'Connor, 'Why the Baby-in-the-buggy Factor makes Property Best Bet Long-term', *IT*, 22 November 2007.
2 M. Coleman, 'We Need these Expert Scaremongers', *SI*, 23 September 2007.
3 P. Honohan and B. Walsh, 'Catching-up with the Leaders: The Irish Hare', *Brookings Papers on Economic Activity*, 2002, vol. 1, pp. 1–79, researchrepository.ucd.ie/bit stream/handle/10197/1596/walshb_article_pub_012.pdf?sequence=3 (accessed 10 December 2013); C. Ó Gráda and K.H. O'Rourke, 'Irish Economic Growth Since 1945', in N.F.R. Crafts and G. Toniolo (eds) *European Economic Growth*, Cambridge: Cambridge University Press, 1996, pp. 388–426.; S. Ó Riain, *The Politics of High Tech Growth: Developmental Network States in the Global Economy*, Cambridge: Cambridge University Press, 2004; *The Rise and Fall of Ireland's Celtic Tiger: Liberalism, Boom and Bust*, Cambridge: Cambridge University Press, 2013; K. Allen, *Ireland's Economic Crash: A Radical Agenda for Change*, Dublin: Liffey Press, 2009, pp. 31–34; D. Finn, 'Ireland on the Turn? Political and Economic Consequences of the Crash', *New Left Review*, 2011, vol. 67, pp. 5–39; D. O'Hearn, 'Macroeconomic Policy in the Celtic Tiger: A Critical Assessment', in C. Coulter and S. Coleman (eds) *The End of Irish History? Critical Reflections on the Celtic Tiger*, Manchester: Manchester University Press, 2003, p. 37.
4 P. Honohan, 'The Irish Banking Crisis: Regulatory and Financial Stability Policy 2003–8. A Report to the Minister for Finance by the Governor of the Central Bank', 2010, pp. 24, 30–31, www.bankinginquiry.gov.ie (accessed 27 December 2012); P. Nyberg, 'Misjudging Risk: Causes of the Systemic Banking Crisis in Ireland: Report of the Commission of Investigation into the Banking Sector in Ireland', 2011, p. 20, www.bankinginquiry.gov.ie/ (accessed 22 February 2013); M. Kelly, 'Whatever Happened to Ireland?' Discussion Paper No. 7811, London: Centre for Economic Policy Research, May 2010, p. 4; Central Bank of Ireland, 'Section 2: The Irish Housing Market: Fundamental and Non-fundamental Influences', Financial Stability Report, 2004, p. 65, cb3.weblink.ie/data/FinStaRepFiles/ The%20Irish%20Housing%20Market%20-%20Fundamental%20and%20Non-Fund amental%20Influences%20.PDF (accessed 9 December 2013); D. Coates and M. Everett, 'Profiling the Cross-border Funding of Irish Banking System', Economic Letter Series, vol. 2013, no. 4, Central Bank of Ireland, www.centralbank.ie/publ ications/Documents/Economic_Letter_2013_V4.pdf (accessed 25 January 2014).
5 Nyberg, 'Misjudging Risk', p. 21; Honohan, 'The Irish Banking Crisis', pp. 25–27.
6 Nyberg, 'Misjudging Risk', pp. 12–16; Kitchin *et al.*, 'Placing Neoliberalism: The Rise and Fall of Ireland's Celtic Tiger', *Environment and Planning A*, 2012, vol. 44, p. 1308.
7 F. O'Toole, *Ship of Fools: How Stupidity and Corruption Sank the Celtic Tiger*, London: Faber and Faber, 2009, p. 120; the Mahon Tribunal's final report (March 2012), www.planningtribunal.ie (accessed 25 August 2013).
8 Kelly, 'Whatever Happened to Ireland?' p. 3.
9 D. Baker, *Plunder and Blunder: The Rise and Fall of the Bubble Economy*, Sausalito, CA: PoliPointPress, 2009; K. Case and R. Shiller, 'Is there a Bubble in the Housing Market?' *Brookings Papers on Economic Activity*, 2003, vol. 2, pp. 301–62; 'Castles in Hot Air', *The Economist*, 31 May 2003, www.economist.com/node/1794899 (accessed 8 July 2013).

10 'Special Report: Going through the Roof – House Prices', *The Economist*, 30 March 2002, www.economist.com/node/1057057 (accessed 8 July 2013); 'Castles in Hot Air', *The Economist*; 'In Come the Waves', *The Economist*, 16 June 2005, www.economist.com/node/1794899 (accessed 8 July 2013).

11 D. McWilliams, 'Irish Economy Mirrors Asia's before the Bust', *IT*, 16 January 1998.

12 M. Kelly, 'On the Likely Extent of Falls in Irish House Prices', UCD Centre of Economic Research Working Paper series, WP07/01, February 2007, p. 1, figure 4, www.ucd.ie/economics/research/papers/2007/WP07.01.pdf (accessed 9 December 2013); M. Kelly, 'How the Housing Corner Stones of Our Economy could Go into a Rapid Freefall', *IT*, 28 December 2006.

13 Nyberg, 'Misjudging Risk', p. iii.

14 The data were obtained from the *Nexis* and *NewsBank* databases. Note that although the trend showed by the two charts is the same, the absolute number of articles is not directly comparable. This is because the *Irish Times* is only published six days per week whereas the *Irish Independent/Sunday Independent* are published seven days per week (thus inflating their numbers relative to the *Irish Times*). Also, the two charts are not derived from the same databases: Figure 3.1 is from *Nexis* (which offered the best coverage of the *Irish Times*) and Figure 3.2 from *NewsBank* (which covered the *Irish Independent/Sunday Independent* back to 1999). The two databases nevertheless give similar results.

15 More precisely, for the *Irish Times*, a search was performed in *Nexis* for articles published from 1995 to 2011 including 'Europe' or 'Ireland' as index terms and containing three or more occurrences of 'housing bubble', 'property bubble' or 'real estate bubble'. For the *Independent/Sunday Independent*, a search was performed in *NewsBank* for articles published from 1999 to 2011 the lead/first paragraph of which included 'housing bubble', 'property bubble' or 'real estate bubble', together with 'Ireland' or 'Irish' anywhere in the article. Multiple variations of those two searches were performed and the results were always essentially the same as those presented in Figures 3.1 and 3.2. The *Sunday Business Post* was excluded because it only goes back to 2007 on *Nexis* and no other database that contains it could be found. The *Sunday Times* was also excluded because it is often impossible to identify its Irish edition on *Nexis*. There is no reason to believe that those two newspapers would have revealed different trends in media coverage.

16 The starting year of 1999 for the *Irish Independent/Sunday Independent* was determined by the fact that this was the earliest year covered by the *NewsBank* database. The starting year of 1996 for the *Irish Times* was chosen because this was the first year when the newspaper began talking about the bubble.

17 O. O'Connor, 'Irish Property Market has Strong Foundations', *IT*, 29 October 1999; J. Suiter, 'Study Refutes Any House Price "Bubble"', 18 November 1999; C. Johns, 'Bricks and Mortar Unlikely to Lose their Value', *IT*, 11 December 2002; E. O'Carroll, 'Prices to Rise as Equilibrium is Miles Away', *IT*, 18 March 2004; M. Coleman, 'House Prices "Set for Soft Landing"', *IT*, 22 November 2005; U. McCaffrey, 'Property Market Unlikely to Collapse, says Danske Chief', 2 February 2006; D. Coyle, 'House Prices Rising at Triple Last Year's Rate', *IT*, 29 June 2006.

18 D. Murphy, 'NCB Rejects House Value Threat from Burst Bubble', *II*, 11 February 1999; C. Power, 'Property "Bubble" is Not Yet Ready to Burst', *II*, 23 April 2003; 'The Property Bubble Never Looked like Bursting in County Roscommon', *II*, 16 May 2003; S. Dodd, 'House Prices Not About to Fall Soon, Insist Auctioneers', *II*, 1 June 2003; J. O'Keeffe, 'Dire Predictions of Collapse in Value of Homes Dismissed', *II*, 5 October 2003; P. Boyle and B. Keenan, 'Price of Houses "Not Overvalued" Says New Report', *II*, 19 December 2003; 'There is No Property Bubble to Burst, Despite Doomsayers', *II*, 27 June 2005; B. Tyson, 'Influx of Workers Gives Big Boost to Property', *II*, 25 January 2006; C. O'Donoghue, 'Property "Bubble" could Continue Expanding', *II*, 10 February 2006.

19 M. Carragher, 'There's a Billion Reasons to Buy', *SI*, 5 November 2006.
20 K. Bielenberg, 'The Irish Buy-aspora', *II*, 9 September 2006, www.independent.ie/opinion/analysis/the-irish-buyaspora-26364012.html (accessed 2 July 2013).
21 McWilliams, 'Irish Economy Mirrors Asia's before the Bust'; M. Kelly, 'How the Housing Corner Stones of Our Economy could Go into a Rapid Freefall'; 'Banking on Very Shaky Foundations', *IT*, 7 September 2007. Data on article numbers on the economy obtained from the *Nexis* database.
22 C. Taylor, 'IMF Points to "Significant Risk" of Overvaluation on House Prices: The Irish Property Market May be in "Bubble Territory". Or Then Again Maybe it's Not. Even the IMF Can't Make Up its Mind', *IT*, 7 August 2003.
23 D. Brawn, *Ireland's House Party: What the Estate Agents don't Want you to Know*, Dublin: Gill and Macmillan, 2009, ch. 29.
24 'Focus on Prime Locations and Bargains', *IT*, 28 November 2007.
25 '2007: The Property Pundits Predict', *IT*, 7 December 2006.
26 J. Suiter, 'Study Refutes any House Price "Bubble"', *IT*, 18 November 1999.
27 K. MacDonald, 'Property Market's No House of Cards', *SI*, 25 March 2007.
28 'Second-hand House Prices Fell 6.8% Last Year', *IE*, 3 January 2008; 'Buyers Reclaim the Market', *SBP*, 17 February 2008; B. O'Connor, 'The Smart, Ballsy Guys are Buying Up Property Right Now', *II*, 29 July 2007; K. O'Connor, 'Why the Baby-in-the-buggy Factor makes Property Best Bet Long-term', *IT*, 22 November 2007; The *Prime Time* segment with Morgan Kelly is www.youtube.com/watch?v=Gd6ZwqLePC0 (accessed 2 September 2013).
29 K. O'Connor, 'Bargains Out there for Shrewd Investors', *IT*, 24 January 2008; I. Morton, 'Talking Property', *IT*, 24 April 2008; D. McConnell, 'More House Price Falls before Recovery Comes', *SI*, 20 April 2008.
30 M. Coleman, *The Best is Yet to Come*, Blackrock: Blackhall Publishing, 2007.
31 M. Coleman, 'We Need these Expert Scaremongers', *SI*, 23 September 2007.
32 M. Coleman, 'Market View', *IT*, 1 March 2007.
33 M. Coleman, 'Market View', *IT*, 15 March 2007.
34 M. Coleman, 'Housing Demand Set to Stay Strong', *IT*, 28 September 2005; 'Risk from Collapse in House Prices "has Receded"', *IT*, 2 November 2005; 'House Prices "Set for Soft Landing"', *IT*, 22 November 2005; '"Ryanair" Effect Adds to Confidence in Housing Market', *IT*, 25 January 2006; 'Legalisation of Contraception a "Major Factor" in House Price Rise', *IT*, 1 May 2006; 'Economists Forecast 15 More Years of Strong Growth', *IT*, 23 March 2006; 'Housing Market Set for "Soft Landing"', *IT*, 28 February 2007; 'Market View', *IT*, 14 June 2007; 'Let's Fight the Battle Closest to Home', *SI*, 12 October 2008.
35 Coleman, *The Best is Yet to Come*, pp. 50–51.
36 *Prime Time* has played twice a week since 1992. Each 40-minute programme is dedicated to in-depth investigations of selected subjects. The analysis here covers the period 2000–7 and includes *Prime Time* and *Prime Time Investigates* (a spinoff show playing a few episodes throughout the year). The programmes can be watched www.rte.ie/news/player/prime-time/ (accessed 2 June 2013).
37 Quoted in Brawn, *Ireland's House Party*, p. 308.
38 S. Ross, *The Bankers: How the Banks brought Ireland to its Knees*, London: Penguin, 2009, p. 160.
39 C. O'Donoghue, 'Future Shock – Property Crash – the Reaction', *II*, 20 April 2007; Coleman, 'We Need these Expert Scaremongers'; *Future Shock: Property Crash* can be watched www.youtube.com/watch?v=ZOE43_YnlOQ (accessed 2 June 2013).

4   Saving the banks

> The primary interest for the government to take into account is that of Ireland Inc.
>
> (Richard Curran, *Sunday Business Post*, 30 November 2008[1])

The collapse of the housing bubble and associated economic downturn put overextended banks into serious difficulty. There were a number of ways in which the Irish government could have dealt with the banking crisis in 2008 and 2009, with varying degrees of fairness in the distribution of costs between the public and financial institutions. However, the chosen strategy turned out to be perhaps Europe's most generous one for the banks. Those two years were 'a time when the controlling forces within Irish society revealed themselves in a way that had not been seen for decades', as Conor McCabe put it in his historical account of the period.[2] The government's reaction was not a mistake, or a series of irrational moves, or symptomatic of a lack of leadership. On the contrary, from the perspective of financial interests, it was a very rational response. The corporate sector supported the socialization of private losses through the bank guarantee, bank recapitalizations, and the establishment of the 'bad bank', NAMA (National Asset Management Agency), in contrast to the majority of the population, which wanted the financial sector to be treated more harshly and more cost-effectively. The media largely supported the government and business agenda, endorsing the guarantee, recapitalization with few strings attached, and NAMA. On the other hand, the press gave relatively limited support to Scandinavian-style nationalization, which would have been fairer than the government plan. Likewise, the establishment of a 'good bank', which would have been an even fairer strategy, received little attention in the news, usually to discredit it.

On 30 September 2008, the Irish state guaranteed all liabilities (except shareholders' equity) of the six largest Irish banks. The guarantee included all deposits (retail, commercial, interbank and institutional), senior debt, dated subordinated debt and covered bonds. It applied to all existing liabilities and those that were to be issued after the guarantee was announced and thus made Irish taxpayers responsible for €365 billion of liabilities, almost 2.5 times the country's GNP. However, the guarantee did not stabilize the financial sector, as the government had hoped. The latter thus orchestrated successive bank recapitalizations and nationalizations, and by 2011 had taken control of five of the six Irish banks. The accepted figure for the direct cost of the bailout is €64 billion, but this does not even include the contingent liabilities associated with NAMA, set up by the government to buy financial institutions' toxic loans. It is not clear whether NAMA will break even, make a profit, or incur losses on those loans, but the exchequer is liable for any future shortfalls.

The IMF conducted a survey of 147 banking crises between 1970 to 2011 and found that Ireland's response to the crisis has been a complete failure. It concluded that the country has had 'the costliest banking crisis in advanced economies since at least the Great Depression [of the 1930s]. And the crisis in Ireland is still ongoing'.[3] The banking rescue has been the most costly in Europe, according to a number of measures. For example, Ireland has incurred the highest absolute fiscal cost on the continent, €41 billion, for bailing out its banks. As a proportion of GDP, the country is still further ahead, at a cost of 25 per cent of GDP (see Figure 4.1). Finally, Ireland is also number one in Europe in terms of costs per capita, at almost €9,000, compared to a relatively low average throughout the EU of €192 (Figure 4.2). Moreover, importantly, those figures do not even include the €20.7 billion taken from

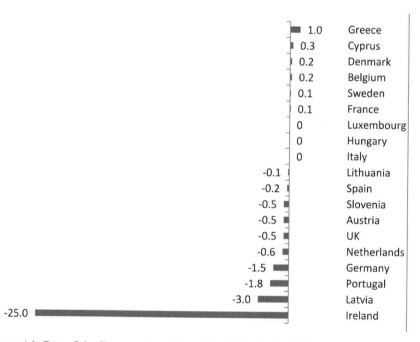

1.0	Greece
0.3	Cyprus
0.2	Denmark
0.2	Belgium
0.1	Sweden
0.1	France
0	Luxembourg
0	Hungary
0	Italy
-0.1	Lithuania
-0.2	Spain
-0.5	Slovenia
-0.5	Austria
-0.5	UK
-0.6	Netherlands
-1.5	Germany
-1.8	Portugal
-3.0	Latvia
-25.0	Ireland

Figure 4.1 Cost of the European banking crisis, 2007–11 (% of GDP)
Source: M. Taft, Unite's Notes on the Front, 15 January 2013, notesonthefront.type pad.com

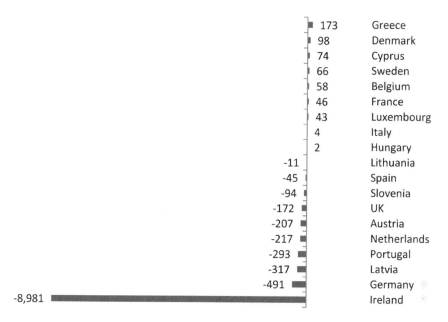

173	Greece
98	Denmark
74	Cyprus
66	Sweden
58	Belgium
46	France
43	Luxembourg
4	Italy
2	Hungary
-11	Lithuania
-45	Spain
-94	Slovenia
-172	UK
-207	Austria
-217	Netherlands
-293	Portugal
-317	Latvia
-491	Germany
-8,981	Ireland

Figure 4.2 Cost of the European banking crisis per capita, 2007–11 (€)
Source: M. Taft, Unite's Notes on the Front, 15 January 2013, notesonthefront.type
pad.com

Ireland's pension reserve (see below) to recapitalize banks. As economist Michael Taft concluded, 'Ireland may not win football's European Championship but when it comes to banking debt we are Barcelona, Bayern Munich and Manchester United all rolled into one with Real Madrid for a bench'.[4]

The bank bailout has had several consequences. First, it has increased public debt. By pushing the private debts of the financial industry onto the government's balance sheet, it eventually forced the state to accept an EU-IMF bailout in November 2010, which will be discussed in the next chapter. In 2007, just before the crisis erupted, Irish sovereign debt amounted to about a quarter of GDP, or €47 billion. This was lower than Germany's debt, which amounted to about two-thirds of its GDP. Following the bank bailout, the debt surged to 117 per cent of GDP, or €192 billion, by 2012. This principal carries heavy interest payments, which amounted to €6.1 billion in 2012, or 3.7 per cent of GDP.[5] Not all of this debt is a result of the bank bailout, but the latter accounts for at least 20 per cent of the total stock of outstanding government debt. The recession and collapse of the housing bubble that have reduced government revenues are also important factors behind the debt increase.

Second, government reserve funds that had been allocated to pay for future pensions have dried up, having been used to support the banks. Almost €20.7 billion was taken from the National Pension Reserve Fund (NPRF) to buy shares in AIB and Bank of Ireland, but after they were purchased, their values dropped significantly. Karl Whelan estimated that total losses incurred by the government in buying bank shares to recapitalize the financial system will amount to about €17 billion, or 10 per cent of GDP, involving a large loss of funds that should have been used to pay for pensions.[6]

A third consequence is that NAMA has resulted in maintaining the dependence of the Irish state on the property market and developers. Through NAMA, the Irish state paid €31.6 billion for loans with a nominal value of €74 billion. In order to recoup that money from developers who had received the loans, the government has cooperated with them. This has led to a 'strange alliance between NAMA and some of the developers', which has unfolded in a variety of ways. For example, NAMA decided to provide €3.5 billion to developers through generous loan facilities to bring some of their projects to completion. Also, 66 developers have been paid salaries exceeding €100,000 a year to work with NAMA, while 41 debtors received over €1 million each on average in 'overhead costs' for renovating or improving their properties. Finally, rent collection from developers' properties has been very flexible. NAMA properties in Ireland generate €9 million in rent every month, but these revenues are not automatically appropriated to pay off the loans held by NAMA. Instead, developers appear to be able to keep a significant amount for repairing and maintaining their properties.[7]

As will be seen below, European authorities endorsed the Irish strategy. Much has been made in the media of the annoyance of European officials at the Irish decision to offer a blanket guarantee to all domestic banks without much consultation with other countries. For example, Christine Lagarde, the then French finance minister, reportedly exclaimed 'Oh my God' when told about the guarantee, and her British counterpart was supposedly alarmed as well.[8] However, the Irish scheme could not have been implemented without the sanction of European authorities. Indeed, three days after the Irish government announced the guarantee, the ECB specified that it 'expects to be consulted on any proposed implementing legislation … that materially influences the stability of financial institutions and markets' and that such legislation must 'fully comply with the relevant provisions of Community law', while it was also assumed that the European 'Commission's opinion will be appropriately taken into account and reflected' in such legislation. Throughout the bank bailout, the ECB and European Commission issued 'opinions' and statements effectively giving their approval and recommendations to the Irish government as it enacted various pieces of legislation to support the banks.[9] It is thus not surprising that a large portion of the costs of bank rescues in 2008–9 in Europe have been shouldered by the public. This has been particularly true in Ireland. As the Honohan report noted, the policy of 'no failure' for Irish banks 'took the question of optimal loss-sharing off the table. In contrast to most of the interventions by other countries … the blanket cover offered by the Irish guarantee pre-judged that all losses in any bank becoming insolvent during the guarantee period – beyond those absorbed by some of the providers of capital – would fall on the State'.[10]

What follows first reviews three main approaches for handling banking crises: (1) the 'bad bank' proposal; (2) nationalization; and (3) the 'good bank' proposal. The first shifts the burden of adjustment on the state and the last is the most favourable to taxpayers, with nationalization somewhere in between, although a lot depends on the specific ways in which the proposals are implemented. For clarity, the three alternatives are described below as separate and ideal types, but in practice, variations and combinations of the schemes have been implemented. In particular, all schemes normally involve the state recapitalizing the banks, and the more stringent the conditions attached to this funding are, the fairer the deal is for taxpayers. The discussion thus contextualizes the decisions taken in Ireland, which favoured the bad bank strategy, recapitalization and nationalization, but with few strings attached. The media largely supported government policy.

Bad bank

This is what the Irish government did by establishing NAMA. In this proposal, the state sets up a bad bank into which the bad assets of banks in trouble are transferred. The rationale is that institutions facing difficulties, now cleansed of their toxic assets, will be able to resume their normal operations and lend again to the domestic economy, providing it with the credit needed. The bad bank is owned and funded by the government. The state purchases banks' toxic assets and then manages them in the bad bank, either by selling them on the market at the best possible price or by holding them to maturity. The idea is that by buying those assets from the banks, the latter will be recapitalized and free of non-performing assets.

However, one obvious problem is to set the price paid by the government for the assets. If it buys them at their current market price, which will be significantly lower than their face value (since they are performing poorly), the banks will not receive enough capital to return to solvency. They will merely receive the small amount of cash that their assets are actually worth, which was the problem in the first place. It would amount to substituting one type of asset (cash from the government) for another (bad loans). On the other hand, if the government purchases the toxic assets well above their market price, this will meet the banks' needs for capital, but will constitute a bad deal for the taxpayer, now stuck with bad assets for which the state overpaid. Therefore, valuing and buying toxic assets to transfer them into a bad bank is in effect a lose-lose situation for the state, as noted by a number of analysts (see below).

Setting up the kind of bad bank described here is a way for the state to channel funds to the banks to recapitalize them, in return for toxic assets. If the state overpays for the toxic assets, say by €10 billion, the banks effectively receive funds of €10 billion at taxpayers' expense. Alternatively, if the state purchases the toxic assets at their market price, this must be followed by a straight recapitalization of €10 billion to reach the same outcome on the banks' balance sheet. In fact, if the government's goal is to recapitalize the banks by €10 billion, it would be more efficient not to set up a bad bank and simply give the €10 billion to the banks, avoiding all the pricing issues involved and the management of the toxic assets over a number of years.

What happened in the United States provides a concrete illustration. In 2008, US Treasury Secretary Henry Paulson's goal was to provide money to the banks in trouble as quickly as possible and with as few conditions as possible through the TARP (Troubled Assets Relief Program). Paulson's initial strategy was to ask Congress to give $700 billion to the Treasury which would then buy toxic assets from the banks. The banks faced acute difficulties because they held many mortgage-backed securities that were going bad rapidly, implying that much of their capital would be wiped out. Paulson's initial plan would have had the government purchase a large portion of such bad assets from the banks, cleansing their balance sheets and allowing them to resume lending. However, buying the toxic assets at market price would only have changed the type of assets held by the banks without providing them with the extra funds they needed. In order to do this, the state would have had to buy the assets at above their market price, with all the inefficiencies that this involves. As Dean Baker noted, it would have made more sense to give the capital needed to the institutions directly, and attach strict conditions to such support, like an ownership stake in the banks. In fact, this is the path that Paulson ended up following after Congress rebuffed his initial plan. When Paulson began to spend the TARP funds, he gave capital directly to the banks, and his plans to purchase the banks' toxic assets were placed on hold indefinitely. In Ireland, however, the government's strategy of buying toxic assets from banks and putting them into a bad bank was implemented.[11]

Nationalization

Nationalization, whereby the state takes control of banks in difficulty, can set the stage for exacting strict conditions on them. The idea is that if the government is to assume responsibility for a bank's assets and liabilities and recapitalize it, it may as well receive an ownership stake in the firm and remodel its operations. For example, the top management can be sacked with no 'golden parachutes' and replaced with newly appointed officials; fees can be charged to the banks to be paid to the state; executives' salaries can be axed; more stringent regulations can be put in place on operations; banks can be obligated to follow specific policies, such as reaching agreements with individuals in arrears over their mortgage payments, stopping home repossessions, increasing lending to the domestic economy, and so on. The effectiveness and stringency of such conditions depend on their details and the capacity and willingness of elected officials to pressurize banks to abide by their obligations. In Ireland, very few strict conditions were attached to the banks' rescue.

The benefits of nationalization for the public also depend on a number of other issues. First, the state may or may not force bank shareholders and creditors to be wiped out or absorb significant losses before the government invests funds in the institutions. Second, the state may or may not direct bank operations towards socially productive ends. Third, a key advantage of nationalization is that once the economy recovers, the state's shares in the banks rise in value. If they are sold back to the private sector at an opportune moment, the state can recoup much of the costs it incurred in the bailout, and may even generate a profit.

One example of nationalization which has received much attention before and during the current global crisis, in Ireland and elsewhere, is that of Scandinavia in the early 1990s. Nordic countries then faced a financial crisis during which their governments intervened to rescue the banks. In the 1980s, Sweden, Finland and Norway all deregulated their financial systems and suffered booms in asset prices that ended in a bust. The scale of the turbulence was comparable in all three countries and the state intervened heavily in each one of them. Finland's five largest banks, Norway's four largest banks, and three main banks in Sweden received capital support from the government, while other institutions received private capital support from their owners.

There were similarities and differences in the details of the respective national rescue plans. Banks were not liquidated in any of the three countries, except for two small ones in Norway. However, government take-overs were common and the largest one was executed by the Norwegian government, which took control of the three biggest commercial banks. In general, all three countries responded rapidly to the crisis and did so in a transparent fashion, while state support for banks had relatively severe conditions attached. In all countries, the banks' boards and top management were largely replaced. The consequences for banks' shareholders, creditors and leadership varied, but in general, were all punitive. In Norway, share capital was written down to zero before the government moved to take control of the banks. In Sweden and Finland, depending on the institution, private shareholders either suffered no losses, got wiped out completely, or absorbed some losses without losing everything. Significantly, creditors did not lose anything in Sweden and Finland thanks to the blanket guarantee put in place in those countries. With one small exception, creditors in Norway suffered no losses either.[12]

Finland and Sweden issued blanket guarantees that covered all liabilities except equity, but Norway did not. All three countries' central banks provided liquidity to domestic banks. Finland and Sweden set up bad banks that managed toxic assets to enable the healthy parts of the firms in trouble to continue their normal operations while the bad banks worked on recovering as much value as possible from the non-performing assets. Norway did not use this approach, but similar structures were set up within some of the core banks. The reasons why Norway did not set up a bad bank included the fact that it would have had to be financed by the state, which could potentially have absorbed further losses. Also, it was thought that the responsibility of handling the non-performing loans should remain with the banks, since they had the most to gain from successful management of the toxic loans.[13]

The Swedish model has been held by some as a template to address the current European and Irish crises.[14] Sweden's financial system was heavily regulated for many years after World War II. Insurance companies and banks faced lending ceilings and had to follow placement requirements constraining them to invest in bonds issued by mortgage institutions and the government. However, starting in the 1980s, deregulation altered those prudent guidelines. Liquidity ratios were abolished, interest ceilings were raised, and banks' lending limits and insurance companies' placement requirements were abandoned. Competition set in and new lending increased significantly, while all actors raised the level of risk involved in their operations. This fed an asset price boom, in the real estate market in particular. Eventually, the real estate bubble collapsed and the Swedish economy was subjected to a significant increase in interest rates. The crisis rapidly spread to the banks, which incurred rising losses.

Starting in 1992, the crisis was dealt with as a systemic one. The Swedish government extended a blanket guarantee (except equity) to all banks, which was maintained until 1996. The banks were divided into three categories. The first included those whose situation might deteriorate but which would eventually be able to remain solvent on their own. The second included those that were in more serious difficulty but would also still recover eventually. The third was for those beyond hope. Category 1 banks were encouraged to find private solutions to their problems. For instance, shareholders were asked to inject additional capital if possible. Category 2 banks could receive some state support, such as capital contributions or loans, in order to restore solvency. Category 3 banks required extensive state involvement. For example, the state took over Nordbanken, a major insolvent bank, and created a bad bank capitalized by the government called Securum into which Nordbanken's bad assets were transferred. Securum was charged with liquidating the toxic assets it had received. The rescue was expensive, but by and large, the state 'followed the principle of saving the banks but not the owners of the banks', even though the bank guarantee, indirectly, saved one or more banks and hence a part of shareholders' wealth as well.[15] However, there are other features of the Swedish rescue that undermine assessments which paint it as a strategy protecting the taxpayer. For example, although shareholders incurred losses, a general principle 'was that no bank creditors, including holders of subordinated debt, were allowed to suffer losses'. Moreover, 'owners of a failing bank were also to some extent compensated. The owners of Första Sparbanken – a foundation – received an interest subsidy of SEK 1 billion. The private minority owners of *Nordbanken* were paid SEK 21 per share in the summer of 1992 when the market price was only SEK 18. The value of this subsidy amounts to SEK 300 million'. The government later tried to persuade Första Sparbanken to pay back the subsidy it had received, without success.[16]

Although there are a number of variables and methods to calculate the costs incurred by the state to rescue banking systems, there is a consensus that the costs that the Scandinavian bailouts entailed, although significant, were low compared with many other countries that have faced similar crises.

Estimated costs were significantly higher in Finland, while Norway's rescue was the cheapest. It has been estimated that gross fiscal costs amounted to 8.9 per cent of GDP in Finland, 3.6 per cent of GDP in Sweden and 2.0 per cent of GDP in Norway. However, once the economy and the banking system recovered, the shares held by the state rose in value, which constitutes a form of payback for the government. Taking this and other factors into consideration, the net costs attached to the crisis have been estimated at 5.2 per cent of GDP in Finland, 0.2 per cent of GDP in Sweden and about 0.0 per cent of GDP in Norway, which clearly shows the financial advantage for the state to own shares, if the operation is well executed.[17]

It is difficult to disentangle the precise reasons explaining the differences in costs, although they could be accounted for by the nature of the respective rescue operations, such as the fact that Norway did not use a bad bank or a blanket guarantee. Another important factor accounting for the relatively successful recovery in all three countries is the devaluation of their currencies in 1992 (they had until then been pegged to baskets of currencies). The ensuing depreciation counteracted the downturn faced by the three economies. The recovery began in 1993 and lasted for over a decade and the main engine behind it was a remarkable growth in exports. The current account surpluses, which had previously been in chronic deficit, turned to what looked like permanent surpluses. For example, between 1992 and 2008, Sweden's exports doubled as a share of GDP.[18] The parallels with and lessons for Ireland have been noted by David McWilliams, who commented that although there has been much discussion of the Scandinavian experience in Ireland, what 'most of this discussion fails to mention is that the devaluation and subsequent printing of money by … central banks did the trick'. Indeed, when the crisis struck, the orthodoxy 'was that the government must reduce spending and the hard currency link to the Deutschmark must be preserved at all costs', but this did not work, and eventually the 'governments broke their currency arrangements and reflated the economy by allowing both currencies to fall. The countries recovered quickly and again, against all conventional wisdom, the competitive edge the countries garnered endured'.[19] It is true that the Scandinavian countries benefited from the fact that the crisis from which they emerged was regional in scope with no global impact, and that the rest of the world was not in recession, which kept up demand for Nordic exports. However, this is also an argument to reflate European national economies through stimulus packages instead of fiscal consolidation. The potential benefits of leaving the eurozone for Ireland and other peripheral countries and use new, devalued national currencies will be discussed in more detail in Chapter 7.

Good bank

The good bank proposal, as presented by economist Willem Buiter and others, posits that instead of the government attempting to save banks in difficulty, it is better for the state to create one or many new 'good' banks, all initially owned and funded by the government, with the possibility of privatization at a later point in time.[20] All existing banks not viable without public support, as determined by 'stress tests' or other methods, would be classified as bad banks. The deposits and good assets of the bad banks would be acquired by the newly created good banks. All business activity, such as lending to the wider economy, would from then on be undertaken only by the new good banks. Their lending and investment could be facilitated by government guarantees or insurance. Existing assets would no longer be guaranteed, either in the new or legacy bad banks. If needed, the new banks would be capitalized by the state, or by a combination of public and private capital. The new banks could obtain more funding by issuing bonds that would be bought by the state or the private sector or through loans from the government.

The bad banks would be prevented from operating as banks, which means that they could not lend or invest, nor could they accept new deposits. This could be easily accomplished by taking away their banking licences. Their purpose would be strictly to manage the portfolio of bad assets left on their balance sheets and ultimately to run them down, either by selling them or holding them to maturity. The bad banks could continue operating with their existing ownership, but would not receive state funds or support, being left on their own. If they were able to remain solvent, their owners would benefit, but if they became insolvent, they would be subjected to the regular insolvency procedures for financial institutions. Their shareholders would be wiped out and their creditors could enter a debt-for-equity swap and absorb the losses. Many, if not all, of the creditors would remain much better off than most taxpayers, even after incurring losses on their investments in banks. If the bad banks failed, this would not be of systemic importance, just as if any other asset manager went bankrupt. When all the bad banks' assets had been sold or reached maturity, the old banks would cease to exist.

Among the assets of the bad banks that would be purchased by the new good banks would be the physical infrastructure required to run the banks, such as the branch network, offices and equipment. Also, many of the legacy banks' staff would be hired by the new banks (except for the top management). The bad banks would keep a small number of their existing staff or hire new employees to manage their bad assets. Bank customers would therefore at first only notice the name change of the bank. According to Buiter, the whole transformation could be implemented over a weekend once old banks' assets had been valued and deposits to be transferred identified. When the economy returned to normal, perhaps after a few years, the new good banks could be privatized. The government would sell its shares to private investors and thereby make a hefty profit.

From the perspective of fairness, the good bank proposal is superior to the other schemes discussed above, principally because it forces shareholders and bondholders to absorb losses and because it allows the government to take a lucrative stake in new clean banks. As such, it does not involve a transfer of wealth from the public to shareholders or creditors. One central problem in the current European crisis is that creditors, to borrow Willem Buiter's words, have become the 'sacred cows of the financial crisis'. The assumption is that 'if there is either a further default on bank debt, or a restructuring involving a significant debt-to-equity conversion, or a significant write-down of the claims of bank bond holders, this will be the end of the world'. However, if bond-holders like insurance companies and pension funds take a hit large enough to make them fail, the economy as a whole would not be affected catastrophically.[21] Moreover, a systematic IMF study of the use of blanket guarantees by governments found that such measures had virtually no effect on stemming the outflows of foreign liabilities from domestic banks. In other words, non-resident investors in banks 'continue withdrawing resources even after a guarantee is put in place'.[22]

In Ireland, the good bank proposal received support from the progressive think tank TASC, which stated that 'the fundamental principle underpinning any resolution to the banking crisis' should be that the 'public, whether Irish or Europeans, should not be obliged to pay for the private debts of the European banking system'. It added that the transfer of debts from the banks to the public has been 'amongst the largest per capita social transfers in modern economic history and is deeply inequitable'. TASC argued that non-systemic insolvent banks (Anglo Irish and INBS) should not have been supported by the state and allowed to fail. Regarding the other, systemically important banks, publicly owned and operated good banks should have been created and assumed the latter's deposits. The new good banks would also have acquired some of the good assets and the physical infrastructure of the legacy banks (such as AIB and Bank of Ireland). The legacy banks' creditors could have become, through a debt-for-equity swap, owners of the banks. Their remaining assets could have been sold off with the proceeds distributed to the creditors and bondholders. It is true that in Ireland, the good bank proposal faced one apparent complication – namely, that the blanket guarantee made the government responsible for the banks' liabilities. However, the guarantee could simply have been repudiated and replaced with a guarantee covering deposits only, as argued by TASC and others. Alternatively, the government could have paid banks' debts until the guarantee expired (originally in September 2010) without renewing it.[23]

Professor of Economics Terrence McDonough also endorsed the good bank proposal for Ireland. He reasoned that nationalizing essentially insolvent banks like Anglo Irish does not maximize returns for the government and taxpayers, although it benefits bondholders who do not incur losses. Likewise, nationalizing such banks or the whole banking system also nationalizes their obligations, with the state ending up paying the tab. He remarked, correctly, that all proposals debated in the media have had one common point: they protect bondholders. However, the good bank proposal, virtually ignored by the press, pushes losses on the bondholders. McDonough added that the proposal allows a range of outcomes as to which kind of banking system will emerge from it once the economy returns to normal. For conservatives, the banks can eventually be privatized and the state may be able to make a profit by selling its shares. For social democrats, the new banks could remain in government hands and run like utilities which would provide the basic credit infrastructure necessary in the private economy. For those who are more radical, the new banks could underpin a public development strategy.[24]

The latter alternative was advanced by Kieran Allen. He proposed that the new good bank(s) remain owned and managed by the state. The financial system would not operate primarily as a profit-making enterprise, but to meet the economy's need for credit and banking services. This would socialize credit for the benefit of society. It would imply a more tightly regulated financial system that prioritizes the allocation of credit for projects that benefit society as a whole. For example, job creation schemes and services for society at large would be prioritized over investments that are speculative or benefit mostly the wealthy. Such a nationalized banking system is often criticized as opening the door to cronyism among state officials. However, cronyism can also arise in private enterprise, as banks like Anglo Irish have demonstrated. Much would depend on the extent to which the political system is democratic and able to organize the control of financial activities in a transparent and accountable way.[25]

Finally, in 2009, Fine Gael, while not in power, proposed a good bank strategy. It will be seen below that the Irish media gave short shrift to the proposal. Richard Bruton, the party's spokesman on finance, wrote that bank losses should be 'absorbed first and foremost by those who took on the risk of funding the risky lending policies of the banks. These are not just the ordinary shareholders', but also bondholders: 'They did the lending and made the investments; they should now share in the losses'. The party proposed to create new, clean banks – which could be called 'New AIB' and 'New Bank of Ireland' – out of the banks facing difficulties. The latter 'would no longer engage in any new lending' and would manage their bad assets 'in the interest of the existing capital owners and other creditors'.[26] However, once in power, Fine Gael did not implement this scheme and proceeded to push the burden of adjustment onto ordinary people instead.

European guidelines, Irish strategy

The Irish strategy fitted within the parameters of the broad European plan of action to address the financial crisis adopted in October 2008. The plan gave guidelines to individual countries to facilitate the funding of banks and recapitalize them. It stated that the situation 'requires European Union and Euro area governments, central banks and supervisors to agree to a coordinated approach', and that governments 'remain committed to support the financial system and therefore to avoid the failure of relevant financial institutions' through recapitalization.[27] By March 2009, EU member states had earmarked a total of €2.8 trillion, equivalent to 22 per cent of the EU's GDP, toward packages to save banks. About €300 billion was made available to recapitalize them and €2.5 trillion for state guarantees of liabilities. It is clear that the European plan of action favoured saving the banks over protecting taxpayers. Indeed, a study by the Central Bank of Austria concluded that 'the European approach imposes a particularly high share of the losses on taxpayers'. In other words, 'the bank packages entail passing on the costs of overcoming the crisis to the taxpayers, while the banks' creditors are not required to make a contribution'. This could be seen when the packages were introduced: banks' credit default swap (CDS) spreads then fell significantly but the sovereign spreads of many EU countries, including Ireland, increased, which 'implies a transfer of risk from bank shareholders to taxpayers'.[28]

Ireland's state guarantee was generous when compared to that of other countries. It applied to existing and newly issued securities as well as wholesale deposits and interbank loans. Others, like Germany and Sweden, only guaranteed new issues of short-term securities but not interbank loans, while Belgium guaranteed new but not existing short-term securities and interbank loans. In fact, only Ireland's and Denmark's guarantees covered bank bonds issued before the financial rescue packages were established. Nonetheless, all EU countries implicitly protected bondholders of 'systematically important banks' as the EU determined that the latter should not be allowed to fail. Eight member states' recapitalization packages provided for the possibility of restricting dividend payments, but the Irish plan contained no such clause.[29]

When the Irish government announced it would guarantee all Irish bank liabilities, economists like Willem Buiter observed that guaranteeing 100 per cent of deposits was 'over the top'. A more modest guarantee, say of all deposits up to €100,000, would have been enough to prevent a run on the banks and the dreaded queues at their doors. Similarly, guaranteeing all bank debts is unnecessary and unfair to taxpayers. Bondholders and shareholders were seemingly unconcerned by the banks' risky property lending during the housing bubble years and benefited handsomely from their investments. It is thus legitimate for them to absorb the losses when the economic situation changes. Punishing the debt holders would act as a warning sign for others to adopt more prudent lending practices in the future. Further, stimulating lending to the wider economy should only require a government guarantee of new lending and of new liabilities, while the existing stock of liabilities should be left without guarantees. This is what other countries like Britain have done. In short, there was 'no upside for the taxpayer in this arrangement … it is a straight transfer from the Irish taxpayer and the competitors of the Irish banking system, to the shareholders and other creditors of the Irish banks'. While it is true that governments can charge fees to the banks in return for guarantees, this is a much smaller reward for the taxpayer.[30]

Nevertheless, the media endorsed the blanket guarantee with no hesitation, declaring that 'We had to act to save the entire system'. An *Irish Times* editorial stated that 'the government has acted decisively to underpin the banking system' and 'few can argue that [the guarantee] was not justified by the circumstances'. To 'support all the banks' was 'the best option as the clock ticked down to the opening of European markets and the possible collapse of an Irish bank'. Doing nothing would have resulted in 'catastrophe'. As soon as the guarantee was announced, the press pointed to signs that supposedly confirmed that it was the correct decision: 'bank shares are recovering, but more significantly the Irish banks are gaining access to credit lines' and 'Ireland has retained its AAA credit rating – the highest possible', which 'reflects the sophistication of the guarantee package' that 'may never be called upon and thus cost tax payers next to nothing'. The media often neglected to mention that both banks' deposits *and borrowings* were guaranteed by the government. In many references to the scheme, only deposits were mentioned, perhaps because it made the strategy appear less favourable to creditors and kinder toward ordinary savers. For example, an *Irish Times* article referred to the plan as the '€400 billion deposit guarantee scheme' while another described the 'government's decision to guarantee around €400 billion of savings deposits'. Ireland was very generous toward the financial sector, as no other country's bank rescue package included subordinated debt. For example, Denmark's blanket guarantee had specifically excluded it. The Danish package, unlike Ireland's, also required that the banks themselves insure their deposits, with the state intervening only if more support was needed. It also prohibited banks from paying dividends, issuing stock options to their management or buying back their shares. Those facts were virtually ignored by the Irish press.[31]

Many claims were made that the guarantee was likely to be cheap, costless, or even profitable for the government. The media announced that the guarantee was the 'cheapest bailout in the world' compared to other countries' rescue packages, according to Brian Lenihan, the minister for finance, who added: 'Look at what happened in Iceland – if we have no viable banking system in this country or we allow the banking system to fail, we won't have an economy'. It was asserted that the scheme incurred 'no cost to taxpayers' and that it 'will, in theory, see a net gain to the exchequer'. This, it was maintained, contrasted with 'the situation in Belgium, Denmark, France, Germany, Iceland, Luxembourg, the Netherlands, Britain and the US, where banks have been nationalised, either de jure or de facto, with taxpayers being handed the tab'. One columnist wrote that thankfully, the government 'made the decision promptly' to offer a blanket guarantee: 'weak or insecure leaders … might have opted for delay. Overly cautious leaders might have persuaded themselves … that they could afford to wait', but 'this would have been fatal'. In fact, 'Ireland could end up being the only country affected by this crisis which will not have had to spend public money buying a bank', and if the guarantee is not called upon, 'the Government finances will turn a substantial profit from the levy charged for the guarantee'.[32]

It was often implied that catastrophic outcomes would follow if the guarantee was not implemented. An article entitled 'Banking system on brink of "collapse"' relayed the government view that 'Ireland's banking system would have "totally collapsed" if the Government had not introduced legislation to underwrite the banks'. A *Sunday Independent* piece entitled 'We don't appreciate the massive carnage we've just survived' said that the government 'took clear, brave, decisive and seismic action' and must be congratulated for averting what 'would have been far worse for Ireland than the aftermath of 9/11 was for the US' if no action had been taken. In short: 'we had no choice, so get over it.rsquo;.[33] An editorial declared that 'Brian Cowen's [the prime minister] words bordered on the apocalyptic last week, and rightly so. Ireland faced disaster on Monday night ... It was as close to a Doomsday situation as any Irish government is likely to get, and Mr Cowen's response was a bold one ... Immediate disaster was averted and Ireland can, for the moment at least, boast the safest banking system in Europe'. An *Irish Times* article opined that 'a banking collapse was avoided' thanks to Brian Lenihan's 'decisive intervention' as 'he faced the stark choice of letting one Irish bank go down, with incalculable consequences for the entire banking industry, or implementing his guarantee scheme', although we may 'never know the scale of the potential calamity that has been avoided' if the guarantee turns out to be successful. Columnist Brendan Keenan wrote that the government guarantee decision may 'come to be admired, even copied, by others' and that 'the reaction of several reputable foreign observers' was favourable. He stated that undoubtedly, 'something had to be done' because 'the system had collapsed and some of those smaller Irish lenders – Anglo, Permanent TSB, Irish Nationwide and EBS, could have gone down with it. Indeed, all of them could have gone down with it'.[34]

The media emphasized the interests of the business sector, as in a *Sunday Business Post* article that asked: 'What should Lenihan be trying to achieve? The primary interest for the government to take into account is that of Ireland Inc. The optimum solution to the banking crisis for Ireland Inc is to plot a course which will ensure a strong banking sector that is actively lending money to consumers and businesses. A further goal is to achieve this with minimum cost and risk to the Irish taxpayer'. The priority was clear. The corporate sector immediately gave 'a broad welcome' to the guarantee. IBEC, the main Irish business group representing 7,000 companies, said it 'strongly supported the Government's "decisive move"' because 'it helped to remove the uncertainty of recent times and sent a very positive message to the domestic and international business community', adding that the 'Government has shown sound leadership'. Small and medium-sized enterprise group ISME said the government decision was a 'good move' for business. Irish bankers were pleased with the package. Sean FitzPatrick, chairman of Anglo Irish Bank, 'defended the government guarantee and said that the financial system had been days from collapse'.[35]

Likewise, endorsements from the global banking community were displayed prominently, as in an article entitled 'Bank experts heap praise on Irish solution to meltdown'. It mentioned that 'Global banking experts and international finance specialists believe that Ireland's solution could be the model for beleaguered bankers and governments around the world', and quoted a 'leading international analyst' as saying that 'the Irish government faced "total chaos" and a failure of the financial system if they hadn't moved to underwrite the banks'. Deutsche Bank described the plan as 'an elegant solution to the crisis of liquidity and confidence facing the banking system', while the Royal Bank of Scotland stated that 'Ireland has engaged in the smartest move so far by a central bank'. The Irish strategy could even 'be a template for troubled banks in other countries'. The guarantee was allegedly 'being lauded by analysts as the safest system in Europe, and possibly the world'. Even economist David McWilliams, who had warned previously about the housing bubble, praised the measures now taken, describing them as a 'wise choice' and a 'unique, Irish plan' that ensured that 'Irish banks are now safe'. He asserted that in time, the blanket guarantee would be seen as 'a masterstroke and a practical blueprint for the new financial architecture which will emerge from this global crisis'. Similarly, an opinion article in the *Irish Times* characterized the government's actions as 'brave and necessary', and declared that 'Europe should follow suit'. The article even claimed that the Irish guarantee 'is the only such initiative – right across the globe – that has demonstrably worked'. Therefore, 'Europe needs the kind of radical thinking that underpins the Irish initiative'.[36]

European authorities endorsed the Irish guarantee. The European Commission stated that it 'agrees' with the measure because it 'is apt to remedy a serious disturbance in the Irish economy'. It even cautiously supported some of the guarantee's most controversial details, such as its application to dated subordinated debt, because in 'the current exceptional circumstances, the Commission notes that the inclusion of subordinated debt into the guarantee may be necessary'.[37]

Government statements were often reported uncritically and not challenged, as when the *Irish Times* mentioned, in an article entitled 'Emergency Bill safeguards economy, says Lenihan', that the minister for finance had said that the bill's objective was 'to protect the long-term interests of the taxpayer'. Lenihan also told the parliament that the guarantee 'was not about protecting the interests of the banks but about safeguarding the economy and everyone who lived and worked in this country', adding that the guarantee 'was not "free" and taxpayers would be remunerated for the value of the support provided'. The newspaper also related without challenging it Lenihan's statement that there was 'understandable concern that the Exchequer is potentially significantly exposed by this measure. I want to reassure the House and the Irish people that this is not the case'.[38]

The media painted a positive and flattering picture of government officials' actions. It was recounted how an 'emotional' Brian Cowen, the prime minister, 'passionately defended' the blanket guarantee in the parliament. The 'decisiveness' of political leaders was deemed 'reassuring'. Analysts praised the 'innovative and timely interventions of the Department of Finance', which 'must be applauded'. The *Sunday Business Post* asserted that Brian

Cowen and Brian Lenihan 'demonstrated leadership and projected authority all week', and that 'Cowen has taken a lot of grief and abuse for his €300,000 salary over the past few months but, last week, he was earning his money'. An *Irish Times* opinion piece was effusive, asserting that the 'Government gained some credibility by the way it has handled matters since last Monday night ... the decisiveness of its response to a crisis was impressive'. Lenihan 'enhanced his reputation by deciding on a clear strategy to deal with the problem and by the calm and competent manner in which he explained it to the Dáil and the public'. Dissent would have been inappropriate: Fine Gael, the opposition party, 'put the country first' by backing the government guarantee, by which 'it has shown that it is capable of being an alternative government', while the Labour Party, which voted against the measure, was deemed 'populist'.[39]

It is significant that the decision to guarantee all bank liabilities was not democratic, taken in the utmost secrecy by a handful of officials during a nightly meeting, the details of which are still not fully known. The public's opinion was never solicited. In fact, the media seemed to equate the interests of the population with those of the bankers, so presumably there was no need to ask the Irish people what they thought. An *Irish Times* editorial that 'commended' Brian Cowen and Brian Lenihan 'for their leadership' stated that in relation to the guarantee, 'the interests of the banks' and 'the welfare of Irish workers ... were so closely entwined as to be indistinguishable'. However, a nationwide poll revealed that the population thought differently and ranked 'politicians' and 'bankers' as the professions lowest in their estimation. Only 40 per cent felt 'more confident about the future' as a result of the guarantee and 96 per cent felt that banks should make a 'full and independently verified disclosure to the Government of the exact extent of all potential losses on their loan books', while 84 per cent said that 'senior banking personnel who have indulged in reckless or irresponsible behaviour should be fired' and 91 per cent 'felt that golden handshakes for executives fired in those circumstances should be axed'.[40]

Opposition to the scheme received very limited coverage. For example, SIPTU, Ireland's largest union, stated that the guarantee amounted to a 'golden parachute' for banks, which was unfair to taxpayers. It was also hypocritical, because the plan entailed state aid for financial institutions which 'have insisted for years on a ruthless free market for everyone else, but are not able to play by the same rules themselves'. The *Irish Independent* reported these views in a 174-word article. Likewise, few commentators were fundamentally opposed to the scheme. One was Economics Professor Morgan Kelly, who described the bailout as 'the wrong solution to the wrong problem'. The problem with Irish banks, he explained, was that so many of their property loans would not be paid back by borrowers and the banks would most likely see their capital wiped out. Instead of the guarantee, he endorsed the Swedish solution, saying that the Irish government 'should have offered new capital to four of the institutions, and left the others, where the real problems lie, to fend for themselves'. He argued that the guarantee 'serves only to keep zombie banks going while starving their customers of credit; and helps nobody apart from some developers and bankers'. Such ideas contrasted with the prevailing opinion in the media, which was opposed to nationalization. An article outlined some of the reasons for keeping the banks in private hands, stating that the 'spectacle of one bank after another being nationalised, with all the messiness that such action entails, would have generated far more uncertainty than guaranteeing liabilities. That would have undermined the confidence that remains in the economy'. However, the most important 'reason to avoid nationalisation is that it is far from clear that such a step was necessary, given that the immediate crisis was one of liquidity, not solvency'. Subsequent events would show how Morgan Kelly was correct and the latter position too optimistic.[41]

While the media supported state intervention to bail out the financial sector, they distrusted intervention that would reduce the latter's freedom and prerogatives. In 2008, there were few calls for nationalizing banks. Debate was limited to discussing the terms of possible recapitalization plans, such as the fees and controlling stakes that should accrue to government if it provided banks with capital. The press warned that 'State intervention must not stifle banks' and conveyed the 'fears over excessive policing of banks' held by the Irish Association of Corporate Treasurers, whose members deal with borrowing in large Irish companies and multinationals. Their concerns included the fact that under the guarantee scheme, 'limits could be set on maximum loan-to-value ratios', which 'will end up stifling any bit of creativity in business'. The *Irish Times* editors argued that although other countries like Britain had taken direct stakes in banks, the Irish 'exchequer can ill-afford' it, even though it would be profitable in time. There was also opposition to replacing the bank managers who had led their firms into deep difficulties. John McManus, the *Irish Times* business editor, said that there was 'a need to be pragmatic' when dealing with the banks' problems and that 'the unpalatable truth is that the people who steered the banks into this mess may be the best people to get them out of it'. Indeed, 'the extent to which everybody in the State bought into the property boom makes it hard really to single out one or two individuals without making them into nothing more than scapegoats', and after all, 'we all bought into the property market story'.[42]

As if to reinforce the idea that the banks were subjected to overly restrictive government action, a number of articles conveyed the impression that the conditions attached to state support were stringent and that financial institutions were paying dearly for their excesses. A piece entitled 'Banks facing a €1bn charge and stringent controls' quoted Brian Lenihan as saying that this 'would amount to at least 10 per cent of the banks' annual profits'. An article entitled 'Clamp tightens on bankers' asserted that 'financial institutions can only look on in horror as power slips' away from them to the politicians as Brian Lenihan provided 'details of the pound of flesh he would seek in return' for the guarantee. It claimed that bank 'boardrooms will never be quite the same again' as 'many of the terms proposed by Lenihan are suitably onerous' and the 'restrictions on banks that want the guarantee are not pretty. No bank director will welcome the forced imposition of up to two so-called "public interest" representatives on each board'. In fact, as was simultaneously reported elsewhere, the guarantee was cheap for banks as it would have cost more than twice what the government intended to charge them if they had obtained the insurance on the market. Moreover, unlike Britain's bailout scheme, the Irish government did not ban banks from paying dividends during the two years of the guarantee and the two directors appointed 'in the public interest' to banks' boards did not have any voting rights.[43]

When Anglo Irish was nationalized in January 2009, the *Irish Times* reported the government line without questioning it. A piece related that the minister for finance had said that 'if Anglo Irish Bank had been permitted to fail there would have been catastrophic consequences for the economy'. Another article quoted the minister as claiming that Bank of Ireland and AIB were 'fundamentally sound and solvent institutions' and that nationalizing Anglo Irish was 'in the national interest' because it would 'safeguard the economic future of the country' since the government is 'determined to protect the taxpayers' interests'. Morgan Kelly dissented and reacted to the government's decision to inject €1.5 billion into the bank by asserting that it would be 'better to incinerate €1.5bn than squander it on Anglo Irish Bank', which, together with Irish Nationwide, 'were purely conduits for property speculation. They fulfil no role in the Irish economy and their absence would not be noticed'.[44]

Finally, it is interesting to note that discussion of the resolution of the banking crisis soon included calls for austerity. For example, the *Sunday Business Post* claimed that the government needed to address the economic crisis thus: 'To be credible, a plan needs to cover the two areas. Asking public sector employees to take pay cuts, while at the same time pumping billions into our banking system, has obvious political difficulties. Yet this is what needs to be done'. Similarly, a *Sunday Independent* editorial commented on a small pay raise in the public sector by saying that it was 'quite simply, a scandal' and that it demonstrated that 'the state sector of this economy operates in a parallel universe where normal economic constraints do not apply'. The *Sunday Times* was impatient with the slow pace of government action, lamenting that 'still we await action from the government. Where are the details of Brian Cowen's plan to cut €2 billion from the public spending bill in 2009, and where is the small print on the recapitalisation plan for the country's two biggest banks?' Labour unions, which are 'as greedy as any banker', should not interfere with the process: 'The social partners should have been dumped last summer after talks on a new pay deal collapsed. To do so would have marked Mr Cowen out as his own man and given his administration a fresh start ... Mr Cowen should cut these unelected trade unionists out of the picture, roll up his sleeves, make his own decisions, and live with the consequences'.[45]

NAMA

The range of alternatives considered in the media to address the banking crisis was relatively narrow. Any scheme that involved letting the banks fail or forcing bondholders to incur losses was virtually excluded from the debate. As the *Irish Times* business editor's discussion of the available options stated: there 'are two options on the table. One is to recapitalise the banks, and the other is to nationalise them. There really is not much point dwelling on the third option – letting either of them go bust – as the Government has made it clear it will not let that happen'.[46]

An article in the same newspaper outlining possible strategies also illustrated the limited debate in the press:[47]

- 'Proceed with recapitalisation' (the government injects taxpayers' funds into financial institutions)
- 'Seek outside capital' (private investment funds could inject capital into banks)
- 'Protect banks from exposure to toxic assets' (the state absorbs losses related to banks' toxic assets, for example, through the establishment of a bad bank)
- 'Nationalisation' (the state takes control of banks and becomes responsible for their assets and liabilities)

In early 2009, discussion of a bad bank became more prominent in the media, which supported the idea. The *Irish Independent* described the scheme as 'the holy grail' and explained that 'setting up a "bad bank" to absorb lenders' "toxic" assets … now seems to be one of the few plausible options open to the Government'. It was deemed to be a 'bold and imaginative idea' that should be 'implemented as soon as possible in order to enable Banks to begin lending again'. It was claimed that 'the pain will be shared between the developers, who will be pursued in full by NAMA, and by the Banks, who will be obliged to sell their assets at a discounted value', but the 'pain' that was going to be suffered by taxpayers was not mentioned. The *Irish Times* announced that '"Bad" bank is best bet as recapitalisation clearly not enough', and an article entitled 'Nama scheme brings benefits to banks, Government and taxpayers' clearly supported NAMA. A *Sunday Times* editorial was also explicit, stating that 'No option now but to bank on the Nama deal', while another, entitled 'Be positive: NAMA might just work', opined that the government 'must get the benefit of the doubt on Nama', even if it is not perfect. Government pronouncements were often repeated without careful scrutiny, as in an *Irish Times* article entitled 'Inaction would have brought greater risk than Nama – Cowen'. Also, the ESRI's (Economic and Social Research Institute) Alan Barrett said that 'We think Nama, and the principles behind Nama, are quite right'.[48]

The corporate sector supported NAMA. Bankers 'welcomed' it and IBEC 'supported' it and 'believe[d] the measure will further stabilise the banking sector and will help re-establish lending to businesses and households'. ISME said the bad bank was 'a welcome development', while Chambers Ireland, the umbrella group for Irish local chambers of commerce, said that it could potentially 'underpin the national banking system and deliver enhanced credit flows at reasonable terms for businesses and the economy'. This contrasted with the point of view of the trade union SIPTU, which believed that NAMA 'represents the socialisation of the toxic debt accumulated by the banks through reckless lending and contrasts sharply with the imposition of the 2 per cent levy and the doubling of the health levies on middle and lower income families'. This quote was all that was reported in the article mentioning it and appeared at the very bottom of it. Likewise, progressive opposition to NAMA was given short shrift, although it included a range of groups like the United Alliance Against Cuts, Grand Theft Nama and the People Before Profit Alliance. Civil society groups stated that NAMA was 'flawed' because the multi-billion-euro 'gift to banks is likely to undermine the State's finances and public services for years to come while failing to secure credit for businesses'.[49]

The *Sunday Independent* interviewed a dozen of 'the so-called "big beasts" of Irish business, the most influential and most powerful people at the very top of the corporate ladder' to know their views about NAMA. They were largely favourable to it, and only one preferred nationalization. For example, David Went, former boss of financial firm Irish Life and Permanent and now chairman of the *Irish Times* board, is 'unequivocally in favour of Nama' and 'does not favour state ownership'. Tony Garry, Davy Stockbrokers chief, said that 'Nama is, by some distance, the best option available'. Myra Garrett, a corporate lawyer, said that 'Nama is the only realistic solution', while Niamh Brennan, a former Ulster Bank director, said that 'Nama is the only game in town'.[50]

European authorities supported the approach, which fitted within their broader strategy to address the crisis. European Commissioner for Economic and Monetary Affairs Joaquin Almunia said he wanted the NAMA legislation 'passed as soon as possible'. The ECB stated that NAMA was 'broadly consistent' with the eurosystem's guiding principles and agreed with the Irish government that 'the preservation of private ownership is preferable to nationalisation' and that NAMA 'should help to avoid' both the 'high costs involved in nationalisations' and the 'risk of banks' objectives being diverted from profit maximisation to alternative goals', which presumably include providing credit to socially useful projects.[51] The OECD agreed that NAMA 'should be implemented swiftly' and did not support nationalization, which it thought 'would carry significant costs and risks and should only be undertaken with the utmost reluctance'. It argued that the 'recapitalisation of the banks and the creation of NAMA are important steps in resolving the banking crisis in an effective way' and should 'enable future lending on a sound footing'. Commenting on the NAMA bill, the IMF said the definition of long-term economic value used to price banks' toxic loans was 'masterful' and that 'Overall, it looks pretty good'. An IMF report stated that the Irish 'government's guarantee to depositors and creditors and the capital injections have helped banks obtain market funding', and that the 'extensive and ongoing support has been vital to maintain financial stability'. Moreover, 'translating NAMA from concept to reality is pivotal to the orderly restructuring of the financial sector and limiting long-term damage to the economy'. A year later, the IMF praised NAMA and Ireland's 'ambitious fiscal consolidation', stating that such 'aggressive measures have helped gain policy credibility and stabilize the economy', and 'reassured the global community and international financial markets'. Moody's, the global ratings agency, also deemed NAMA to be 'a positive development'.[52]

Elite views contrasted sharply with those of the public, which favoured nationalization, as reported in several opinion polls. 'The public is deeply sceptical about Nama', according to a *Sunday Independent* survey. 'An overwhelming majority believe the Nama concept to be nothing other than another a bail-out for the banks and builders and expect the taxpayer will never get a financial return. A clear majority, 60 per cent, also say they would prefer the banks be nationalised', against 40 per cent favouring NAMA (the survey was seemingly restricted to those two alternatives only). Significantly, 85 per cent believed that NAMA was 'another bail-out for the banks'. This was even 'after months of preparation' on the government's part, including favourable media coverage of the bad bank option. When asked 'who they believed would benefit most from Nama, a significant majority (65 per cent) said the banks, 27 per cent said property developers, while only eight per cent felt that taxpayers would ultimately benefit'.[53]

A later poll confirmed the findings, as only 26 per cent of voters showed support for NAMA compared to 40 per cent against it. It is interesting that 'in terms of social class, the strongest support for Nama comes from the best-off', with 32 per cent in favour and 42 per cent against. On the other hand, the 'strongest opposition comes from the poorest', with 19 per cent for and 39 per cent against. Conversely, the 'strongest opposition to nationalisation comes from the best-off', with 44 per cent against and 40 per cent in favour, while 'the most support for the proposal comes from the least well off', with 36 per cent for and 35 per cent against.[54] It is revealing, however, to examine how the *Irish Times* editors interpreted those findings as being supportive of NAMA. Commenting on the poll's results, they wrote that although 'taxpayers do not welcome the bailout of the developers nor the banks at their own expense', nevertheless, 'deep down in their consciousness, the poll suggests that there is an acceptance that something has to be done. Otherwise, Nama would be rejected by 90 per cent of the electorate and nationalisation would be accepted with a vengeance'. The editors were unclear as to how they could access the electorate's 'deep consciousness'.[55]

Three weeks later and following debate in the parliament, another survey revealed that popular support for NAMA had declined further: 48 per cent opposed it, up eight points since the last poll, while only 29 per cent supported it, up three points. The strongest support still came from the best-off social group, with 43 per cent in favour and 38 per cent against, while the strongest opposition came from the poorest group, with 19 per cent in favour and 52 per cent against. Moreover, 65 per cent thought that the state was paying too much for banks' toxic loans while only 2 per cent believed it paid too little and 7 per cent thought the price was about right.[56]

Those who attacked government plans were accused of engaging in 'populist rhetoric and scare-mongering', but this did not prevent Nobel Prize winning economist Joseph Stiglitz from calling NAMA 'a fraud' and 'criminal' because it involved 'a massive transfer of money from the public to bankers'. He said that the government 'should have let Irish banks go to the wall instead of "squandering" public money' on the bad bank. He stated that the 'rule of capitalism says that when firms can't pay what they owe, they go bankrupt'. When this happens to banks, their shareholders get wiped out and the bondholders incur losses. If this doesn't happen, 'then you have privatised profits and socialised losses'. Another isolated voice was Morgan Kelly. In January 2009, his position was that the government should 'perform a ruthless triage' and separate the 'worthwhile banks' from the others. The government should save the banks that are of systemic importance to the economy and let the others fail. In practice, this meant that the 'State must do everything to rescue AIB, Bank of Ireland and Permanent TSB, and let Anglo Irish and Irish Nationwide sink. The Government must continue to guarantee all deposits at Anglo Irish while announcing that, in the light of continuing revelations of misconduct in the bank and shortcomings in its auditing procedures, it will enter into negotiations with senior and unsecured bondholders'. However, at that stage, Kelly did not call for all bondholders to take losses, only those of Anglo Irish and Irish Nationwide.[57]

Kelly explained the transfer of resources from the public to the banks and bondholders implied by the guarantee and subsequent nationalization of Anglo Irish by pointing out that it would 'saddle Irish taxpayers with Anglo's bad debts, which could easily exceed €20,000 per household, and starve the other, worthwhile, banks of the capital they need to survive'. He also provided an antidote to the exaggerated warnings that letting Anglo Irish fail would result in dire consequences for the broader economy. In fact, Anglo had no systemic importance in Ireland's financial system and 'existed purely as a vehicle for a few politically connected individuals to place reckless bets on the commercial property market. These property speculators may be of systemic importance to the finances of Fianna Fáil, but their significance ends there'. Accordingly, if Anglo had been allowed to sink, 'very little' would have happened: 'Developers would have gone bust and commercial property would have become more or less worthless, but that is going to happen anyway, with or without Anglo Irish. Depositors of Anglo Irish would have been paid off in full, and the hit would have been taken by the international financial institutions that hold around €22 billion of its bonds'. It is important to note that bondholders are investors who lent to Anglo hoping to capture higher returns to compensate them for the higher risk to which they were exposed.

Moreover, bondholders are already insured against potential losses through credit default swaps, a type of insurance contract. As Kelly noted, this 'is the central point about the bailout of Anglo Irish, and one that has not received any attention: the only effect of a bailout is that the Irish taxpayer will make up the losses of Anglo Irish's bondholders instead of the insurers who had already been paid to underwrite the risk. Why it is necessary to transfer Anglo's losses from the writers of Credit Default Swaps to the Irish taxpayer is something that the Government has not thought to justify'.[58]

During the months leading up to the establishment of NAMA, the government's preferred strategy of establishing a bad bank predominated in the media, but the alternative of nationalization also drew significant attention. The 'good bank' proposal, however, was very little mentioned. On the few occasions that it was, it was usually criticized as impractical and doomed to failure, as will be seen below. Likewise, the option of letting banks fail was little discussed, usually only to be rebutted. For example, an article in the *Sunday Business Post* argued that 'we need to be careful of those who argue loudly that this bank and that bank should be "let go". The problem here is that most of the liabilities of the banks are protected – closing a bank would trigger the guarantee in some form'. Repudiating the guarantee, however, was not an option considered by the media.[59] The range of opinions voiced was thus narrow, pitching the bad bank option against that of nationalization. Debate revolved around the details of NAMA's workings, such as the price that should be paid by the agency to purchase the banks' bad loans. Paying too little would force the state subsequently to pump more funds into the banks to recapitalize them, while paying too much would directly increase NAMA's costs. This debate, which took much space in the press, was thus somewhat futile, because either way, the taxpayer was bound to lose.[60]

As Anglo Irish management's corrupt practices were becoming blatantly clearer, some calls could be heard simply to wind down the bank. However, such reactions were specific to Anglo Irish and did not suggest a general strategy of letting any insolvent bank fail if it was not able to stand on its own. For example, the *Sunday Independent* editors stated that 'Anglo Irish is a dead bank walking ... Anglo must be wound down ... The government must discover the courage to confront Anglo's problems head-on, negotiating aggressively with its bondholders so that they, too, pay part of the price of the bank's failure'. Anglo came to be seen by some as a 'rogue bank' of no systemic importance, and 'the scale of its mismanagement has reached a point where it poses a real threat to our financial system ... An orderly wind-down represents the best option to protect the interests of the State and the taxpayers'. In short, the removal of a bad apple was acceptable once it became too obvious to ignore, but the preservation of the political economic system as a whole was still upheld. Further, the negative image that Anglo Irish projected on the financial and corporate sectors needed to be rectified and removing what had become a pariah institution could only help in that regard. Nevertheless, some still believed that Anglo Irish, in as bad a condition as it was, should nevertheless not be allowed to fail, as it 'is a bank with no future but it is too expensive to kill off ... Perhaps we will just have to learn to live with it in some shape or form'.[61]

Commentary favourable to NAMA went so far as denying that it was a bailout for bankers, asserting that 'Not a shred of evidence was produced to back up this posturing. The evidence, little though there is, points the other way'. Similarly, the *Sunday Times* called for a 'reality check': NAMA 'is not a taxpayer bailout for the banks'; rather, it is a 'carefully structured rescue of the Irish economy, mitigating the need for the International Monetary Fund to do the same'. Thus, there should be no discussion of whether NAMA should go ahead or not, only what a 'good Nama or bad Nama' would look like. Others claimed that creating NAMA was 'a decisive pro-active move' that would clean up banks' balance sheets 'at no expense to the taxpayer' who will be 'fully protected'. In short, NAMA is the beginning of 'a difficult, but a very important, journey towards finally bringing the banks back to financial health'. It appeared to be such a good strategy that some analysts asserted that 'many serious people now suspect that Nama could be a model to be copied elsewhere' in Europe and the United States.[62]

The claim that 'there is no alternative' was often heard, as in an analysis piece entitled 'Bank rescue may be risky but we don't have an option'. Readers were told that 'nobody supporting Nama is doing so with any enthusiasm or out of any ideological commitment. It is being done out of necessity ... No sane politician would embark on this project were it not for the absence of any workable alternative'.[63] It was urgent to pass NAMA, as the *Irish Independent* editors insisted:

> The more time that passes before the agency is seen as a real, working entity, the more likely it is that our banks would find it increasingly difficult to raise finance in the marketplace. If "Operation NAMA" were to be allowed rot on the vine, the markets would regard it as a chimera without substance. The danger is that deposits would flow out of the banks and the Government's €440bn guarantee would be called into play. Ireland Inc would then be seen as bankrupt and the Government would find it even more expensive, perhaps impossible, to borrow, with all the appalling consequences that implies.[64]

The dire consequences that would allegedly afflict Ireland if NAMA were not passed urgently was a running theme in media coverage. An article entitled 'Solution isn't perfect but it's no time for bickering' claimed that 'if we don't feed NAMA, even if it means cutting off an arm to do so via austerity measures, we will wind up in a greater mess'. Otherwise, 'the international markets – the people we borrow from to pay our nurses, guards and teachers – will conclude that lending to Ireland is no longer a safe bet. In future they may no longer advance us money, or do so with penal interest rates attached'. In short, 'if we don't rescue the banks, the economy will collapse'. However, as Morgan Kelly argued, actions such as burning the bondholders would probably have done more to improve the state's credit rating than shouldering it with even more private debt.[65]

Dr Alan Ahearne, a professor of economics who became adviser to Minister for Finance Brian Lenihan, praised NAMA as a 'bold and radical action' and asserted that 'commercial banks function better than State-owned banks', and that nationalization can be dangerous as it is often perceived by the markets 'as a sign that a bank has failed completely'. He maintained that nationalized banks have more difficulty raising funds in global markets and that this could undermine their attempts at lending to the domestic economy. Among the 'intractable and dangerous pitfalls' of nationalization is that 'international confidence in Ireland' could be affected negatively. He also alleged that it is 'difficult to see a credible exit strategy' once banks have been nationalized. Elaborating on the reasons why he believed NAMA-type bad banks are the best option, Ahearne asserted that such a scheme was 'a proven way of solving banking crises' and, in particular, has three main benefits. First, it 'protects taxpayers'. Second, banks do not have the expertise to manage distressed assets. Third, removing bad assets from banks' balance sheets allows them to increase lending to the domestic economy. However, such arguments have been debunked by economists favourable to nationalization (see below). First, NAMA does not protect taxpayers, as it is one of the strategies least favourable to the public purse. Second, banks do have the expertise to manage distressed assets, with which they deal regularly, and if they do not have this expertise, it is not a reason for the state to pick up the tab for them. Third, removing bad assets from banks' balance sheets is no guarantee of increasing lending to the domestic economy. Even if it did have that effect, it would not justify dealing with banks' problems through one of the most regressive schemes available when other options are possible.[66]

Another argument advanced against nationalization is that it leads to cronyism as government officials managing banks are inevitably subject to political pressures and are often involved in clientelist networks. For example, financier Dermot Desmond declared that nationalization would leave the economy in 'dire straits for several decades' and the banks open to 'political interference, skulduggery and cronyism'. It has also been claimed that 'the policy that sees the State intervene the least must be the one that will work best' because allegedly, in the private sector, the 'level of accountability is higher and the consequences of poor performance graver than in the public service'. Nationalization 'would result in lethargy at best and unconscious sabotage at worst'. That such statements can still be made in the media after light (i.e., no) regulation of the financial sector and cronyism in the private financial sector led to the crash is remarkable.[67]

One myth repeated by some NAMA supporters is that it was a good strategy because Irish people would not even have to pay for it, since 'the money for NAMA is coming from Europe'. However, as Karl Whelan noted, this is false: 'Nama will pay for its assets with bonds that are obligations on the Irish taxpayer'. The banks would then be able to use these bonds as collateral for loans from the European Central Bank.[68]

Another misleading way of describing NAMA appeared repeatedly in the press and consisted in asserting that it had to be established, but in a way that protects taxpayers' interests. However, this is logically impossible, as NAMA is inherently harmful to the interests of taxpayers, being one of the most regressive measures that can be adopted in a bank rescue package. To posit that there is a way for NAMA to be implemented in a way that safeguards taxpayers' money must thus be considered political spin. For example, the *Sunday Business Post* stated that it 'is essential that, as the plan for the National Asset Management Agency is finalised, the interests of the taxpayer and the wider economy are paramount ... we need to get back to a functioning financial system at the lowest possible cost to the taxpayer'. An article entitled 'Nama must be accountable to the taxpayer' falls into the same category: it implies that it is indeed possible to make NAMA accountable to the taxpayer. Similarly, many pieces asserted that it was not possible to know if NAMA would work, because not enough details were made available in its early stages. However, the point is that NAMA is an inherently regressive strategy, whatever its details. Even if 'it works' and leads to new lending in the domestic economy and removes toxic assets from the banks' balance sheets, this does not justify it as a policy, since the same results could have been accomplished through a more progressive path. Nevertheless, articles made statements such as: 'It will be some time before one can say whether Nama will work' because we don't know yet how much the government will pay for the banks' bad assets.[69]

Another way to support government actions implicitly is to protect those responsible for the economic downturn by claiming that assigning responsibility will lead nowhere. An article in the *Sunday Independent* asserted that 'Blaming people and scoring points off each other and expressing our anger and talking about our feelings, and demanding the bankers and politicians go through some kind of 12-step programme involving us all confronting them and them apologising for everything they've ever done, all of that is all very well and kind of satisfying in the short term. But it's not going to help us'. Similarly, columnist John Waters wrote that NAMA should not display 'the kind of moralistic desire for retribution' since the point 'is not to punish developers for the collapse of the Celtic Tiger' because when the economy starts growing again, 'property developers, including many of those on Nama's visiting list, will be a vital component of the recovery process'. Marc Coleman said that 'denouncing the banks and builders is puerile since others are also to blame' for the crisis. Cathal O'Loghlin, a former assistant secretary of the Department of Finance and director of the IMF, penned an article entitled 'We are all also culpable for excess'. He asserted that it is a 'delusion' to believe that 'ordinary citizens contributed nothing to the current difficulties'; in fact, they played a 'major role' in it by buying houses in the years previous to the crisis, and were also 'substantially responsible for the emergence of budget problems'. Therefore, it is another 'delusion' to believe that society shouldn't have to pay to fix the economy.[70]

The option of nationalizing the banks was favoured by the Labour Party and received some support in the media. For example, the *Sunday Times* editors stated prudently that they 'remain to be convinced that the banking problem can be fixed without first taking the key players in the sector into temporary state ownership'. The clearest presentation of this view was provided by a number of Irish economists, including Brian Lucey and Karl Whelan, who showed convincingly that nationalization was a more progressive approach than NAMA. They demonstrated that temporary nationalization of the banking system, or at least of those institutions of systemic importance, was preferable to the government's strategy of combining a bad bank to limited recapitalization, for several reasons. First, nationalization offers more protection to the taxpayer. This, among other things, is because the government takes an equity stake in the bank, and therefore can sell its shares back to the private sector when their value recovers, which does 'substantially reduce the underlying cost to the taxpayer'. Second, nationalization is more transparent, mostly because in a bad bank scheme, the pricing of toxic loans purchased from the banks involves a significant element of arbitrariness, giving rise to a range of issues related to fairness and opacity. By contrast, with nationalization, such problems do not arise because the government owns the banks. A bad bank can then be created if the state so desires, but because it would also be owned by the government, transferring assets to it makes their pricing somewhat irrelevant. Third, nationalization provides the opportunity to fire the banks' top management and replace them with 'highly independent boards of senior figures of the utmost integrity'.[71]

As Karl Whelan explained, 'Nama is a conscious policy of transferring billions of euro through overpayment from the taxpayer to bank shareholders. These are the same bank shareholders who appointed and cheered on the boards of directors that contributed to bringing the Irish economy to its knees'. The bad bank proposal and its variations are simply 'indirect methods of recapitalising the banks without giving the Government any further control' over the institutions in the form of equity. If the state must recapitalize the banks, 'it is only fair that the Government take control and temporarily nationalise the banks'. Finally, 'scaremongering comments ignore the fact that a number of troubled financial institutions around the world have been nationalised without unleashing the plagues of frogs and locusts suggested by the Minister for Finance and his stockbroker supporters. It is noteworthy that in the US, the Troubled Assets Relief Program, which had originally been based, like Nama, on the idea of overpaying for bad assets, was altered to be a programme of equity investments by the US government'. In August 2009, the same economists reiterated their view that the banking system should be nationalized, but this time they added that as part of that process, not only should shareholders be wiped out, but also that 'certain classes of bondholders' be required to absorb some losses. However, they still did not call for the repudiation of the guarantee, suggesting that bonds covered by it until September 2010 should be honoured by the state.[72]

The good bank proposal, however, was repeatedly criticized on the few occasions it was mentioned in the media. Patrick Honohan, who later became head of the Central Bank, wrote that although the proposal 'may seem theoretically to be the cleanest and it can be the fairest', in practice, if implemented, it 'would cause a significant shock to the overall economic system' and would most likely result in 'alarm and disruption'. Marc Coleman said that the good bank proposal 'involves a collapse in property values and land values that would not only be traumatic, but the consequences of which, economic and political, could be potentially uncontrollable and disastrous'. Others have claimed that a good bank 'would end up completely supplanting the existing banks' and would 'create a huge domestic banking monopoly'.[73]

Likewise, those proposing strategies that involved forcing bondholders to take up losses or repudiating the guarantee constituted a small minority. For example, Morgan Kelly, who in July 2009 seemed to have shifted his position from his earlier calls for the government to do whatever it takes to save all banks except Anglo Irish and Irish Nationwide, now explained that the bad bank and nationalization schemes, while different in detail, both lead to the same outcome: 'Irish taxpayers will be stuck with a large bill'. He thus proposed that instead, bondholders of AIB and Bank of Ireland be forced to undertake a debt-to-equity swap, in which a portion of their bonds would be converted into shares. This would recapitalize the two institutions and would 'not cost the taxpayer a cent'. It is one way in which bondholders would shoulder some of the losses. Economist Constantin Gurdgiev also proposed a scheme, which he referred to as 'Nama Trust', under which shareholders and bondholders would incur losses before taxpayers. He suggested that the banks first needed to estimate the full extent of losses on their loans to obtain an idea of how much capital will be wiped out. Then, shareholders and bondholders would absorb losses in legal order of priority, and only 'after the private avenues for recapitalisation are exhausted, should Irish taxpayers provide capital to the banks in exchange for equity'.[74]

Economist David McWilliams, in 2009, also called for the bondholders to absorb losses. This represented a shift in his position for dealing with the banking crisis. In September 2008, he saw the guarantee as the best option, as seen above. At that time, he rejected the alternative of nationalization, a 'discredited idea from abroad', because 'it will alert investors ... that the Irish banking system is in tatters ... This will lead to contagion, and the system unravels'. Neither did he agree with letting banks fail, claiming that 'This is not an option for Ireland, as only failed states have failed banks'. He wrote that with a blanket guarantee in place, things will eventually settle down, the 'crisis will pass, and Ireland will become a model of financial innovation', no less. He continued: 'If we act now, quickly and with confidence, a potential insolvency won't escalate beyond a temporary problem of illiquidity and will be sorted without panic or long-term consequences'. However, by 2009, his position had evolved and in an article entitled 'Time to wind down the banks', he asked: 'Why should a democratic government broker a deal which bails out stockholders and unsecured bond holders, both of whom have no right to be treated with such generosity?' He proposed that bank 'shareholders, unsecured, and senior bond holders would take the hit'. He explained that there 'is no evidence from the world of finance and banking which says that a winding up of the banking system in a country and replacing it with a new banking system has any lasting effect on the economic performance of the country. In the US this year alone 300 banks and finance houses have gone to the wall and, according to the latest data, the US economy is tentatively recovering. Sweden wound up its worst banks without adverse effect'. Significantly, he moved from advocating a blanket guarantee to one covering only deposits: 'Banks are like any other business: new ones replace old ones, and if we install a national deposit guarantee rather than a blanket guarantee, which can be allowed to lapse, we can prevent chaos'.[75]

In sum, the media, just like the business community, endorsed the government's strategy for rescuing the banks, while reserving some space to debate the option of nationalization. The good bank proposal, however, received little attention, let alone support. In any case, public finances continued to deteriorate and in late 2010, the EU and IMF had to bail out the government.

Notes

1 R. Curran, 'Riding to the Banks' Rescue', SBP, 30 November 2008.
2 C. McCabe, *Sins of the Father: Tracing the Decisions that Shaped the Irish Economy*, 2nd edn, Dublin: The History Press, 2013, pp. 176–77.
3 L. Laeven and F. Valencia, 'Systemic Banking Crises Database: An Update', International Monetary Fund Working Paper, WP/12/163, 2012, p. 20, www.imf. org/external/pubs/ft/wp/2012/wp12163.pdf (accessed 4 December 2013); P. Honohan, 'The Irish Banking Crisis: Regulatory and Financial Stability Policy 2003–8. A Report to the Minister for Finance by the Governor of the Central Bank', 2010, p. 19, www.bankinginquiry.gov.ie/ (accessed 27 December 2012).
4 M. Taft, 'A Really Really Special Case Requires a Really Really Special Solution', Unite's Notes on the Front, 15 January 2013, notesonthefront.typepad.com/politi caleconomy/2013/01/with-considerable-speculation-about-an-impending-deal-on-ba nk-debt-with-the-taoiseach-and-the-german-chancellor-jointly-sta.html (accessed 1 December 2013). For discussion of the costs of the bank bailout, see T. Healy, 'Private Bank Debts and Public Finances: Some Options for Ireland', NERI Working Paper 2013/01, February 2013, www.nerinstitute.net/download/pdf/neri _wp20131_private_bank_debt_public_finances_.pdf (accessed 4 December 2013); S. Coffey, 'Deficit-, Debt- and Expenditure-Impacting Banking Measures', Economic Incentives, 1 February 2013, economic-incentives.blogspot.ie/2013/02/deficit-debt-and-expenditure-impacting.html (accessed 20 November 2013); K. Whelan, 'What is Ireland's Bank Debt and What Can Be Done About it?', Karlwhelan. com, 7 June 2012, karlwhelan.com/blog/?p=471 (accessed 4 December 2013).
5 National Treasury Management Agency, 'Debt Projections', www.ntma.ie/business-areas/funding-and-debt-management/debt-profile/debt-projections/ (accessed 23 November 2013); 'Interest Costs', www.ntma.ie/business-areas/funding-and-debt-management/debt-service/ (accessed 23 November 2013).

6 Whelan, 'What is Ireland's Bank Debt and What Can Be Done About it?'; see also S. Barnes and D. Smyth, 'The Government's Balance Sheet After the Crisis: A Comprehensive Perspective', Irish Fiscal Advisory Council, September 2013, www.fiscalcouncil.ie/wp-content/uploads/2013/09/Balance-Sheet1.pdf (accessed 22 November 2013).

7 K. Allen and B. O'Boyle, *Austerity Ireland: The Failure of Irish Capitalism*, London: Pluto, 2013, p. 9; 'Correspondence from NAMA to Public Accounts Committee', 20 September 2012, www.oireachtas.ie/parliament/media/committees/pac/correspondence/2012-meeting512009/%5bPAC-R-589%5dCorrespondence-3A. 3.pdf (accessed 15 November 2013); 'Written Answers: National Assets Management Agency', Dáil Éireann Debates, Vol. 760, No. 2, 22 March 2012, debates. oireachtas.ie/dail/2012/03/22/00069.asp (accessed 15 November 2013).

8 Allen and O'Boyle, *Austerity Ireland*, p. 11.

9 European Commission, 'Opinion of the European Central Bank of 3 October 2008 at the Request of the Irish Minister for Finance on a Draft Credit Institutions (Financial Support) Bill 2008', CON/2008/44, 3 October 2008, pp. 2–3, www.ecb. europa.eu/ecb/legal/pdf/en_con_2008_44.pdf (accessed 12 October 2013).

10 Honohan, 'The Irish Banking Crisis', p. 135.

11 D. Baker, *False Profits: Recovering from the Bubble Economy*, Sausalito, CA: PoliPointPress, 2010.

12 K. Sandal, 'The Nordic Banking Crises in the Early 1990s – Resolution Methods and Fiscal Costs', in T. Moe, J.A. Solheim and B. Vale (eds) *The Norwegian Banking Crisis*, Norges Bank's Occasional Papers no. 33, Oslo, 2004, pp. 77–115.

13 B. Vale, 'The Norwegian Banking Crisis', in T. Moe, J.A. Solheim and B. Vale (eds) *The Norwegian Banking Crisis*, Norges Bank's Occasional Papers no. 33, Oslo, 2004, pp. 1–21.

14 L. Jonung, 'The Swedish Model for Resolving the Banking Crisis of 1991–93. Seven Reasons Why it was Successful', Economic Paper 360, Brussels: European Commission, 2009, ec.europa.eu/economy_finance/publications/publication14098_ en.pdf (accessed 13 November 2013).

15 P. Englund, 'The Swedish Banking Crisis: Roots and Consequences', *Oxford Review of Economic Policy*, 1999, vol. 15, no. 3, p. 92.

16 P. Englund and V. Vihriälä, 'Financial Crisis in Finland and Sweden: Similar but Not Quite the Same', in L. Jonung, J. Kiander and P. Vartia (eds) *The Great Financial Crisis in Finland and Sweden: The Nordic Experience of Financial Liberalization*, Cheltenham: Edward Elgar, 2009, pp. 107–8.

17 Sandal, 'The Nordic Banking Crises in the Early 1990s'.

18 Vale, 'The Norwegian Banking Crisis'; Jonung, 'The Swedish Model for Resolving the Banking Crisis of 1991–93'; 'Lessons from the Nordic Financial Crisis', Report for the American Economic Association meeting of January 2011, www.aeaweb. org/aea/2011conference/program/retrieve.php?pdfid=413 (accessed 10 October 2013).

19 D. McWilliams, 'Time for Us to Start Singing from a Different Hymn Sheet', *SBP*, 25 January 2009.

20 W. Buiter, 'The "Good Bank" Solution', *FT*, 29 January 2009, blogs.ft.com/maver econ/2009/01/the-good-bank-solution/#axzz2mY2X9r6i (accessed 4 December 2013); 'Good Bank/New Bank vs. Bad Bank: A Rare Example of a No-brainer', *FT*, 8 February 2009, blogs.ft.com/maverecon/2009/02/good-banknew-bank-vs-bad-bank-a-rare-example-of-a-no-brainer/#axzz2mY2X9r6i (accessed 4 December 2013); '"Good Banks" are the Cost Effective Way Out of the Financial Crisis', *WSJ*, 21 February 2002, online.wsj.com/news/articles/SB123517593808837541 (accessed 4 December 2013); 'How to Set up a New "Good Bank"', *FT*, 21 February 2009, blogs.ft.com/maverecon/2009/02/how-to-set-up-a-new-good-bank/ #axzz2mY2X9r6i (accessed 4 December 2013); 'Insuring Toxic Assets: Throwing

Good Tax Payers' Money After Bad Private Money', *FT*, 26 February 2009, blogs. ft.com/maverecon/2009/02/insuring-toxic-assets-throwing-good-tax-payers-money-a fter-bad-private-money/#axzz2mY2X9r6i (accessed 4 December 2013); 'Don't Touch the Unsecured Creditors! Clobber the Tax Payer Instead', *FT*, 13 March 2009, blogs.ft.com/maverecon/2009/03/dont-touch-the-unsecured-creditors-clobber-the-tax-payer-instead/#axzz2mY2X9r6i (accessed 4 December 2013). See also A. Evans-Pritchard, 'Let Banks Fail, says Nobel Economist Joseph Stiglitz', *DT*, 2 February 2009, www.telegraph.co.uk/finance/newsbysector/banksandfinance/4424418/Let-banks-fail-says-Nobel-economist-Joseph-Stiglitz.html (accessed 4 December 2013); George Soros, 'We Can Do Better than a "Bad Bank"', *WSJ*, 4 February 2009, online.wsj.com/news/articles/SB123371182830346215 (accessed 4 December 2013); P. Romer, 'Let's Start Brand New Banks', *WSJ*, 6 February 2009, online.wsj.com/news/articles/SB123388681675555343 (accessed 4 December 2013).

21 Buiter, 'Don't Touch the Unsecured Creditors! Clobber the Tax Payer Instead'; 'Slaughtering Sacred Cows: It's the Turn of the Unsecured Creditors Now', *FT*, 18 March 2009, blogs.ft.com/maverecon/2009/03/slaughtering-sacred-cows-its-the-turn-of-the-unsecured-creditors-now/#axzz2mY2X9r6i (accessed 4 December 2013).

22 L. Laeven and F. Valencia, 'The Use of Blanket Guarantees in Banking Crises', IMF Working Paper WP 08/250, 2008, p. 4, www.imf.org/external/pubs/ft/wp/2008/wp08250.pdf (accessed 20 February 2013).

23 T. McDonnell, 'The Debt and Banking Crisis: Progressive Approaches for Europe and Ireland', TASC Discussion Paper, May 2011, pp. 2, 6–8, www.tascnet.ie/upload/file/DebtBanking190511.pdf (accessed 25 February 2013); T. McDonough, 'NAMA: If You Want to Play "Solve the Irish Banking Crisis", there are Several Games in Town', Progressive Economy Blog, 1 September 2009, www.progressive-economy.ie/2009/09/if-you-want-to-play-solve-irish-banking.html (accessed 10 February 2013).

24 T. McDonough, 'Stop Bailing Out Bad Banks and Build a Good One', *IT*, 24 March 2009.

25 K. Allen, *Ireland's Economic Crash: A Radical Agenda for Change*, Dublin: Liffey Press, 2009.

26 R. Bruton, 'New Approach Needed Over Recapitalisation', *IT*, 11 February 2009.

27 Euro Area Countries, 'Declaration on a Concerted European Action Plan of the Euro Area Countries', Summit of the Euro Area Countries, 12 October 2008, ec. europa.eu/economy_finance/publications/publication13260_en.pdf (accessed 12 March 2013).

28 M. Posch, S.W. Schmitz and B. Weber, 'EU Bank Packages: Objectives and Potential Conflicts of Objectives', Financial Stability Report 17, Austrian Central Bank, June 2009, pp. 63, 72, oenb.at/en/img/fsr_17_special_topics02_tcm16-140532.pdf (accessed 2 January 2013).

29 Posch *et al.*, 'EU Bank Packages', pp. 72, 78.

30 W. Buiter, 'The Irish Solution: Unlawful, Beggar-thy-neighbour and Short Sighted, but Apart from that OK', *FT*, 2 October 2008; 'A Damp Squib from the G-7 in Washington DC', *FT*, 11 October 2008.

31 '"We had to Act to Save the Entire System"', *II*, 1 October 2008; 'Beholden to the State', *IT*, 1 October 2008; 'Cowen Warns Against abuse of scheme', *IT*, 4 October 2008; 'EU Mixed Reaction to Irish Strategy', *SBP*, 5 October 2008; S. Molony, 'Taxpayer "Picking Up €10bn in Risky Bad Debt"', *II*, 9 October 2008; P. Gillespie, 'EU Regulatory Frailties Need Restructuring', *IT*, 11 October 2008.

32 S. Carswell, 'Irish Bailout Cheapest in World, Says Lenihan', *IT*, 24 October 2008; D. O'Brien, 'Bailout Comment: Radical Problem, Right Solution', *SBP*, 5 October 2008; N. Whelan, 'The Cowen Government Comes of Age', *IT*, 4 October 2008.

33 M. O'Halloran, 'Banking System on Brink of "Collapse"', *IT*, 2 October 2008; G. Duffy, 'We Don't Appreciate the Massive Carnage We've Just Survived', *SI*, 5 October 2008.

34 'Pain and Hope in Equal Amount', *SI*, 5 October 2008; S. Collins, 'Banking Collapse Averted but Guarantee Rankles with Public', *IT*, 2 October 2008; 'A Stroke of Genius, Perhaps, but Don't Bank on it Just Yet', *II*, 1 October 2008.

35 R. Curran, 'Riding to the Banks' Rescue', *SBP*, 30 November 2008; F. Black, 'Business Groups Give Backing to Guarantee', *II*, 1 October 2008; 'Minister Tells Banks to Come Clean on Debts', *SBP*, 5 October 2008.

36 'Bank Experts Heap Praise on Irish Solution to Meltdown', *II*, 1 October 2008; 'Panic Turns to Relief in Long Night of Drama', *II*, 1 October 2008; D. McWilliams, 'Lenihan's Masterstroke has Bought Us Time to Sort Out Our Own Problems', *II*, 1 October 2008; R. Kinsella, 'EU-wide Approach Needed', *IT*, 3 October 2008.

37 European Commission, 'State Aid NN 48/2008 – Ireland', Brussels: European Commission, 13 October 2008, pp. 11–12, ec.europa.eu/eu_law/state_aids/comp-2008/nn048-08.pdf (accessed 4 December 2013).

38 M. O'Halloran and M. O'Regan, 'Emergency Bill Safeguards Economy, Says Lenihan', *IT*, 1 October 2008; S. Collins, S. Carswell and M. Hennessy, 'Bill Allows State to Take Stake in any Financial Institution Given Aid', *IT*, 1 October 2008.

39 'We had to Act to Save the Entire System', *II*, 1 October 2008; S. Collins, 'State Intervention Yields at Least Short-term Gains', *IT*, 1 October 2008; D. O'Leary, 'Ireland is a Very Queasy Passenger on the Global Financial Rollercoaster', *II*, 2 October 2008; 'In at the Deep End', *SBP*, 5 October 2008; S. Collins, 'Handling of Seismic Events was Good for Irish Politics', *IT*, 4 October 2008.

40 'Paying for their Excess', *IT*, 2 October 2008; 'Bankers Run Out of Political Capital as Public Rages: Poll', *SI*, 12 October 2008.

41 '"Golden Parachute" for Banks Unfair to Taxpayers – SIPTU', *II*, 1 October 2008; M. Kelly, 'Bailout Inept and Potentially Dangerous', *IT*, 2 October 2008; M. Kelly, 'Things are Going to Get Much Worse', *IT*, 24 October 2008; D. O'Brien, 'Bailout Comment: Radical Problem, Right Solution', *SBP*, 5 October 2008.

42 'Little Credit on the Banks', *IT*, 16 December 2008; M. Flynn, 'State Intervention must not Stifle Banks', *SBP*, 19 October 2008; 'Fears Over Excessive Policing of Banks', *SBP*, 19 October 2008; 'Banks and their Capital', *IT*, 24 October 2008; J. McManus, 'No Reason to Expect Bank Chiefs to be Held to Account', *IT*, 6 October 2008.

43 S. Carswell, 'Banks Facing a €1bn Charge and Stringent Controls', *IT*, 16 October 2008; D. Clerkin, 'Clamp Tightens on Bankers', *SBP*, 19 October 2008; 'Banks Get Guarantee on the Cheap', *SBP*, 19 October 2008; 'All Banks Will Bear the Cost if One Defaults on State Loan', *II*, 16 October 2008.

44 F. Gartland, 'Warning of Consequences if Bank had Failed', *IT*, 19 January 2009; M. O'Regan, 'State Wants Both Banks to Stay Independent – Lenihan: Bank of Ireland and AIB "Solvent Institutions"', *IT*, 21 January 2009; M. Kelly, 'Better to Incinerate €1.5bn than Squander it on Anglo Irish Bank', *IT*, 23 December 2008.

45 'Time Running Out for Government Action', *SBP*, 18 January 2009; 'ESB Pay Rise is a Call to Arms', *SI*, 18 January 2009; E. O'Hanlon, 'Unions are as Greedy as Any Banker', *SI*, 1 March 2009; 'It's Time to Part Company with the Unions', *ST*, 1 February 2009.

46 J. McManus, 'To Nationalise or Not, that is the Question for Government', *IT*, 26 January 2009.

47 A. Beesley, 'Where does the State Go from Here?' *IT*, 21 January 2009.

48 J. Brennan, 'Establishing a New "Bad Bank" to Absorb Toxic Debt could Solve Crisis', *II*, 21 January 2009; M. Hayes, 'Agency to Manage "Risky Bank Loans" a

Bold Idea', *II*, 8 April 2009; S. Carswell, '"Bad" Bank is Best Bet as Recapitalisation Clearly Not Enough', *IT*, 11 February 2009; J. Kelly and E. King, 'Nama Scheme brings Benefits to Banks, Government and Taxpayers', *IT*, 19 September 2009; 'No Option Now but to Bank on the Nama Deal', *ST*, 20 September 2009; 'Be Positive: NAMA Might Just Work', *ST*, 18 October 2009; S. Collins, 'Inaction would have Brought Greater Risk than Nama – Cowen', *IT*, 1 August 2009; L. Slattery, 'Lenders May Overreact and Adopt "Innate Conservatism"', *IT*, 16 July 2009.

49 C. Keena, 'Banking Sector Welcomes Decision to Set Up Asset Agency', *IT*, 8 April 2009; P. McGarry, 'State's Approach to Fiscal Crisis Flawed, Says Justice Group', *IT*, 29 September 2009; H. McGee, 'Left-wing Alliance to Oppose Nama Set-up', *IT*, 19 August 2009.

50 S. Ross and N. Webb, '"Beasts of Business" Give Verdict on Nama', *SI*, 13 September 2009.

51 S. Carswell, 'Almunia wants Nama to be Passed Quickly', *IT*, 10 October 2009; European Central Bank, 'Opinion of the European Central Bank of 31 August 2009 on the Establishment of the National Asset Management Agency', CON/2009/68, 31 August 2009, pp. 6–7, www.ecb.europa.eu/ecb/legal/pdf/opinion_con_2009_68_f_sign.pdf (accessed 29 May 2013); European Commission, 'Communication from the Commission on the Treatment of Impaired Assets in the Community Banking Sector', European Commission, 2009, ec.europa.eu/competition/state_aid/legislation/impaired_assets.pdf (accessed 25 April 2013).

52 P. Boyle, 'Nationalising Banks Must be Last Resort, Warns OECD', *II*, 5 November 2009; OECD, 'Economic Surveys: Ireland 2009', Paris: OECD Publishing, November 2009, pp. 10, 33; S. Carswell, 'Nama Definition of "Long-term Value" Masterful, Says IMF', *IT*, 19 December 2009; IMF, 'Ireland: 2009 Article IV Consultation – Staff Report', IMF Country Report No. 09/195, June 2009, pp. 15–16, www.imf.org/external/pubs/ft/scr/2009/cr09195.pdf (accessed 20 June 2013); IMF, 'Ireland: 2010 Article IV Consultation – Staff Report', IMF Country Report No. 10/209, July 2010, pp. 1, 3, www.imf.org/external/pubs/ft/scr/2010/cr10209.pdf (accessed 12 July 2013); J. Brennan, 'NAMA Plan is a Positive Development – Moody's', 19 September 2009.

53 J. Corcoran, 'Public No to Nama "Bail-out for Banks"', *SI*, 2 August 2009.

54 S. Collins, 'Just 26% of Voters Show Support for Setting Up Nama: One-third have No Opinion about Asset Agency, Poll Shows', *IT*, 5 September 2009.

55 'Attitudes to Nama', *IT*, 5 September 2009.

56 S. Collins, 'Support for Nama has Fallen Since Dáil Debate on Issue', *IT*, 28 September 2009.

57 N. Whelan, 'Addressing Banking Crisis was Crucial to Budget's Credibility', *IT*, 11 April 2009; 'State Should have Let Banks Fail, Says Nobel-winning Economist', *II*, 8 October 2009; C. Keena, 'Fairness Needed when Dealing with Crisis, Says Stiglitz', *IT*, 9 October 2009; M. Kelly, 'Piling Anglo Losses on to National Debt Risks Bankrupting the State', *IT*, 20 January 2009.

58 Kelly, 'Piling Anglo Losses on to National Debt Risks Bankrupting the State'; see also G. Kerrigan, 'Servile Surrender Sowed Seed of Doom', *SI*, 31 May 2009.

59 C. Taylor, 'Fixing the Broken Banks', *SBP*, 10 May 2009.

60 Variations on the NAMA scheme were also discussed, such as the 'Honohan amendment', which consisted in keeping NAMA's basic mechanism with the difference that government payment for banks' toxic assets would be made not in one lump sum, but in two stages. The first payment would be made up front when the assets are transferred to NAMA, and the remainder would take the form of a claim on whatever revenues NAMA obtains from the toxic loans it acquires. This, Honohan argued, would share the pricing risk more fairly between taxpayers and the bank shareholders. If NAMA did not make a large revenue on its toxic assets,

shareholders would correspondingly only receive a small payment. See P. Honohan, 'Banking Debate has been Reduced to False Dichotomy', *IT*, 21 May 2009.

61 'How Much Worse Can it Get?' *SI*, 31 May 2009; J. McManus, 'High Time for State to Make a Killing – Anglo Irish Bank', *IT*, 8 June 2009; T. Molloy and J. Brennan, 'Anglo Irish – the Bank with No Future that's Too Expensive to Kill Off', *II*, 4 June 2009.

62 B. Keenan, 'It is in All Our Interests to Give Assets Agency a Chance', *SI*, 12 April 2009; B. Carey, 'Nama Can Bring Ireland in from the Cold', *ST*, 16 August 2009; P. Stronge, 'First Step Taken on Long Road to Recovery for Banks', *SI*, 12 April 2009; B. O'Connor, 'We Could Get Angry Over this Mess ... or Get Real', *SI*, 23 August 2009.

63 T. Molloy, 'Bank Rescue May Be Risky but we don't have an Option', *II*, 15 May 2009; N. Whelan, 'Nama Must have Checks and Balances', *IT*, 1 August 2009.

64 'NAMA Must Not Rot on the Vine', *II*, 16 May 2009.

65 M. Devlin, 'Solution isn't Perfect but it's No Time for Bickering', *II*, 20 August 2009; M. Kelly, 'Brought to Our Knees by Bankers and Developers', *IT*, 3 July 2009.

66 M. Parsons, 'Ahearne Wary of Bank Nationalisation', *IT*, 24 April 2009; A. Ahearne, 'Nationalised Banks would Find it Harder to Get International Funds', *IT*, 25 April 2009; A. Ahearne, 'Asset Management a Proven Way of Solving Banking Crises', *IT*, 20 May 2009.

67 'Desmond Warns Against Nationalising the Banks', *II*, 28 April 2009; S. Carey, 'Banking on Nama May Be Safest Option to End the Crisis', *IT*, 29 April 2009.

68 M. Devlin, 'Solution isn't Perfect but it's No Time for Bickering', *II*, 20 August 2009; K. Whelan, 'Government Must Change Flawed Nama Strategy', *IT*, 2 October 2009.

69 'Protect the Taxpayer in Banking Reform', *SBP*, 3 May 2009; E. Byrne, 'Nama Must Be Accountable to the Taxpayer', *IT*, 4 August 2009; S. Carswell, 'Bill Makes it No Clearer if Nama Will Work or Not', *IT*, 31 July 2009.

70 B. O'Connor, 'Playing the Blame Game won't Help Create Jobs', *SI*, 15 February 2009; J. Waters, 'A Moralising Nama would not be Fit for Purpose', *IT*, 17 April 2009; M. Coleman, 'Bankers May Be Slimy but Economy Still Needs Them', *II*, 26 April 2009; C. O'Loghlin, 'We are All Also Culpable for Excess', *SBP*, 2 August 2009.

71 'A Better Route to Bolstering the Banks', *ST*, 19 April 2009; K. Whelan *et al.*, 'Nationalising Banks is the Best Option', *IT*, 17 April 2009.

72 K. Whelan, 'Nama a Good Deal Only for the Banks' Shareholders', *SI*, 9 August 2009; K. Whelan, 'Stay Away from Bad Banks and Risk Insurance', *IT*, 27 February 2009; see also 'Fairer Way to Ease the Crisis', *IT*, 3 April 2009; K. Whelan, 'Government Must Change Flawed Nama Strategy', *IT*, 2 October 2009; B. Lucey *et al.*, 'Nama Set to Shift Wealth to Lenders and Developers', *IT*, 26 August 2009.

73 P. Honohan, 'Bank Rescue Package: More to Come', *SBP*, 15 February 2009; M. Coleman, 'Bankers May Be Slimy but Economy Still Needs Them', *II*, 26 April 2009; G. Garvey, 'Opposition Proposals Need Meat on their Bones before Dail Debate', *II*, 22 August 2009.

74 M. Kelly, 'Brought to Our Knees by Bankers and Developers', *IT*, 3 July 2009; C. Gurdgiev, 'NAMA Needs Tweaking or it Could Destroy Us', *II*, 28 August 2009. See also more details on his proposal on his blog: 'NAMA 3.0: A Real Alternative', 1 August 2009, trueeconomics.blogspot.ie/2009/08/nama-30-real-alternative.html (accessed 15 August 2013); 'NAMA 3.0 – More Weight', 17 August 2009, trueeconomics.blogspot.ie/2009/08/nama-30-more-weight.html (accessed 15 August 2013).

75 D. McWilliams, 'State Guarantees Can Avert Depression', *SBP*, 28 September 2008; 'State Must Act as a Safeguard', *SBP*, 21 September 2009; 'Time to Wind Down the Banks', *SBP*, 13 September 2009; 'We're the Hostages to Fortune in NAMA Drama', *II*, 16 September 2009.

5 The EU-IMF bailout and the default option

The recession caused by the collapse of the housing bubble and the expenses associated with the bank guarantee and recapitalizations put such pressure on public finances that the Irish state was soon unable to service its debts and lost access to international capital markets in 2010. In need of external financing, and under pressure from the ECB, it agreed to a €67.5 billion loan package from the EU and IMF to finance government borrowing and recapitalize the Irish banking system. Of this package, €50 billion was directed towards the fiscal position and €35 billion was aimed at recapitalizing the banks, €17.5 billion of which would come from the government's own resources.[1]

The bailout is often described as an 'Irish bailout' or a 'bailout for Ireland', but in fact, it was a bailout of European financial institutions which had lent to Irish banks and were now looking to recoup their money. As Vincent Browne observed, in a rare example of such an interpretation in the press, 'The main point of this bailout is not the bailout of Ireland but the bailout of the European Central Bank and of privately owned banks around Europe that have poured tens of billions of euro into the Irish banks. The plan is to lend money to the Irish State to pay back some of this lending ASAP and all of it if possible. So essentially what is involved is a second bank bailout at potentially further enormous cost to this society'. This situation is not unique to Ireland and also applies to the rescue packages for Greece, Portugal and Spain. As David McWilliams observed, all these bailouts were 'nothing more than parachutes for the banks and other creditors who had lent money unwisely in the great euro-credit binge'. The 'bailouts of the periphery have been nothing more than the transfer of more and more private debt to ordinary people who had nothing to do with the debt in the first place'. In short, we 'are seeing the gradual socialization of private debt all over Europe'.[2]

There was a tension in Irish elites' attitudes toward the bailout and it was reflected in media coverage. On one hand, when it became apparent that the government would have to accept financial help, elites were very much opposed to it as it entailed a loss of sovereignty and control over their country's economy and politics. The bailout meant that European officials and the

IMF would be able to exert more leverage over Irish affairs and domestic elites would have to operate by following externally imposed guidelines on government spending, taxation, privatization and a host of other conditions attached to the bailout. On the other hand, the fact that such guidelines and the values underpinning them were largely similar to those espoused by Irish elites made them easier to accept, sometimes even with enthusiasm. After all, the EU and IMF may be more effective at driving through changes bound to generate popular opposition.

However, as a few critical commentators observed, with or without the EU and IMF, policy would remain essentially the same and favour the corporate sector and the wealthy, to the detriment of the rest of the population. As Vincent Browne put it, 'It hardly matters whether we have to be rescued by the EU or the International Monetary Fund in a few months. The outcome will be more or less the same – aside from the humiliation of having to acknowledge that we are not capable of running our own country'. Gene Kerrigan added dryly: 'Yes, people will die from IMF policies. They'll die on the same hospital waiting lists they'd have died on as a result of Mr Cowen's [the prime minister] policies'.[3]

In other words, the debate in the press about the 'loss of sovereignty' that a bailout would entail was misleading. States are not homogeneous entities; they are internally divided by class. However, the only 'sovereignty' that mattered in the media was the sovereignty of Irish elites to control Ireland, not the sovereignty of Irish people to have a say over economic policies that affect their lives. There was a serious democratic deficit in the decisions surrounding the bailout and the possibility of defaulting. This will be discussed below by reference to Ecuador, which conducted a debt audit only a few years ago to identify which of its debts were 'odious', an idea virtually never discussed in the Irish press.

The possibility of peripheral states defaulting on their accumulating debts eventually became an issue discussed in the media. It will be seen that news organizations, just like economic and political elites, have been opposed to any drastic debt default, claiming that catastrophic consequences would follow. However, this is in direct contradiction with the available evidence that shows that default usually does not result in significant negative long-term consequences – in fact, it is likely to lead to positive outcomes. Nevertheless, peripheral states have been forced to repay their debts by their own elites and European leaders, who have acted in a loose alliance throughout the crisis. However, default would have resulted in no negative consequences whatsoever in some significant cases, notably on the promissory notes. Moreover, there is a considerable degree of irony in Germany telling the Greeks, Portuguese, Irish and Spaniards that they must repay all their debts to prevent catastrophe. Indeed, after World War II, Germany had a lot of its debts cancelled, which allowed it to become Europe's leading economy. Also, in 2012, the eurozone witnessed the largest default in modern history when Greece restructured some €200 billion of its debts – but Armageddon has not yet arrived.

Towards the EU-IMF bailout

Apprehensions about IMF and EU intervention were clearly visible in the media. The government led a campaign to avoid a bailout and a 'serious rift' reportedly developed with European authorities, in particular the ECB, which tried to pressurize Ireland to agree to financial support measures. Minister for Finance Brian Lenihan countered that Ireland was taking a 'step-by-step' approach in order 'to build up credibility in the markets' and so 'there was no need' for the bailout because the state was well funded up to June 2011 thanks to 'substantial reserves'. In those circumstances, he said that 'it doesn't seem to me to make any sense' to apply for a bailout because it 'would send a signal to the markets that we're not in a position to manage our affairs ourselves'. Labour Party leader Eamon Gilmore called on the government to defend Ireland's economic independence, declaring that 'We fought hard for our independence, and we should not hand it away'. A *Sunday Independent* editorial stated that being pushed into the arms of the IMF 'is not something we can be relieved about'.[4]

The threat of a possible rescue was used extensively in the media to reinforce the case for austerity. This was made all the more natural as discussion of the bailout coincided with debate on the 2011 budget, delivered to the parliament in early December 2010. Specifically, the main argument heard in the press was that the budget needed to be a tough one, in order to demonstrate Ireland's ability and willingness to reduce its deficit and hence avoid the need for financial support. For example, Peter Sutherland, the chairman of Goldman Sachs International and former attorney general of Ireland and EU commissioner, warned that it was 'imperative' that a 'robust' budget be passed by the Irish parliament to avoid IMF intervention, which is 'neither inevitable nor desirable', and that he was 'happy' that a €6 billion 'savings' package had been decided upon in that respect. It was reported that 'leading economists have warned that Ireland must cut spending by at least €7 billion in the budget for 2011 to avoid intervention' by the IMF. If the deficit reduction targets were not reached, 'it was very likely the bond markets would stop lending to Ireland or they would raise interest rates to impractical levels'. One economist, Colm McCarthy, said that the impending budget 'is our last chance for sovereignty' and warned that the IMF 'will be running Ireland by February [2011] if the Budget "fails to convince the financial markets"'.[5]

The issue of the bailout was also used to pillory the Fianna Fáil party for its poor economic performance, a tactic which was convenient given that the watershed elections of February 2011 were fast approaching. They resulted in the collapse of Fianna Fáil in one of the worst defeats by a sitting government since the birth of the Irish state in 1922. Fianna Fáil had presided over the Celtic Tiger expansion, but because of its association with the economic downfall, was replaced by a coalition government led by the Fine Gael party with the Labour Party as junior partner. Dissatisfaction with the ruling party's mismanagement of the economy led to much infighting among elites, including criticism for making a bailout inevitable. However, this was counterbalanced by a common elite interest in preserving national sovereignty over possible EU and IMF control over the country.

An *Irish Times* article, while lamenting the fact that Ireland would have to receive European financial support, which signified 'Ignominy heaped on catastrophe', argued that now, 'Honour demands that those at the helm who have failed to navigate away from this national humiliation should concede their failure and stand down'. However, it lamented the fact that 'they have no intention of doing so. Worse still, Government representatives display contempt for citizens with their bare-faced denials of a bailout when it is so patently happening'. Similarly, in a strongly worded editorial, the *Irish Times* asked 'whether this is what the men of 1916 died for: a bailout from the German chancellor with a few shillings of sympathy from the British chancellor on the side. There is the shame of it all. Having obtained our political independence from Britain to be the masters of our own affairs, we have now surrendered our sovereignty to the European Commission, the European Central Bank, and the International Monetary Fund'. The editors concluded that to bring the state this low 'and make it again subject to the decisions of others is an achievement that will not soon be forgiven. It must mark, surely, the ignominious end of a failed administration'. The level of dissatisfaction with the government was reflected in a poll that revealed that the public believed that the IMF was more capable of solving the crisis than Irish politicians.[6]

There were others, like the People Before Profit Alliance, who opposed the bailout, but not because it took away some of the power of Irish elites or because it stained the sense of patriotism the latter use to rally the country. Rather, their opposition was motivated by the fact that the EU and IMF intervention would reduce the already limited democratic input into governmental decisions on the economy and further entrench the 'free' market ideology that played a significant role in causing the collapse, in addition to reinforcing the implementation of austerity policies. However, such views received very limited coverage in the media.[7]

On the other hand, some articles suggested that an EU-IMF bailout, although undesirable, would not be so dramatic. For example, an *Irish Times* article entitled 'Signs suggest IMF is in tune with Ireland' argued that a 'bailout must be avoided if at all possible. But it would not be the end of the world if it happened' and would most likely 'not be as bad as feared'. Another piece, weighing the pros and cons of IMF intervention, noted that resorting to the IMF 'would do one very positive thing immediately. It would ensure that Ireland had access to money it needed', while another 'big positive is that it provides political cover for painful and difficult cuts to be introduced on issues like reform of the public sector'. However, the 'downsides are obvious. There is a loss of economic sovereignty'.[8]

Others went further and said that European elites taking control of the country would be beneficial because they would be able to implement reforms better than the Irish government itself: 'Putting our economy in the hands of the Germans and the Dutch for a period does not guarantee complete reform. But it provides an opportunity to break the power of the insiders while radically reducing our dependence on borrowed money in a planned way'. Furthermore, it 'would focus minds quickly. The executives of the IMF have seen it all before. They have dealt many times with the kind of rotten system operated in Ireland over the past decade'. The IMF would allegedly be able to remove the obstacles posed by the trade unions and the rich to needed reforms: 'Who else will tell lawyers that €1,000 a day is enough for anyone who purports to serve the state? Who else will dislodge the Services, Industrial, Professional and Technical Union (Siptu) hacks and left-wing luvvies that have inserted themselves at the top of the poverty industry on salaries of €120,000 a year?' Similarly, one commentator said that previous IMF annual consultations about Ireland 'conjure up nothing but a picture of reason: a property tax, reform of the social-welfare system to stop benefits being paid to those who do not need them, pensions reform, a structured mechanism to help those in mortgage arrears, with genuine reform and slimming down of the public sector'. In short, the IMF 'has basically suggested many of the measures that politicians and civil servants here are too cowardly or incompetent to implement'.[9]

Michael Casey, a former chief economist with the Central Bank of Ireland and a former IMF board member, wrote that an IMF programme may actually turn out to be a 'miracle' that would improve the economy, and is thus a 'no-brainer'. Such a programme is 'like sanctuary in a church' because the 'country is protected from the markets'. Another positive is that the IMF does not bother about democratic input into policy, nor does it worry about popular resentment caused by its prescriptions, which is important because, allegedly, 'Good economic policies are almost always unpopular'.[10]

Irish corporate circles espoused similar views about the impending aid package. In mid-November 2010, an article summarized the perceptions among business circles by stating that while most 'think intervention by an outside agency would harm Ireland, others argue that it could be exactly what is needed'. Danny McCoy, the director general of IBEC, said that 'there was cause for concern' about 'suggestions that the country was insolvent', and he believed that the government should try not to resort to a bailout. Mark Fielding, chief executive of ISME, was also opposed, because it 'would be an absolute disgrace for our sovereign government to throw in the towel ... We are a resilient nation and we roll up our sleeves and get stuck in when times are hard. We don't go knocking on doors looking for a bailout from anybody'. Finally, a partner in an investment firm said that 'Ireland's reputation would suffer if it was bailed out, but the country could recover'. Nevertheless, among some business owners, a growing feeling could be detected that 'the IMF-backed EFSF [European Financial Stability Facility] would force through politically difficult changes – pushing public sector reform and savings, and possibly cutting the minimum wage and dole payments'. An analyst at NCB Stockbrokers said that a bailout 'could actually be welcome' because it would bring certainty and stability to the way in which the economy would be managed and 'corporations like to make decisions in a stable world'. 'Crucially', it would also 'enable the country to focus on correcting the deficit, regaining competitiveness and promoting its virtues', such as 'a pro-business environment'. Sir Michael Smurfit, former chief executive and chairman of Jefferson Smurfit, the first big Irish multinational corporation (MNC), thought that the IMF 'might not be such a bad thing' because it 'will do things that the government can't do themselves, that politically they can't achieve'.[11]

As the bailout came closer to reality, the bitter pill was not so difficult to swallow, because in practice, EU-IMF prescriptions were in line with Irish elites' interests. IBEC now seemed to be more favourable to the aid, which it 'welcomed' because 'it provided much-needed certainty around Ireland's public finances and the path to recovery'. SIPTU, however, still opposed the plan, which it branded 'a shameful indictment of the right-wing policies that informed the Government's approach for the last 13 years and which now dominate thinking in European Union institutions'. An *Irish Times* article saw some positive aspects in the bailout. For example, on 'one level, intervention by the EU and the IMF is no bad thing. It means that rational decisions on how we can live within our means will now be forced down the throats of the competing interests who have stymied any genuine national response to the crisis'. Another piece, entitled 'Firm hand of the IMF will keep us steering in right direction', argued that measures proposed by the IMF would be what the Irish government intended to do anyway, such as 'the introduction of a property tax, higher university fees/charges, further reductions in the size of the public sector payroll and some widening of the tax base'. Therefore, outside intervention is tolerable, because it will simply be a 'nudge to keep our shoulder to the wheel and do what we mostly all agree has to be done in any event'. A more explicit article, entitled 'I'd choose the IMF over this ailing government any day', argued that 'these IMF overseers will ensure that the Government will do what it has failed to do so far, and that is to bite the bullet on cutbacks and reform. It will ensure that we stick to the timetable promised, or else we won't get further cash'.[12]

Nevertheless, there was still resentment on the part of Irish elites. One official said tersely that the 'ECB f—ked us', and Michael Noonan, then soon to be minister for finance, suggested that 'Germany was benefitting from the crisis' and he wanted to tell the European Commission that 'Ireland was not a colony'. One issue on which Irish and European elites clashed was Ireland's low, 12.5 per cent corporate tax rate. Irish elites and the media were adamant that this had to be defended at all costs. A *Sunday Independent* poll among the chief executives of Ireland's top 200 companies revealed that 93 per cent of them believed that the 12.5 rate should not be changed. A *Sunday Times* editorial argued strongly in favour of including the IMF in any aid package that would be requested because it was more likely to support Ireland's low tax regime than European authorities: 'The strong voting position of America within the IMF could assist Ireland in keeping its corporate tax structure, provided it fights the case properly. Retaining low profits tax and a strong flow of inward investment is critical if the country is to create an export-led recovery'. Irish elites were united in their defence of the tax rate. Minister for Enterprise Batt O'Keeffe and Minister for Education Mary Coughlan said that it was 'non-negotiable' and opposition parties were 'unanimous in their call for the rate to remain'. Business groups agreed, such as the American Chamber of Commerce in Ireland, which represents US multinationals in the country, the Irish Taxation Institute, as well as Chambers Ireland, which represents Irish chambers of commerce. Lionel Alexander, a Hewlett-Packard executive and the American chamber's president, said that 'the fiscal success of Ireland's corporate tax policy is clear' in that it attracts foreign investment. Bill Doherty, the executive vice-president of Cook Medical, an American multinational, said about the rate that it 'would rock the MNC community if it changed. Just like the rain, the corporation tax rate is a constant in Ireland'. Accordingly, a survey of MNCs was released at that time which reiterated the view that 'the rate was crucial in attracting investment'. Pfizer Vice-President Paul Duffy warned that US multinationals 'may stop investing in Ireland or pull out completely' if the tax rate were increased as part of the bailout.[13]

The default option

The accumulation of sovereign debt in the peripheral countries gave rise to suggestions that defaulting on (parts of) it would be preferable to repaying it entirely, as the Irish government has insisted on doing. The media and European governments have repeated numerous times that default would lead to a variety of negative consequences, ranging from recession to Armageddon.

However, the literature on sovereign debt restructuring finds that countries which choose to or are forced to cancel the repayment of their debts usually suffer only short-term economic costs, while negative consequences over a longer period of time are not significant. A number of states have even benefited from default, such as Argentina and Ecuador, where post-default growth has been remarkable, as will be seen below. A systematic IMF study concluded that the 'most robust and striking finding is that the effect of defaults is short-lived, as we almost never can detect effects beyond one or two years'. This is a strong rebuttal of the official line from governments and the media. For example, 'there is by now agreement on the fact that default does not lead to a permanent exclusion from the international capital market. Although there is some capital market exclusion period following a default, countries that defaulted in the last three decades have regained access to international capital markets fairly quickly'.[14] Other studies have confirmed that default 'does not reduce significantly the probability of tapping the markets' and find that 'the average exclusion from international credit markets following a default declined from four years in the 1980s to two years in the 1990s'. Some have also been 'unable to detect strong punishment of defaulting countries by credit markets'. Likewise, capital inflows to a defaulting country increase as time elapses after the default. Moreover, the level of bilateral trade between a defaulting country and its creditor countries tends to decrease initially, but it eventually recovers. Similarly, 'Reputation of sovereign borrowers that fall in default, as measured by credit ratings and spreads, is tainted, but only for a short time'. One would need to look hard in the media to find statements that even approach those established findings about default.[15]

Debt restructurings may have a negative effect on output growth, but it is not as large as is commonly perceived, as there is no 'statistically significant effect after the year in which the default takes place' although there is a negative effect on GDP growth 'ranging between 0.6 and 2.5 percentage points' immediately after default.[16] Furthermore, some argue that the impact of default on growth is in fact even less negative than the consensus in the literature maintains. Using a fine-grained analysis relying on quarterly GDP data (instead of annual data), such studies conclude with 'a simple and sobering message: contrary to what it is typically presumed, defaults have not been followed by output contractions. In fact, we find that the opposite seems to be the case: the default quarter coincides with the trough of the output contraction, and marks the start of the economic recovery'. This means that the negative output effects of default are likely related to its anticipation rather than to the default itself – and once it has happened, growth picks up quickly. This finding has one important policy implication: once the market anticipates a default, the formal decision to stop servicing the debt actually 'does not entail any additional cost', and at that point, 'default is therefore optimal (or even overdue)'. Finally, it could be maintained that the unemployment rate is a more meaningful measure of social well-being than growth and that a default's impact on employment should be assessed. It turns out that the same results hold – namely, that whatever negative consequences on unemployment default may have, they materialize before a country formally stops servicing its debts, and unemployment starts decreasing just as the event takes place.[17]

In short, default tends not to involve significant long-term economic costs, which seriously puts into question claims by European elites and the media that it only leads to negative consequences. However, it also raises the additional question of why countries repay their debts, if the consequences of not doing so are not as catastrophic as is often claimed. In the case of the European sovereign debt crisis, the answer has to do with power. Countries like Spain, Greece, Ireland and Portugal repay their debts because the troika and international creditors in core countries like Germany and France put pressure on domestic elites in the debtor country to do so, and in turn, domestic elites are usually happy to go along while implementing austerity programmes that cut welfare spending and increase taxes. There is thus a loose alliance between creditors and domestic elites whose aim is to squeeze ordinary people and repay sovereign debts, many of which are private debts that have been socialized. International elites to whom the debts are owed wish to be repaid and national elites in debtor countries collaborate and in turn can increase their relative power within their own societies through structural adjustment programmes that loosen labour regulations, reduce the minimum wage and cut social services. The dynamics can be understood through reference to a 'transnational capitalist class' that has become more prominent over the last several decades, within the context of globalization.[18] The transnationalization of capital thesis has generated much critical debate which has argued that it should not be exaggerated, as domestic and international elites are not homogenous and national dominant classes have not lost all ties to their home country, as implied in some accounts.[19] Nevertheless, the point is that although there are tensions and differences of interests among elites – both within and between nation-states – they still share strong common interests, for example, in the preservation of a (neoliberal) capitalist system and in the repayment of sovereign debts.[20]

The European debt crisis provides an obvious example of such dynamics, but there are also parallels with the experiences of developing countries that have repaid debts to international creditors in the Western world. For example, Joseph Stiglitz explains how the process works in his discussion of the role of the IMF's 'rescue' packages to Russia and Asian countries during their 1990s financial crises. His key point is that such bailouts seek to save creditors at the expense of taxpayers living in debtor countries. This is why 'bankruptcy and standstills were not (and are still not) welcome options, for they meant that creditors would not be repaid'. The bailout funds 'are often used to pay back foreign creditors, even when the debt was private'. In 'the Asian financial crisis, this was great for the American and European creditors, who were glad to get back the money they had lent to Thai or Korean banks and businesses or at least more of it than they otherwise would have'.[21]

Accordingly, the task of reducing popular opposition to the socialization of private debts requires a substantial amount of ideological work. It is here that the media play a role in presenting favourably such policies to the public, as will be seen shortly.[22] In particular, the ways in which news organizations have offered negative views of default will be examined in detail. First, though, the next section reviews the scale and sources of Irish government debt during the crisis.

Ireland's debts

Between 2000 and 2007, Irish government debt was kept at a low level and was even falling, thanks to the economic boom. The gross government debt-to-GDP ratio stood at 37 per cent in 2000, 30 per cent in 2003 and 25 per cent in 2007, making it one of the lowest debt burdens in the EU. However, it then worsened considerably and reached 117 per cent of GDP (€192 billion) in 2012, a four-fold increase over the previous five years. As such, it rose from the second lowest debt-to-GDP ratio in the eurozone in 2007 to the fourth highest in 2012.[23]

Irish government debt has evolved greatly since the onset of the crisis.[24] For example, at the end of 2012, general government debt stood at 117 per cent of GDP and the state had €208 billion of total liabilities. This was composed mainly of €94 billion of government bonds, €62 billion of loans including EU and IMF borrowings, and €25 billion of promissory notes. The February 2013 deal replaced all promissory notes with long-term government bonds, but no debt was cancelled in this process. Bonds thus now account for a larger portion of total sovereign debt. The maturity structure of those debts in 2013 is shown in Figure 5.1. (To this must be added contingent liabilities, estimated at €119 billion in total, including government guarantees for €75 billion of bank liabilities and for €29 billion of NAMA bonds.)[25]

Ireland's debt structure thus reveals the following potential points of default or restructuring.[26] The point is not that Ireland should default uni-laterally in all possible ways, but that over the crisis years, such avenues for restructuring should have been explored more seriously.

- Government bonds: a sovereign default would hit investors holding the bonds. As will be seen below, this option has been dismissed by the media. As of mid-2013, the Irish government had issued €115.5 billion in medium- and long-term bonds, 55 per cent of which were held by for-eigners. This percentage would be over 70 per cent if one excludes the €25 billion of long-dated government bonds issued to the Irish Central Bank in early 2013 to replace the promissory notes.[27]
- Bank bonds: repaying bank bondholders became the responsibility of the Irish government due to the guarantee of liabilities and nationalization of financial institutions. Between 30 September 2008, when the guarantee was introduced, and April 2012, a sum of €103.7 billion was paid to senior bondholders, including €32.5 billion by AIB/EBS, €35.7 billion by Bank of

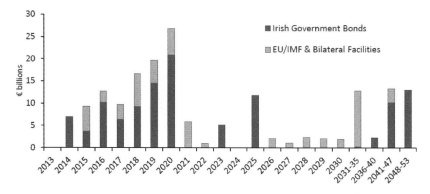

Figure 5.1 Repayment schedule of Irish government debt, August 2013
Source: Barnes and Smyth 2013

Ireland, €10 billion by IL&P and €25.5 billion by the IBRC (Irish Bank Resolution Corporation), the successor of Anglo Irish Bank and Irish Nationwide Building Society (INBS).[28]

The government does not publish a list of bonds paid and outstanding, which reveals its interest in reducing criticism of such repayments. The alternative news websites NAMAWineLake and Bondwatch have put together, to this author's knowledge, the only list available, although it is not perfectly reliable due to a number of bond market changes difficult to document.[29] Analysts estimate that as of early 2014, there are only a few bonds outstanding. Therefore, defaulting on such bonds would not alleviate Ireland's debt burden as much as it would have earlier in time. The bonds have effectively been replaced on banks' balance sheets by funding from the ECB and the Central Bank of Ireland, whose refinancing has allowed the bonds to be repaid. Irish banks, and thus the Irish government, must now pay back or roll over this Central Bank funding. As will be seen below, the media have not been very forceful in exposing the costs incurred by the state to pay bondholders. However, there has been some discussion in the press of possible haircuts that could be applied to bond repayments, in particular to Anglo Irish bonds.

• Promissory notes and related bonds: promissory notes were replaced in February 2013 by long-term government bonds, but the debate that took place about them over the previous two years is instructive. The details related to the notes are complex, but can be summarized as follows. The IBRC was formed in 2011 by merging Anglo Irish Bank and INBS. In order to pay those institutions' creditors, the Central Bank of Ireland printed money in the form of Extraordinary Lending Assistance (ELA). However, such monetary financing not being allowed under eurozone legislation, the Irish government agreed to repay the funds to the Central Bank of Ireland in annual instalments totalling €47.9 billion until the year 2031, through the vehicle of promissory notes. In short, money was first created, then used to pay the IBRC's creditors, and must now be repaid over a number of years by the state.[30]

One significant point about the notes is that not repaying them would have only resulted in more euros in circulation, giving rise to worries about inflation. The point of repaying them was only to mop up the excess money first created to repay the IBRC's creditors. No creditor or investor would have been hit by defaulting on the notes – the only concern was inflation. Politically, even if the amount of money initially printed was very small relative to the size of the eurozone, the ECB did not want to allow Ireland to default and set a precedent that could be followed by other countries. It is a matter of speculation as to how the ECB and European authorities would have reacted to a unilateral Irish default on the notes. Some alarmist commentators have claimed that the ECB could have withdrawn the large amount of funding it provides to Irish banks, leading to a collapse of the Irish financial system, or that Ireland could have been expelled from the eurozone. However, others have maintained that the ECB would not have retaliated because widespread bank failures in one member country, or expulsion, would have had devastating political consequences for the euro project. In any case, it is clear that an Irish default on the notes would have had no significant negative economic impact at all, their amount being too small to create inflation in the eurozone.[31]

In February 2013, the IBRC was dissolved by the Irish government and the promissory notes arrangement restructured. The new deal is complex but boils down to the following. The notes have been eliminated and replaced by long-term government bonds. The repayment of the latter by the Irish government will take place over a longer time frame – 40 years – than the promissory notes. This is a benefit for the government, but there has been no debt cancelled, so that its nominal value remains the same, although extended maturities will lighten the burden.[32]

- Central bank loans (ECB and Central Bank of Ireland): the ECB and Central Bank of Ireland have provided large amounts of liquidity to Irish banks. For example, ELA was provided to the IBRC in order to pay its bondholders. In 2013, ECB refinancing of Irish banks amounted to about €36 billion, down from a peak of nearly €160 billion in both ECB and Central Bank of Ireland refinancing in early 2011.[33] The possibility of defaulting on those loans has been largely ignored by the media, with the exception of a few analysts. Yet, a default or restructuring would not hit any investor directly, and would only result in leaving more euros in circulation, as in the above case of the promissory notes repayments.
- IMF, EU and bilateral loans: the EU-IMF bailout included loans from the IMF (€22.5 billion), EU (European Financial Stability Mechanism/EFSF) and the United Kingdom, Denmark and Sweden (€45 billion). A default on these loans would affect these creditors and the losses would ultimately be shared by member governments of the EU and IMF. There has been little discussion in the media of defaulting on such loans beyond calls for minor restructurings.

The media on default

In order to examine the opinions circulated in the media on the question of default, several searches were conducted on the *Nexis* database in the five main Irish newspapers for the period 2008–13. The first search identified all pieces that contained the phrase 'sovereign default' or 'sovereign debt default' anywhere in the articles. This ensured that virtually all references to the idea would be captured, and a total of 503 articles were returned.[34] Three other searches were conducted, for mentions of 'default', 'bondholders' and 'promissory notes' appearing at the start of articles in the opinion and business sections. These searches together returned a total of 1,256 articles.[35] The four searches combined provided a relatively comprehensive dataset to examine press coverage of the default option.

A first observation is that default has not been discussed in the media as much as could have been expected. The number of articles returned by the searches may seem large, but a number of those pieces were either descriptive or not related to default for the case of Ireland. Approximately 500 articles on 'sovereign default' in five newspapers over five years is equivalent to roughly 20 articles per year per newspaper. Considering that a significant portion of those do not voice any clear opinion on the subject, or are related to another country (e.g., Greece), or mention the topic only in passing, it can be concluded that there has been relatively little engagement with the option of a sovereign default on Ireland's debts, which demonstrates implicitly the media's opposition to it.

When the subject of sovereign default has been discussed, it has gathered almost invariably negative connotations.. It has been described as a possible 'cataclysm', an 'evil day', 'an unmitigated disaster', 'hugely damaging', a 'doomsday scenario' and the harbinger of 'intolerable contagion effects' throughout the eurozone. It has also been alleged that it would bring 'hyper-inflation, increased unemployment, ravaged public services', with the result that 'We wouldn't be trimming services in one hospital. We would be closing hospitals'.[36]

An alarmist article entitled 'What would happen to your money if Ireland defaulted?' emphasized the dire consequences that individuals would allegedly face if Ireland did not repay its debts or if it left the euro. It stated that a default would result in 'pensions and savings wiped out' and 'mortgage bills at sky-high levels', while it could 'blast a hole in your pocket'. The Irish pound could be reintroduced following a euro exit, but it would 'plummet', plunging the country into a 'currency crisis'. Ordinary people's savings 'would be worth between 50 and 70 per cent less in punts than they would have been worth in euro', or worse, 'You could lose your savings if your bank or credit union went bust'. Pensions would be threatened like in Argentina, which 'expropriated pension funds' when it defaulted. Further, hyperinflation would emerge: in countries that have defaulted, prices have 'exploded' and the 'same would probably happen here'. Moreover, 'Your child benefit and dole' would be threatened because if Ireland defaults on its EU-IMF loans, it would not have the necessary funds to meet its budget deficit. The government would then need 'to unleash spending cuts of €18bn', which could mean to 'slash child benefit, dole payments, state pensions and public sector wages by about a third'. Also, if the country defaulted, 'our reputation might never recover' and multinationals could 'pull out of Ireland, leading to major job losses'. Daily lives would be affected immediately: 'Paying by credit card could be impossible' and we could be 'forced to barter for food and petrol', while the black economy would thrive, and 'we'd become a third-world country'.[37]

Prime Minister Enda Kenny ruled out a default, asserting that there was 'no case for a sovereign default here under any circumstances … You simply don't do that as a country'. He also declared that 'We will not have "defaulter" written on our foreheads. We will pay our way'. Moreover, while EU leaders were advancing a plan to cut half of the Greek national debt, Kenny was 'adamant' that Ireland 'will not renege on any obligations to its international creditors'. The point was that 'any move to follow the Greek example would be self-defeating and would hamper Ireland's growth prospects', while it would bring 'huge' damage to Ireland's reputation and 'delay Ireland's return to markets'. In short, the elite consensus, as outlined by the prime minister, has been not to default, but to make minor modifications to the terms of repayment: 'We will not unilaterally repudiate the agreement with our partners, but will instead continue to improve its terms to make it more affordable'.[38]

The media have contributed to make this strategy the preferred one. Some messages have been sensationalist, as when one analyst wrote that 'Ireland may have, via the last default wild card, a finger on the fiscal equivalent of the nuclear button. However, the problem any future government faces is that if we do press the button, will we blow ourselves up first?' There have been repeated calls not to antagonize other European countries and the ECB, whose role in the crisis is perceived as helpful to peripheral countries, along with many references to 'contagion' that would 'spread rapidly' if bondholders were not paid, which would add 'fuel to the fire of an Irish debt-spiral'. The *Irish Times* complained about a 'widespread public delusion that there is some relatively painless way out of our current woes', whereas the 'reality is that we have got to implement the EU-IMF programme as any alternative will be far worse'. 'Snake oil' solutions like unilateral default or leaving the euro are just 'populist rabble rousing' and will make things 'a whole lot worse and would plunge the country into a serious long-term decline'. A sovereign default would 'impose immediate cuts in public spending that would be five times greater than all the budget "adjustments" since 2008 taken together'. The case for austerity surfaced again, as the 'only coherent alternative to the doomsday scenario is a determined effort to get the exchequer finances under control'.[39]

Professor John McHale, the head of economics at the National University of Ireland, Galway, is also strongly opposed to default. In a piece entitled 'Putting brakes on default bandwagon', he argues that the 'populist urge to blow Ireland Inc's creditors out of the water is a siren call that could land us on the rocks'. He warns of the 'reputational damage' that this would inflict on Ireland and concludes that sovereign and bank debts should be honoured to preserve 'the goodwill of the international community'. Even if some conditions attached to the EU-IMF bailout are harsh, such as the complete protection of unguaranteed senior bondholders, we should still repay to the last cent because without ECB assistance, 'the Irish banking system would have collapsed'. Similarly, Colm McCarthy thinks it would be wrong to 'stuff the bondholders' of banks for which the state has become responsible. Removing the guarantee and letting them take the hit 'is not a unilateral policy option for Ireland' because it 'is ruled out by our agreements with the IMF' and European authorities. Perhaps at some later point in time bondholder haircuts could be advisable, but it 'does not appear to be a viable go-it-alone strategy for Ireland at this stage'. Others have suggested that a default 'would shut the nation out of international financial markets', even though 'Populist economists argue that capital markets have no memory and, consequently, that access to external borrowing would resume quickly'.[40]

The media have highlighted dire prognostics regularly. For example, an article mentioned a report by rating agency Fitch which argued that a default in peripheral countries could damage the economy through disruptions to 'Government payments to firms that supply services', 'Supply chains for companies', 'Firms and their banking facilities', and 'in extremis' disturbances to payment systems. A *Sunday Independent* article discussed a Goldman Sachs report arguing that Irish 'banks would be all but wiped out if the Government was to default or restructure the State's borrowings because of their vast holdings of Irish bonds and sovereign debt'. This 'machine-gunning of the banks' balance sheets by any restructuring or haircuts on state debt is seen as a key reason that the Government is so keen to avoid default'. The article described sovereign defaults or debt restructurings as 'nasty surprises' and quoted ECB officials as saying that 'Restructuring is not a solution, it's a horror story', and that such moves would 'very probably' have systemic consequences 'quite likely more devastating' than the Lehman Brothers collapse.[41]

However, claims that default would lead to 'Armageddon' were disproved when in 2012, Greece defaulted on its sovereign debt in the largest sovereign restructuring in modern history, which 'set a new world record in terms of restructured debt volume and aggregate creditor losses'. The default involved some €200 billion of sovereign debt and applied haircuts of about 60 per cent on bonds held by investors, resulting in a debt relief of more than 50 per cent of GDP. As a careful examination of the default concludes, it 'refuted predictions that the debt restructuring would lead to chaos and financial collapse in Europe' and, in fact, 'it certainly demonstrated the feasibility of orderly sovereign debt restructuring inside the EU'. There has been very little media commentary on this obvious fact.[42]

Neither has the press mentioned the European history directly relevant to the current situation. In particular, Germany's debt was largely cancelled after World War II.[43] The London Debt Agreement of 1953 wrote down its outstanding debt by a significant amount and established a schedule that extended the repayments over 30 years, which allowed the country to recover and become Europe's economic leader. It even postponed the payment of part of the interest until reunification, and the terms of repayment were very accommodating to ensure that Germany could recover and become a strong Western ally. For example, it was decided that only interest payments were due for the period 1953–58. Also, debt service was made dependent on capacity to pay and no more than 5 per cent of export revenues were to be used to reimburse its debts. In the words of one analyst, the agreement was based on the premise that 'Germany's actual payments could not be so high as to endanger the short-term welfare of her people or her long-term ability to rebuild a shattered economy and society'.[44] This came on top of other generous policies to support recovery, such as Marshall Plan aid from the United States, much of it in the form of grants. It was a very different strategy from that employed after World War I, when defeated Germany had been squeezed by being forced to pay heavy war reparations. It was also very different from the way Germany now treats peripheral countries, in one of the great ironies of the current crisis.

It is interesting that even Ashoka Mody, until recently a member of the IMF responsible for designing Ireland's financial rescue programme, has departed clearly from the predominant position in the Irish media. He has opposed austerity and argued in favour of the default option, which he now says is 'economically efficient', 'fair' and 'politically sensible'. In fact, it may be 'the only way to hold together an unsustainable structure that threatens to drive deeper divisions and set back the magnificent integration project on which Europe has embarked'. It should not be difficult to do, as there are 'well-known and orderly ways to bring banks' creditors to the table and engineer debt-equity swaps', just as there exist 'well-established techniques for sovereign debt reprofilings'. He adds that the idea that 'markets would be "spooked" has no good basis', as shown by the fact that the Greek debt restructuring was well received.[45]

Bank bondholders

Because of the guarantee given to the banks, the Irish government became responsible for their liabilities, in particular the debts they owed to bond-holders. The media have regularly described the potential consequences of defaulting on bondholders in negative and scary terms. For example, an *Irish Independent* article entitled 'Here's what is at stake if we don't repay those Anglo bondholders' noted that the ECB could withdraw its funding. Refusing to honour the bonds could have 'knock-on effects' for other banks, which would find it 'far harder' to borrow internationally while Ireland's return to the markets would be 'jeopardised'. Moreover, the cost of borrowing would rise for everybody, including individuals, businesses and banks. Also, 'Stiffing Anglo bondholders would be [a] high-risk strategy' because it could result in 'antagonising the bond markets', echoing the governor of the Central Bank of Ireland, Professor Patrick Honohan, who declared that it would be 'highly risky' to take 'any aggressive action' against Anglo's senior bondholders. Similarly, Leo Varadkar, a minister in the current ruling Fine Gael party, defended the repayment of Anglo bondholders because failure to do so would 'have shaken confidence in Ireland' internationally. He reiterated the govern-ment line when he said that most 'significantly, defaulting would bring us into sharp conflict with the ECB and other EU member states, at a time when we need them most'. The financial sector agreed. A large US brokerage firm warned that forcing Anglo haircuts 'will spook markets' and would result in a negative 'major impact that could last for a decade' and a bond investor writing in the *Irish Times* claimed that burning creditors 'would be extremely dangerous' and 'would completely shatter all confidence' in the banking system.[46]

It is true that there has been support in the press for burning the bond-holders, but such calls have been relatively weak. First, they have usually been restricted to specific kinds of bondholders and specific banks, rather than calling for a blanket default on bank debt. For example, Anglo Irish creditors have received the most attention and opprobrium in the media and default on Anglo bonds has been recommended by a number of commentators, however, bonds of other banks have received much less attention. Second, while there have been calls to default on bonds not covered by the Irish government guarantee, or on those 'junior' in status, media commentators have been in general more reluctant to call for default on bonds covered by the guarantee or 'senior' in status (there have actually been a few defaults on some junior bonds[47]). Third, there is a range of views among analysts favourable to imposing haircuts on bondholders, from those favouring small ones to those believing that larger ones would be more appropriate, and therefore to be in favour of default does not necessarily mean to support any radical losses for bondholders. Fourth, the media never produced a list of bonds paid or out-standing, which would have been a first investigative step to undertake if the press had wished to criticize government policy and inform the public about how state funds are used. Such work had to be undertaken by the efforts of one alternative news website, NAMAWineLake, which drew up a list of out-standing bonds, as mentioned above. Fifth, bond repayments have usually not been covered by the press to any serious degree. A media intent on challenging the government would, for example, have announced in front page articles when bonds were going to be repaid. A countdown to each repayment could even have been included in newspapers every day, but nothing of the sort was conducted by the press.

Finally, it should be noted that some of the calls to burn Anglo's or other banks' bondholders are best seen as populist declarations. For example, in a June 2010 article, economic commentator Marc Coleman denounced with great fanfare the transfer of €22 billion to bondholders, or '€4,888 from each man, woman and child in the Republic to Anglo bondholders', and believed the bondholders should take a hit. Yet, three weeks later, he seemed to have reversed his position in an article entitled 'Why defaulting on Anglo bonds is not an option', in which he said that 'brutal sudden moves – like defaulting on senior debt – could still be highly counter-productive' and that defaulting could scare the markets, which he believed should be treated 'with a mixture of fear and respect'. Coleman hinted at a middle-ground position, writing that 'Between paying those debt holders the whole whack and defaulting is an interim position: negotiating a haircut on their loans, as was done with our domestic banks'. This approach is representative of the position of a significant portion of the media.[48]

In sum, news organizations have reflected the views of political and economic elites. Bondholder losses are part of the normal workings of capitalism, and although international institutions such as the IMF put much effort into ensuring that creditors are repaid in full, when it becomes clear that it is not possible, settling for partial repayment is an accepted second-best alternative. The range of acceptable debate in the media has coincided with the range of debate among elites. For example, the IMF has been more favourable to the option of creditors taking losses than the European Commission and the ECB, which have taken a relatively hard line on defaults. Lorenzo Bini Smaghi, an ECB executive board member, argued that defaulting 'is not a viable option' because 'it would lead to a flight of capital and deeper disaster'. However, more radical options, such as a large, Argentine-style debtor-led default, have not received any significant support in the media.[49]

The narrow spectrum of debate is illustrated by a pair of pieces in the *Sunday Independent* on whether or not Ireland should default. One article makes the case for 'no' and repeats the official line that it would be 'economic suicide' and 'totally undesirable and unnecessary' because the country would lose access to credit markets. Defaulting on all or part of Anglo's debt is 'not worth it' for the same reasons. The other article presents the 'yes' case for default, but by this it means a very limited kind of default, for example, 'defaulting on at least some of the Anglo debt', or guaranteeing banks' future liabilities but not their past ones, or imposing some losses on bondholders that are 'less extreme than wiping them out completely'. However, more drastic alternatives have received scant attention, even if endorsed by Nobel Prize winners like economist Joseph Stiglitz, who described government payments to bondholders as 'unconscionable'. He asked, 'Why should Irish taxpayers have to give up health and education to make good on a loan from a private bank when the previous government failed to do an adequate job of regulation?' He said that the Irish government should not be intimidated by 'threats from creditor banks and political partners' in Europe because they are 'as predictable as they are toothless', while adding that 'They always say if you don't all hell will break lose but the fact is, whenever it's tested, it's never true … Russia defaulted and was back in the market a short time later. And that was a government defaulting, [while] Ireland is socialised debt of an unsecured creditor'.[50]

A *Sunday Independent* survey of the chief executives of the top 200 Irish companies revealed that corporate leaders' views on bank bondholders correspond to media coverage: some believe that all bank bondholders should be repaid, while others call for more flexible terms on Ireland's debt burden. Indeed, 25 per cent of executives think that 'the bondholders should not be touched', 45 per cent believe they 'should be burned', and 30 per cent are 'undecided'. Goodbody's Stockbrokers said that the government should impose 50 per cent losses on all unguaranteed bank bonds to alleviate the costs of the banking bailout (guaranteed bonds, however, would apparently need to be repaid in full). Interviews with top Irish business leaders find similar opinions. Most argue that Ireland's debt situation should be alleviated through concessions such as debt restructuring or interest rate reduction, while the government should pursue austerity in order to show resolve to European authorities and global markets. One CEO thinks that 'We absolutely should not default' but we should 'restructure the debt because, like any business, you can't run anything well if you're relying on short-term funding', while a lower rate of interest would also help. Another executive says that 'We need to restructure by seeking a repayment period far beyond that contained in the EU-IMF bailout agreement', but if 'we are refused a longer repayment period we should notify the EU of our intention to default'. Other executives emphasize the need for fiscal consolidation, as one who declares that 'we need to convince the markets that we have taken the necessary steps to avoid a restructuring' by generating a government budget surplus and not a deficit. Another one suggests to 'cut the €19bn public sector wage bill' and 'take an axe to some of the benefits in terms of pensions' and other areas. Interviews with Irish business leaders operating abroad revealed similar views. One executive believes that all 'unsubordinated bondholders should be cut, but we have to honour guaranteed bank debt', while there is a need to cut the government deficit, especially by taking 'an axe to most of the civil service'. Another thinks that 'We shouldn't default … but restructuring the debt might work as part of a proper business plan for the country'. Another agrees, saying that if 'we default, we risk making ourselves a pariah of the global economy and we'd further damage our international reputation'. However, creditors 'should share some responsibility for the money they lent the banks' by restructuring the debt and extending maturities 'as far as possible'.[51]

Promissory notes

The dominant view conveyed by the media about the promissory notes was that there should not have been a unilateral default on them, although a more flexible repayment arrangement could have been negotiated. The debate in the press reflected tactical divisions among elites similar to those mentioned above. The ECB was mostly opposed to radical changes in repayment terms and the IMF took a more flexible position. In the media, the *Irish Times'* Dan O'Brien believed that the ECB was 'entirely correct to refuse to magic away Ireland's promissory notes', otherwise, the dominoes would start falling: 'If the ECB was to delete some of Ireland's debts at the click of a button, as some people advocate, it would not be long before other governments started issuing promissory notes and looking to Frankfurt for some monetising magic'. Another piece argued that a 'unilateral cessation of payments on the promissory note would also entail risks, given Ireland's current dependence on troika resources for day-to-day budget funding'. However, because 'it is in everyone's interest that Ireland turn out to be a success story', flexibility on the promissory notes 'could significantly cut Ireland's funding requirements over the next few years', which would be positive.[52] This strategy sat well with mild calls for debt flexibility in general, as a *Sunday Business Post* editorial stated:

> The reality is that, to have some chance of getting back into financial markets, an overall deal to restructure the promissory note payments is

needed. If there is to be no actual write-off of any of this debt – as the EU and ECB continue to insist – then the deal must help Ireland in other ways. The repayments must be stretched over a long enough period and on favourable enough terms to allow a cut in the actual burden of our national debt. There is also no reason why, in time, a restructuring of our repayments to the EU and IMF should not be negotiated.[53]

Achieving a rescheduling of the notes was the government's position, and in February 2013, it was agreed with European authorities to replace the notes with long-term bonds. The deal was praised by the media, even if it included no debt cancellation at all. An *Irish Times* editorial stated that the deal marked 'an important landmark in the country's rocky road to recovery' and the prospect of 'an earlier return to growth', while for taxpayers it represented 'the prospect of a real, welcome easing of financial pressures'. The government was congratulated for having 'held its nerve when others despaired' and the deal was deemed to have 'reinforced the image of the competence' of the ruling parties while providing a 'massive boost' for them. The promissory notes agreement was also well received by Irish business leaders interviewed by the *Sunday Independent*. One of them thought the package was 'very positive news' and signified that 'Ireland has turned a corner'. Another was confident that the resulting improvement in Ireland's image internationally would translate into reduced borrowing costs. Yet another believed that the deal would 'undoubtedly' help the economy recover. It was also asserted that it would raise consumer confidence and that an effective reduction of the debt had to be welcomed.[54]

However, the option of a larger default on the notes was brushed aside as 'naïve and a waste of time' because 'the effects of a default could have been catastrophic' for the usual reasons: the ECB could withdraw its funding from the Irish banking system, which would then allegedly collapse, the government would supposedly be excluded from the bond markets, in addition to hurting Ireland's reputation, according to Donal Donovan, a former IMF staff member.[55]

However, this catastrophic scenario was far from certain, indeed unlikely, as others pointed out. For example, David McWilliams wrote that the consequences of not repaying the notes were 'likely to be minimal'. The ECB would most probably not have withdrawn its funding from the Irish banking system because this would have spread contagion throughout the eurozone. In fact, Greece has defaulted four times already within the euro, and the ECB never used the 'nuclear option' in retaliation. Therefore, McWilliams, like other economists, advocated not to repay the notes. Because they were essentially debts Ireland owed itself (the government had to pay back the Central Bank of Ireland), a default would not have involved any other government or investor taking direct losses. The only consequence to not repaying the notes would have been that the liquidity funding in the form of ELA used to repay bank bondholders would not have been expunged from the eurosystem.

Because the notes constituted such a small fraction of the total money in circulation in the eurozone, not repaying them would thus have had no negative effect in that respect, as Constantin Gurdgiev explained.[56]

Another interesting point is that while the media enthusiastically endorsed the deal, they were nevertheless quick to warn that it should not be seen as a pretext to relax austerity. For example, a *Sunday Business Post* editorial reminded its readers that there was a 'risk' that in the wake of the deal, some would start believing that 'we should ease up on "austerity" or find extra money to invest in "job creation projects"', but, the editors maintained, there is 'a need for a dose of reality here', reminding their audience that 'a serious deficit remains' and that we are still 'living beyond our means'. Therefore, we must not falter and must opt for 'sticking with the existing plan' of fiscal consolidation. It would be 'a big mistake to send out a message that the problem of the public finances is, in some way, close to being fixed'. Professor Philip Lane agreed and penned an article entitled 'To slacken austerity would be a big mistake' because Ireland 'would lose credibility and court disaster by taking a break'. The *Sunday Times* stated the same in a bold editorial entitled 'We should continue to toe the troika line', which argued that it 'would be foolish of the government to deviate wildly off course' in its pursuit of fiscal consolidation.[57]

ECB, Central Bank of Ireland, EU/IMF and bilateral loans

During the crisis, Irish banks have received large amounts of funding from both the ECB and the Irish Central Bank. As seen above, in mid-2013 for example, ECB refinancing of Irish banks amounted to about €36 billion, down from a peak of nearly €160 billion in early 2011. The possibility of defaulting on such loans has not been discussed to any significant extent in the media. Yet, it would be one way to alleviate Ireland's debt burden, although the potential write off would have been larger if done earlier in time. Furthermore, in the case of EU, IMF and bilateral loans, the option of defaulting on those borrowings has generated so little discussion in the media that perhaps the most obvious conclusion to draw is that news organizations have, in practice, erased this alternative by remaining silent about it.

Few media commentators have advocated defaulting on ECB loans to banks. Economists Constantin Gurdgiev and Brian Lucey called for restructuring the loans to reduce Ireland's debt burden, perhaps via 'a direct write-down of 20–25 per cent of Irish banks' borrowings from the ECB'. David McWilliams outlined a series of actions to decrease bank debt and offer some protection to taxpayers. First, Ireland should default on bank bondholders or force them into a debt-for-equity swap. Next, the ECB could be told that its loans to Irish banks simply cannot be repaid. It is important to understand that in return for those loans, Irish banks gave the ECB dubious collateral, such as bundles of home and car loans. Therefore, the ECB gave Irish banks real money and Irish banks gave the ECB promises to pay – it is thus the ECB that is in trouble. Contrary to the official story, McWilliams made the plausible argument that if Ireland defaulted on its bank debt, financial markets would not punish the country by taking money out of it. Rather, the 'markets will support this move' because they 'want an economy with less debt and some growth potential, not one that is intent on strangling itself with other people's debts'. In other words, defaulting on bank debt would reduce the Irish debt burden, a first step toward recovery. With (part of) the bank debt removed, the government could go back to the markets and obtain financing more cheaply. Also, in order to negotiate with European authorities about the bank debt, it would help to form an alliance of peripheral countries facing the same problems in order to obtain a stronger bargaining voice with the ECB and push the concept of 'co-responsibility' whereby both creditors and debtors are responsible for banks' inability to repay their borrowings. This strategy has received almost no mention in the media.[58]

Democratic deficit vs. debt audits

An important but often forgotten issue in relation to peripheral countries' debts is that the decision not to default is usually taken with little democratic input, which would reduce elites' privileges. This is why a concept like a debt audit to identify 'odious debts' has received virtually no attention in the media. The notion of odious debt refers to borrowings that were not used to benefit the population and which were often contracted without popular consent.[59]

In 2008, Ecuador became the first country to reduce its debt burden by invoking the odious debt concept. President Rafael Correa announced that interest payments on some bonds would stop and a successful bond buyback was engineered in which the government repurchased its own bonds at a significant discount of 35 cents in the dollar, thus retiring about one-third ($3.2 billion) of the external debt. An audit of Ecuador's past borrowings was conducted and determined that some debts were odious, having been contracted, for example, by the military regime in the 1970s, under corrupt arrangements, for projects which never benefited the population, or under coercive conditions imposed by the IMF and the World Bank. The debt default did not impact negatively on GDP growth; in fact, Ecuador 'suffered only a mild recession during the 2008–9 global downturn' to rebound thereafter, in contrast to Europe, whose economies have been sluggish at best.[60]

Yet, the Irish press has virtually ignored Ecuador's relevant experience, while only a handful of articles have mentioned the possibility of conducting a debt audit in Ireland. A search for the phrases 'debt audit' or 'odious debt' as related to Ecuador in all 64 Irish publications included in the *Nexis* database returned only four articles between 2008 and 2013. A search for articles containing the phrase 'debt audit' as related to Ireland in the same 64 publications returned only six pieces published during the same period. The only article in the *Irish Times* was a short 292-word piece. This is even though a debt audit was actually conducted in Ireland by scholars at the University of Limerick, which received virtually no media coverage.[61]

In sum, the issue of debt repayment illustrates the serious democratic deficit that has characterized the response to the crisis in Ireland and Europe. The implementation of austerity reveals the same state of affairs, as the next chapter shows.

Notes

1 J. FitzGerald and I. Kearney, 'Irish Government Debt and Implied Debt Dynamics: 2011–15', ESRI research article, Dublin: Economic and Social Research Institute, 2011, p. 8, www.esri.ie/UserFiles/publications/QEC2011Aut_SA_FitzGerald. pdf (accessed 5 December 2013).

2 V. Browne, 'We Didn't Need IMF to Tell Us to Target Needy', *IT*, 24 November 2010; D. McWilliams, *The Good Room: Why we Ended up in a Debtors' Prison – and How we can Break Free*, Dublin: Penguin, 2012, pp. 39–40.

3 V. Browne, 'The Country Will Be Ruined, and Nothing Will Change', *SBP*, 14 November 2010; G. Kerrigan, 'Elite Stand Ready to Serve New Overlords', *SI*, 21 November 2010.

4 P. Leahy, 'EU Bailout Pressure Intensifies', *SBP*, 14 November 2010; A. Beesley and S. Collins, 'Government Campaigns to Avoid EU Financial Bailout', *IT*, 13 November 2010; S. Collins, M. O'Regan and A. Beesley, 'Ministers Claim Fiscal Plan and Budget Negate Need for Bailout', *IT*, 15 November 2010; 'Spirit of Nation must be Revived', *SI*, 31 October 2010.

5 'Passing of December Budget Imperative says Sutherland', *IT*, 6 November 2010; S. McInerney, 'Economists: Cut Budget by €7bn', *ST*, 31 October 2010; J. Corcoran, 'McCarthy Warning: IMF is at Our Door', *SI*, 31 October 2010.

6 D. O'Brien, 'Ignominy of Bailout Compounded by Contemptuous Leaders', *IT*, 18 November 2010; 'Was it for This?' *IT*, 18 November 2010; 'IMF would do Better than Parties in Solving Economic Crisis, Poll Shows', *II*, 11 October 2010.

7 S. Carroll, 'Call to Stand Up to EU and IMF "Bullies"', *IT*, 19 November 2010.

8 D. O'Brien, 'Signs Suggest IMF is in Tune with Ireland', *IT*, 1 October 2010; R. Curran, 'Who's Afraid of the IMF', *SBP*, 14 November 2010.

9 D. Kiberd, 'IMF Heavies will Take a Firmer Grip', *ST*, 7 November 2010; B. Carey, 'The Big Bad IMF May Save Us from Europe', *ST*, 14 November 2010.

10 M. Casey, 'Search and Rescue', *IT*, 26 November 2010.

11 G. Daly, 'Weighing Up the Pros and Cons of a Bailout', *SBP*, 14 November 2010; T. Lyons, 'IMF Strictures Might Not Be Such a Bad Thing', *ST*, 21 November 2010.

12 E. Donnellan, 'Plan Doomed to Fail, says Siptu', *IT*, 29 November 2010; S. Collins, 'Surrender of Sovereignty Highlights Political Failings', *IT*, 18 November 2010; D. Donovan, 'Firm Hand of the IMF will Keep Us Steering in Right Direction', *IT*, 19 November 2010; 'I'd Choose the IMF Over this Ailing Government Any Day', *II*, 20 November 2010.

13 D. O'Brien, 'Far from being Calmed, Crisis has Ratcheted to Boiling Point', *IT*, 27 November 2010; 'Burn the Bank Bondholders – 45pc of Bosses', *SI*, 10 April 2011; 'We Must Seek IMF Aid or Face Crushing Defeat', *ST*, 14 November 2010; B. Carey and M. Paul, 'The Big Break-up: The IMF Intervention must Uncouple Ireland's Fate from that of its Banks', *ST*, 21 November 2010; N. Webb, 'Multinationals will Exit if Corporate Tax Rate Jumps', *SI*, 21 November 2010.

14 E. Borensztein and U. Panizza, 'The Costs of Sovereign Default', IMF Staff Papers, vol. 56, no. 4, Washington: International Monetary Fund, 2009, pp. 722, 699, www.imf.org/external/pubs/ft/wp/2008/wp08238.pdf (accessed 5 December 2013); S. Kamalodin, 'To Default, or not to Default: What are the Economic and Political Costs of Sovereign Default?' Utrecht: Rabobank Economic Research Department, April 2011, economics.rabobank.com/PageFiles/7288/SP1102ska% 20To%20default%20or%20not%20to%20default_tcm64-138583.pdf (accessed 5 December 2013). The literature on sovereign default has focused in large part on governments' external debts to private or official creditors, but for a study of default on domestic debt, see C. Reinhart and K. Rogoff, 'The Forgotten History of Domestic Debt', *The Economic Journal*, 2011, vol. 121, no. 552, pp. 319–502.

15 R.G. Gelos *et al.*, 'Sovereign Borrowing by Developing Countries: What Determines Market Access?' *Journal of International Economics*, 2011, vol. 83, p. 243; R. G. Gelos *et al.*, 'Sovereign Borrowing by Developing Countries: What Determines Market Access?' IMF Working Paper WP/04/221, November, Washington: International Monetary Fund, 2004, p.1, www.imf.org/external/pubs/ft/wp/2004/ wp04221.pdf (accessed 5 December 2013); M. Fuentes and D. Saravia, 'Sovereign Defaulters: Do International Capital Markets Punish Them?' *Journal of Development Economics*, 2010, vol. 91, pp. 336–47; for historical studies in line with those findings, see B. Eichengreen, 'The U.S. Capital Market and Foreign Lending, 1920–55', in J. Sachs (ed.) *Developing Country Debt and Economic Performance*, vol. 1, Chicago: University of Chicago Press, 1989, pp. 211–40; and E. Jorgensen and J. Sachs, 'Default and Renegotiation of Latin American Foreign Bonds in the Interwar Period', in B. Eichengreen and P. Lindert (eds) *The International Debt Crisis in Historical Perspective*, Cambridge, MA: MIT Press, 1989, pp. 48–85; Borensztein and Panizza, 'The Costs of Sovereign Default', pp. 722–23; A.K. Rose, 'One Reason Countries Pay their Debts: Renegotiation and International Trade', *Journal of Development Economics*, 2005, vol. 77, pp. 189–206.

16 F. Sturzenegger and J. Zettelmeyer, *Debt Defaults and Lessons from a Decade of Crises*, Cambridge, MA: MIT Press, 2006; B. de Paoli *et al.*, 'Costs of Sovereign Default', Bank of England Financial Stability Paper no. 1, London: Bank of England, July 2006, www.bankofengland.co.uk/publications/Documents/fsr/fs_paper01. pdf (accessed 5 December 2013); de Paoli *et al.*, 'Output Costs of Sovereign Crises: Some Empirical Estimates', Working Paper No. 362, London: Bank of England, 2009, www.bankofengland.co.uk/research/Documents/workingpapers/2009/wp362. pdf (accessed 5 December 2013); Borensztein and Panizza, 'The Costs of Sovereign Default', p. 723, an assessment corroborated by P. Chuhan and F. Sturzenegger, 'Default Episodes in the 1980s and 1990s: What Have we Learned?' in J. Aizenman and B. Pinto (eds) *Managing Economic Volatility and Crises*, Cambridge: Cambridge University Press, 2005, pp. 471–519. See also F. Sturzenegger, 'Toolkit for the Analysis of Debt Problems', *Journal of Restructuring Finance*, 2004, vol. 1, no. 1, pp. 201–23.

17 E. Levy Yeyati and U. Panizza, 'The Elusive Costs of Sovereign Defaults', *Journal of Development Economics*, 2011, vol. 94, pp. 103, 96, 102; E. Levy Yeyati and U. Panizza, 'The Elusive Costs of Sovereign Defaults', Working Paper #581, Washington, DC: Inter-American Development Bank, 2006, www.iadb.org/res/ publications/pubfiles/pubWP-581.pdf (accessed 5 December 2013).

18 W. Carroll, *The Making of a Transnational Capitalist Class: Corporate Power in the 21st Century*, London: Zed Books, 2010; W.I. Robinson, *A Theory of Global Capitalism: Production, Class, and State in a Transnational World*, Baltimore, MD: Johns Hopkins University Press, 2004; L. Sklair, 'Social Movements for Global Capitalism: The Transnational Capitalist Class in Action', *Review of International Political Economy*, 1997, vol. 4, no. 3, pp. 514–38; *The Transnational Capitalist Class*, Malden: Blackwell, 2001; 'The Transnational Capitalist Class and Global

Politics: Deconstructing the Corporate-State Connection', *International Political Science Review*, 2002, vol. 23, no. 2, pp. 159–74; B. van Appeldoorn, *Transnational Capitalism and the Struggle Over European Integration*, London: Routledge, 2002.

19 W. Bello, 'The Capitalist Conjuncture: Over-accumulation, Financial Crises, and the Retreat from Globalization', *Third World Quarterly*, 2006, vol. 27, no. 8, pp. 1345–67; H.J. Chang, *Bad Samaritans: The Myth of Free Trade and the Secret History of Capitalism*, New York: Bloomsbury Press, 2008; R. Desai, 'The Last Empire? From Nation-building Compulsion to Nation-wrecking Futility and Beyond', *Third World Quarterly*, 2007, vol. 28, no. 2, pp. 435–56; H. Macartney, 'Variegated Neo-liberalism: Transnationally Oriented Fractions of Capital in EU Financial Market Integration', *Review of International Studies*, 2009, vol. 35, no. 2, pp. 451–80; *Variegated Neoliberalism: EU Varieties of Capitalism and International Political Economy*, New York: Routledge, 2011; K. van der Pijl, 'A Theory of Global Capitalism, Feature Review', *New Political Economy*, 2005, vol. 10, no. 2, pp. 273–77; M. Hardt and A. Negri, *Empire*, Cambridge, MA: Harvard University Press, 2000.

20 D. Harvey, *A Brief History of Neoliberalism*, Oxford: Oxford University Press, 2005.

21 J. Stiglitz, *Globalization and its Discontents*, London: Penguin, 2002, pp. 208–9; see also R.A. Palat, '"Eyes Wide Shut": Reconceptualizing the Asian Crisis', *Review of International Political Economy*, 2003, vol. 10, no. 2, pp. 169–95.

22 Harvey, *A Brief History of Neoliberalism*.

23 National Treasury Management Agency, 'Debt Projections', www.ntma.ie/business-areas/funding-and-debt-management/debt-profile/debt-projections/; S. Barnes and D. Smyth, 'The Government's Balance Sheet after the Crisis: A Comprehensive Perspective', Irish Fiscal Advisory Council, September 2013, www.fiscalcouncil.ie/wp-content/uploads/2013/09/Balance-Sheet1.pdf (accessed 22 November 2013).

24 For updated figures on the size and maturity profile of the debt, see National Treasury Management Agency, 'Debt Profile', www.ntma.ie/business-areas/funding-and-debt-management/debt-profile/ (accessed 14 January 2014).

25 Barnes and Smyth, 'The Government's Balance Sheet after the Crisis', p. 33.

26 For further discussion, see S. Coffey, 'Ireland's Public Debt – Tell me a Story we have not Heard Yet … ', in B. Lucey, C. Larkin and C. Gurdgiev (eds) *What if Ireland Default?* Blackrock: Orpen Press, 2012, ch. 4; C. Gurdgiev, 'Debt Restructuring in Ireland: Orderly, Selective and Unavoidable', in Lucey *et al.* (eds) *What if Ireland Default?* ch. 3; S. Kinsella, 'A Very Irish Default, or When a Default is not a Default?' in B. Lucey *et al.* (eds) *What if Ireland Default?* ch. 5.

27 National Treasury Management Agency, 'Ownership of Government Bonds', www.ntma.ie/business-areas/funding-and-debt-management/debt-profile/ownership-of-government-bonds/ (accessed 10 November 2013).

28 NAMAWineLake, 'Is Ireland in Line for €100bn Refund after ECB Changes Stance on Bondholders?' 16 July 2012, namawinelake.wordpress.com/2012/07/16/is-ireland-in-line-for-e100bn-refund-after-ecb-changes-stance-on-bondholders/ (accessed 12 July 2013).

29 NAMAWineLake, 'When are Bondholders in Irish Banks Due to be Re-paid?' 3 June 2011, namawinelake.wordpress.com/2011/06/03/when-are-bondholders-in-irish-banks-due-to-be-paid/ (accessed 13 June 2013); and Bondwatch, bondwatch ireland.blogspot.ie/ (accessed 1 December 2013).

30 K. Whelan, 'ELA, Promissory Notes and All That: The Fiscal Costs of Anglo Irish Bank', September 2012, www.karlwhelan.com/IrishEconomy/Whelan-PNotes-September2012.pdf (accessed 16 February 2013).

31 For a detailed discussion, see Whelan, 'ELA, Promissory Notes and All That'.

32 K. Whelan, 'Ireland's Promissory Notes Deal', *Forbes*, 11 February 2013, www. forbes.com/sites/karlwhelan/2013/02/11/irelands-promissory-note-deal/ (accessed 16 February 2013).

33 IMF, 'Ireland: Tenth Review Under the Extended Arrangement', Country report 13/163, Washington, DC: IMF, June 2013, p. 11, www.imf.org/external/pubs/ft/scr/2013/cr13163.pdf (accessed 5 December 2013).

34 The exact *Nexis* search is: BODY("sovereign default!" OR "sovereign debt! default!") for the period 1 January 2008–31 August 2013.

35 The exact *Nexis* search is: HLEAD(default! OR "bond holder!" OR bondholder! OR "promissory note!") AND BODY(debt!) AND SECTION(opinion OR comment OR editorial OR analysis OR business OR finance) for the period 1 January 2008–31 August 2013. (The term 'debt!' in the body of the articles was added to eliminate article not related to the economic crisis.)

36 'Stop-gap for Greece', *IT*, 23 June 2011; A. Beesley, 'EU Leaders cannot Put Sovereign Debt Emergency behind them Just Yet', *IT*, 24 March 2011; R. Curran, 'New Government Forced to Bear the Unbearable', *SBP*, 3 April 2011; D. Clerkin, 'Selling Debt, Buying Time', *SBP*, 26 September 2010; D. O'Donovan and B. Keenan, 'Default a Remote Possibility within Troubled Eurozone, Says Moody's', *II*, 23 December 2010; J. Downey, 'Politicians will Always Seek the Promised Land', *II*, 9 July 2011.

37 L. McBride, 'What would Happen to Your Money if Ireland Defaulted?', *SI*, 15 May 2011.

38 S. Collins, D. de Bréadún and M. Minihan, 'Gilmore Warns Voters against Giving FG Monopoly of Power', *IT*, 22 February 2011; V. Browne, 'Kenny's Big Gaffe was in the Dáil, not in Davos', *SBP*, 29 January 2012; A. Beesley, 'Kenny Adamant State will Honour Rescue Plan', *IT*, 24 October 2011; E. Kenny, 'Government beginning to Deliver Results for State', *IT*, 2 November 2011.

39 J. Drennan, 'Ireland Now Seen as Bad Debt Waiting to Happen', *SI*, 28 November 2010; D. O'Mahony, 'Now is the Time to Pause the National Self-destruct Button', *IT*, 12 November 2010; S. Collins, 'Public must be Told Survival is at Stake', *IT*, 9 April 2011.

40 J. McHale, 'Putting Brakes on Default Bandwagon', *II*, 9 December 2010; C. McCarthy, 'We Need to Stay the Course because there are no Shortcuts to Recovery', *SI*, 2 January 2011; C. Fell, 'Solo Run on Currency would be Economic Suicide', *IT*, 6 August 2010.

41 E. Oliver, 'Ireland's "Real Economy" could be Hurt by a Default Event, Says Fitch', *II*, 6 April 2011; N. Webb, 'State Default would Wipe Out Ireland's Banks', *SI*, 29 May 2011.

42 C. Weston, 'Sovereign Debt Default would Lead to "Financial Armageddon", Says Author', *II*, 5 April 2012; J. Zettelmeyer *et al.*, 'The Greek Debt Exchange: An Autopsy', July 2013 draft, p. 2, scholarship.law.duke.edu/cgi/viewcontent.cgi?article=5343&context=faculty_scholarship (accessed 1 December 2013); 'The Greek Debt Exchange: An Autopsy', 11 September 2012, draft, p. 3, av.r.ftdata.co.uk/files/2012/09/The-Greek-Debt-Exchange-An-Autopsy.pdf (accessed 1 December 2013); see also D. McWilliams, 'Year of the Central Bank', *SBP*, 11 March 2012; R. Janssen, 'The Mystery Tour of Restructuring Greek Sovereign Debt', *Social Europe Journal*, 28 March 2012, www.social-europe.eu/2012/03/the-mystery-tour-of-restructuring-greek-sovereign-debt/ (accessed 30 November 2013); N. Roubini, 'Greece's Private Creditors are the Lucky Ones', *FT*, 7 March 2012, www.ft.com/intl/cms/s/0/f0f0708e-679d-11e1-b6a1-00144feabdc0.html#axzz2m8tzOZ3f (accessed 30 November 2013).

43 R. Kuttner, *Debtors' Prison: The Politics of Austerity versus Possibility*, New York: Alfred Knopf, 2013; 'Economic Historian: Germany was Biggest Debt Transgressor of 20th Century', Spiegel Online, 21 June 2011, www.spiegel.de/international/

germany/economic-historian-germany-was-biggest-debt-transgressor-of-20th-centur y-a-769703.html (accessed 5 December 2013); E. Toussaint, 'Greece-Germany: Who Owes Who?' Committee for the Abolition of Third World Debt, 2012, cadtm. org/Greece-Germany-who-owes-who-1 (accessed 14 January 2013).

44 T. Guinnane, 'Financial Vergangenheitsbewaeltigung: The 1953 London Debt Agreement', Discussion Paper No. 880, Economic Growth Center, Yale University, 2004, p. 24, papers.ssrn.com/sol3/papers.cfm?abstract_id=493802 (accessed 29 June 2013).

45 A. Mody, 'Time for Euro Zone to Revisit Debt Default Option', *IT*, 14 November 2012.

46 L. Noonan, 'Here's what is at Stake if we Don't Repay those Anglo Bondholders', *II*, 2 November 2011; G. Garvey, 'Stiffing Anglo Bondholders would be High-risk Strategy', *II*, 28 September 2010; 'Honohan Warns on "Risky" Action Against Anglo Bondholders', *IT*, 13 October 2010; L. Varadkar, 'Bond Payment May Earn Promissory Note Leniency', *IT*, 26 January 2012; L. Noonan, 'Default on Senior Debt "Would Cost State Dear"', *II*, 21 October 2010; D. Chunilal, 'Too Late Now to Burn Anglo's Bondholders', *IT*, 25 October 2010.

47 T. Healy, 'Private Bank Debts and Public Finances: Some Options for Ireland', NERI Working Paper 2013/01, February 2013, p. 6, www.nerinstitute.net/down load/pdf/neri_wp20131_private_bank_debt_public_finances_.pdf (accessed 4 December 2013).

48 M. Coleman, 'Time to Put Responsibility for Anglo's Black Hole in the Hands of its Creators', *SI*, 20 June 2010; 'Why Defaulting on Anglo Bonds Now is Not an Option', *SI*, 11 July 2010.

49 B. Carey and T. Lyons, 'IMF and EU Divided Over Rescue Plan: Portugal's Plight', *ST*, 28 November 2010; L. Bini Smaghi, 'Debt Default could Trigger Run on Frail Fiscal System', *IT*, 20 December 2010.

50 'We Shouldn't (We Couldn't)', *SI*, 5 September 2010; 'Making the Case for "Yes"', *SI*, 5 September 2010; D. Scally, 'Nobel Economist Criticises Irish Bondholder Payments', *IT*, 27 January 2012.

51 'Burn the Bank Bondholders – 45pc of Bosses', *SI*, 10 April 2011; L. Noonan and T. Molloy, 'Government Must Force Losses on Bondholders, Stockbroker Claims', *II*, 9 February 2011; R. Burke, J. Reynolds and N. Webb, 'Is it Time to Default on our Loan or is there an Alternative?' *SI*, 24 April 2011; J. Reynolds, 'Ireland's Top "Wild Geese" Say Deal with the Debt', *SI*, 15 May 2011.

52 D. O'Brien, 'ECB is Right in Refusing to Magic Away Promissory Notes', *IT*, 16 March 2012; D. Donovan, 'Why Ireland Can't Take the Same Road as Greece', *SBP*, 18 March 2012.

53 'Real Talking on our Debt is Still Ahead', *SBP*, 1 April 2012.

54 'Frankfurt's Way', *IT*, 8 February 2013; S. Collins, 'Coalition Held its Nerve when Others Despaired', *IT*, 8 February 2013; N. Whelan, 'Deal on Promissory Notes is Massive Boost for Down-at-the-polls Coalition', *IT*, 9 February 2013; L. McBride, 'Anglo: Irish Business Gives its Verdict', *SI*, 10 February 2013.

55 D. Donovan, 'Promissory Notes Debt Deal a Step in the Right Direction', *IT*, 11 February 2013.

56 D. McWilliams, 'Why we Should Not Pay the Promissory Note', davidmcwilliams. ie, 7 February 2013, www.davidmcwilliams.ie/2013/02/07/why-we-should-not-pay-the-promissory-note (accessed 25 June 2013), reprinted as 'ECB Won't Go Nuclear if we Default on Promissory Note – Look at Greece', *II*, 6 February 2013; C. Gurdgiev, 'Anglo's Promo Notes – Perfect Target for Debt Restructuring', True Economics, 21 March 2012, trueeconomics.blogspot.ie/2012/03/2132012-anglos-promo-notes-perfect.html (accessed 12 July 2013).

57 'Debt Deal Does Not Rule Out Budget Cuts', *SBP*, 17 February 2013; P. Lane, 'To Slacken Austerity would be a Big Mistake', *IT*, 25 June 2013; 'We Should Continue to Toe the Troika Line', *ST*, 28 July 2013.

58 C. Gurdgiev, 'Debt Restructuring in Ireland: Orderly, Selective and Unavoidable', in Lucey *et al.* (eds) *What if Ireland Default?* Kindle edn location 1490–91; D. McWilliams, 'If I was Taoiseach … What I would Do to Save Ireland', *II*, 8 January 2011. See also D. McWilliams, 'Time to Play the ECB Card', *SBP*, 28 November 2010; and M. Burke, 'Debt-equity Swap for Banks Won't Work', Progressive-Economy@TASC, 21 March 2011, www.progressive-economy.ie/2011/03/debt-equity-swap-for-banks-wont-work.html (accessed 21 July 2013).

59 W. Mansell and K. Openshaw, 'Suturing the Open Veins of Ecuador: Debt, Default and Democracy', *The Law and Development Review*, 2009, vol. 2, no. 1, p. 164; R. Howse, 'The Concept of Odious Debt in Public International Law', UNCTAD Discussion Papers No. 185, Geneva: United Nations Conference on Trade and Development, 2007, unctad.org/en/docs/osgdp20074_en.pdf (accessed 5 December 2013).

60 Mansell and Openshaw, 'Suturing the Open Veins of Ecuador'; Internal Auditing Commission for Public Credit of Ecuador, 'Final Report of the Integral Auditing of the Ecuadorian Debt. Executive Summary', Quito: Internal Auditing Commission, 2008, www.jubileeusa.org/fileadmin/user_upload/Ecuador/Internal_Auditing_Commission_for_Public_Credit_of_Ecuador_Commission.pdf (accessed 5 December 2013); R. Ray and S. Kozameh, 'Ecuador's Economy Since 2007', Washington, DC: Centre for Economic and Policy Research, May 2012, p. 2, www.cepr.net/documents/publications/ecuador-2012-05.pdf (accessed 31 December 2013); M. Weisbrot *et al.*, 'Ecuador's New Deal: Reforming and Regulating the Financial Sector', Washington, DC: Centre for Economic and Policy Research, February 2013, www.cepr.net/documents/publications/ecuador-2013-02.pdf (accessed 5 December 2013).

61 S. Killian *et al.*, 'Au Audit of Irish Debt', University of Limerick, September 2011, www.debtireland.org/download/pdf/audit_of_irish_debt6.pdf (accessed 5 December 2013).

6   Austerity, or class warfare

We should continue to toe the troika line.

(*Sunday Times*, 28 July 2013[1])

Now is the time to roll back the middle-class welfare state. But it also seems unavoidable that more deserving recipients will also have to have their benefits trimmed.

(Dan O'Brien, *Sunday Business Post*, 8 February 2009[2])

those on middle or higher incomes … are among the most hardpressed people in the country in financial terms.

(Matt Cooper, *Sunday Times*, 10 October 2010[3])

Europe embraces austerity

Austerity, or fiscal consolidation, refers to policy packages that seek to reduce government budget deficits by cutting public spending and raising taxes. It is often accompanied by moves to reduce wages and labour protections to make the workforce more 'flexible' and the privatization of state-owned enterprises and assets. Such measures contribute directly to implementing neoliberalism's objective of restoring and maintaining the power of elites over ordinary people. Critical scholars have thus argued that austerity is best conceived as a class project aimed at rolling back the welfare state and redistributing income upwards. This is supported by the media, which in Ireland called for a campaign to 'educate' the public about the need for austerity at the outset of the crisis, as will be seen below. Also, the *Sunday Business Post* announced clearly the media's agenda when it stated: 'Now is the time to roll back the middle-class welfare state. But it also seems unavoidable that more deserving recipients will also have to have their benefits trimmed'.[4]

Spending cuts are usually favoured over tax hikes when austerity is implemented. Spending cuts tend to target programmes on which the poor and vulnerable segments of the population rely to a greater extent, such as welfare, old-age and child benefits, public health care and poverty alleviation measures. Taxes, on the other hand, open the possibility of capturing large portions of the income of the wealthy and the corporate sector. This is why when taxes are increased to reduce the fiscal deficit, regressive taxes on consumption (such as VAT) are often raised in priority over corporate tax rates, which on the contrary, are sometimes even cut, ostensibly to foster investment.

More technically, austerity policies can also be traced to the inability of eurozone countries to devalue their currency or use monetary policy to increase competitiveness and stimulate their economies. 'Internal devaluation', consisting in lowering labour costs through high unemployment, has thus become the default strategy. Such measures, however, do not lead to growth when applied in a downturn, because cutting aggregate demand shrinks the economy and forces businesses to cut back on hiring, investment and production, which typically leads to economic stagnation and unemployment. Nevertheless, fiscal consolidation programmes are rational from the perspective of elites because they contribute to maintaining and extending their prerogatives and power. Because the strategy directly targets the welfare and employment conditions of the majority of the population, there is important ideological work to be carried out in the ongoing deployment of austerity in Europe, which consists in making it acceptable to the public, or at least to reduce popular opposition to it.

The Irish media have been overwhelmingly supportive of the strategy. Indeed, only 11 per cent of the nearly 1,000 opinion pieces examined in this chapter did not support fiscal consolidation. The media have thus fully accepted the principle of austerity, and debate has revolved around how best to implement it. This is even if by now, the fact that it does not lead to economic growth is accepted by a range of individuals whose credentials cannot be dismissed. Nobel Prize winner Joseph Stiglitz said that historically, there might have been 'cases where austerity programmes led to quick recovery'; however, 'there were so few and in circumstances so different to Ireland's that they weren't applicable'. He added that 'internal devaluation' would 'only fan the flames of recession' and described European austerity measures as a 'mutual suicide pact' and 'medieval practice of blood-letting to get rid of bad humours', which only made the patient sicker.[5] It is also interesting that Ashoka Mody, until recently a member of the IMF responsible for designing Ireland's financial rescue programme, has now departed clearly from the dominant position among European elites. He said that 'perpetual austerity seems destined to fail' and that 'the elixir of structural reforms to boost domestic growth is a policy myth'. He observed that Europe, by scaling back its imports from other European countries and Asia, is hurting world trade. Therefore, 'Europe cannot export its way out of this tangle because Europe is helping drag down world trade'.[6]

Furthermore, austerity's lethal effects have become visible around the continent. For example, a major study in the medical journal *The Lancet* examines its impacts on health care in Europe.[7] The report focuses on Greece, Spain and Portugal, which have adopted rigid fiscal austerity policies, including expenditure cuts which have led to increased 'strain on their health-care systems' while 'suicides and outbreaks of infectious diseases are becoming more common in these countries, and budget cuts have restricted access to health care'. In Greece, 'the troika has demanded that public spending on health should not exceed 6 percent of GDP', and 370 specialist units have been eliminated or merged, 2,000 public hospital beds removed and a freeze on hiring new physicians implemented. Meanwhile, there have been reports of 40 per cent cuts to hospital budgets and shortages of staff and medical supplies, amid 'widespread drug shortages' in pharmacies. Some of the effects are already clear. Cases of mental disorders have increased in Greece and Spain, while the number of suicides in the EU has grown, reversing a sustained decrease in many countries in the years before 2007. The report notes that in England, the surge in suicides in 2008 to 2010 was 'significantly associated with increased unemployment and resulted in an estimated 1,000 excess deaths'.

Moreover, Greece has faced an HIV outbreak among drug addicts using needles. Before 2010, there were at most 15 new infections per year, but in 2011, 256 new infections were reported, along with 314 in the first eight months of 2012. The reasons behind this drastic increase are low provision of preventive services and the disruption, since 2008, of needle exchange programmes, which are effective in reducing HIV and other infections. Unfortunately, such outcomes can only be assumed to be the tip of the iceberg, as many of the consequences of spending cuts take time to affect people's health negatively and even more time to be reported in national health statistics.

Interestingly, the report also emphasizes the case of Iceland, which does not seem to have suffered any marked deterioration in its health indicators. *The Lancet* highlights the difference between Iceland and countries like Greece, Ireland, Spain and Portugal: even though Iceland was hit solidly by the financial crisis, it offered a more effective resistance to austerity. How can the positive outcomes be explained? The report lists a few reasons. First, Iceland rejected the advice of the IMF in dealing with the crisis and instead 'invested in social protection'. Second, diet improved because McDonald's left the country due to rises in import prices of the onions and tomatoes it uses in its burgers. Third, restrictive policies on alcohol were maintained, contrary to IMF advice. Eurozone countries should thus pay close attention to the Icelandic alternative to fiscal consolidation. *The Lancet* report makes one last important point by noting the inaction of European governments and health bodies in relation to the deteriorating health outcomes in territories under their jurisdictions. The directorate-general for health and consumer protection of the European Commission has the legal obligation to evaluate health effects of EU policies, but it has not assessed those of the troika's austerity policies. Rather, it has focused on advising national health ministries on how to cut their budgets.

Ireland has distinguished itself among European countries by implementing austerity at the outset of the crisis, whereas most governments reacted by first enacting Keynesian stimulus packages, in parallel to bailing out their banks. For example, in the United Kingdom, between 2008 and 2010, the government partially committed itself to demand management through interventions such as quantitative easing and a credit guarantee scheme, sustained growth in public spending, including larger social protection spending, a reduction in VAT from 17.5 to 15.0 per cent, bringing forward £3 billion in capital spending, financial help for businesses, and a new scheme of subsidies to employers to hire the long-term unemployed. Government expenditure during 2008–9 continued to rise and was directly responsible for increasing public sector employment by over 100,000, partially compensating for the loss of almost a million jobs in the private sector. However, starting in 2010, spending decreased and signalled the beginning of the austerity strategy.[8]

Similar Keynesian measures were taken by other European countries, but the strategy was short-lived.[9] By mid-2010, the *Financial Times* was organizing an 'austerity debate' that 'pitted increasingly on-the-defensive Keynesians against a coterie of conservatives and neoclassicals'. At the same time, 'major German politicians began to join forces with principals at the ECB to send a common message', summarized by ECB chief Jean-Claude Trichet thus: 'Stimulate no more – it is now time for all to tighten'.[10]

Fiscal consolidation's record

There has been much debate about fiscal consolidation. Its proponents claim that government deficits have negative economic consequences and that books must therefore be balanced. For example, Germany's finance minister, Wolfgang Schäuble, declared that fiscal consolidation was the right path to follow because 'restoring confidence in our ability to cut the deficit is a prerequisite for balanced and sustainable growth … Without this confidence there can be no durable growth'. On the other hand, the evidence for the contractionary effects of fiscal consolidation has led some scholars, which this chapter broadly follows, to conceive of austerity within the context of neoliberalism, as a set of policies whose effect is to maintain or reassert elites' privileged socio-economic and political position.[11]

Proponents of fiscal consolidation maintain that public borrowing to make up for budget deficits 'crowds out' borrowing by the private sector that would lead to investment, and pushes interest rates upwards, reducing private investment further. Moreover, politicians are subject to electoral pressures that entail wasteful spending, in contrast to the private sector, which is subject to the efficiency of the market. Furthermore, governments may be tempted to finance their accumulating deficits by printing money, potentially leading to inflation.

Advocates of fiscal consolidation assert that it can be expansionary and pull countries out of a recession. The rationale is that balanced budgets lead people to expect taxes and interest rates to remain low. This should increase the confidence of investors and the public, who will be inclined to spend more, thus stimulating the economy. The confidence of bondholders and international financial interests will also increase as the likelihood of default on sovereign debt is reduced. If investors in government bonds do not have this confidence, interest rates will move upwards, making it more difficult, and eventually impossible, for governments to borrow. Carmen Reinhart and Kenneth Rogoff's influential work claimed that based on historical experience, a debt level of 90 per cent of GDP is the threshold beyond which sovereigns run the risk of facing a debt crisis. The seminal work of Alberto Alesina and collaborators has provided much of the intellectual justification for austerity policies. They attempted to show empirically that cuts in government expenditures have positive impacts on economic growth. They argued that austerity is most expansionary when deficits are reduced primarily by cutting spending instead of raising taxes, and when expenditure is cut in social security programmes like health care and pensions rather than in public investment like infrastructure projects.[12]

However, the case for austerity is undermined by comparative and historical economic evidence, which lends strong support to Keynesian policies. First, history provides virtually no examples of countries growing out of an economic downturn by implementing austerity, as Joseph Stiglitz and others have observed.[13]

Second, there are important examples supporting the value of Keynesian stimulus to fight recessions, such as when US government spending during World War II pulled the country out of the Great Depression and led to the 'golden age' of capitalism in the following decades. Also, since the beginning of the current crisis, the United States has adopted policies that have provided more stimulus to the economy than Europe, and has fared better. Both the United States and Europe had a recession of about a year and a half at the outset of the crisis, but the eurozone then fell into a longer recession in 2011 from which it may only now be exiting. Also, unemployment in Europe is still at near record levels at over 12 per cent (and higher in the periphery), while it is below 7 per cent in the United States. Those different outcomes are explained by different policies. President Obama orchestrated a US$700 billion stimulus at the outset of the crisis, which, although too small, made up for some of the demand lost due to the collapse of the housing bubble. Also, the Federal Reserve has kept short-term interest rates near zero since 2008 and signalled its intention to keep them at that level for a long time. Moreover, the Fed presided over three rounds of 'quantitative easing', amounting to over $2 trillion of money printing. This stimulated the economy by lowering interest rates. Finally, Europe engaged in more and earlier fiscal consolidation than the United States did. In short, on economic policy, Europe has been more right-wing than the United States, and its economic performance has suffered more as a result.[14]

Third, even the IMF stated that fiscal consolidation has contractionary effects in the short run, contrary to Alesina's findings. Typically, a fiscal consolidation amounting to 1 per cent of GDP reduces GDP by about 0.5 per cent within two years and increases the unemployment rate by 0.3 per cent, while domestic demand (consumption and investment) drops by about 1 per cent. Furthermore, 'fiscal contraction is likely to be more painful when many countries adjust at the same time' because curtailed global demand negatively affects exports, as in Europe today. The IMF also argued that the potential impact of austerity on growth should be revised, because 'fiscal consolidation has been associated with lower growth than expected' during the current crisis.[15]

Fourth, other researchers using Alesina and Ardagna's data have shown that fiscal consolidation's effect on growth depends on when the consolidation is undertaken in the business cycle: when it is carried out in an economic downturn, it is contractionary. Also, one of Alesina's co-authors came to the conclusion in a recent paper that new evidence 'cast doubt' on the '"expansionary fiscal consolidation" hypothesis, and on its applicability to many countries in the present circumstances' because currency devaluation is not possible for eurozone countries and a 'net export boom is not feasible for the world as a whole'.[16]

Finally, Ireland's 1987–90 fiscal consolidation is often used as an example of expansionary contraction. The years before 1987 witnessed double-digit government deficits, the national debt exceeded 100 per cent of GDP and the cost of servicing it reached nearly 10 per cent of GDP. However, over the next three years, the government deficit was reduced from 11.4 per cent of GNP to 2.2 per cent of GNP, a remarkable achievement. The government then entered the Celtic Tiger period of unprecedented growth. It is thus no wonder that the fiscal consolidation of the late 1980s has been used to bolster the case for austerity. However, this analogy is invalid. During the adjustment of the late 1980s, government spending actually rose slightly in nominal terms. It is increased tax revenues that accounted for the bulk of the fiscal adjustment. However, this was not due to increases in tax rates or new tax measures, but to economic growth that generated extra government revenues. Why did the economy grow? Because in the late 1980s, Ireland benefited from a number of contextual factors that are absent today. Europe, the United States and Britain experienced significant growth rates and Ireland had devalued its currency sharply in 1986. Those two factors account for the significant increase in Irish exports in the late 1980s. For example, in 1989, 33 per cent of Irish merchandise exports went to the United Kingdom. Moreover, the EU delivered a substantial stimulus package to Ireland by sending more than €1 billion in social and regional development grants over three years, which amounted to 3 per cent of the 1989 GDP. A similar stimulus today would be equivalent to €5 billion over three years. Therefore, such EU grants were a form of Keynesian stimulus, the opposite of the spending cuts that austerity involves. Furthermore, whereas today numerous calls have been made to cut wages to carry out an 'internal devaluation', in the late 1980s wages increased by 4.6 per cent annually on average, just like the public sector's pay bill. These wage increases stimulated the economy by boosting consumption and raised government revenues through taxation.[17]

In sum, the adjustment of the late 1980s does not support today's austerity. In fact, it suggests that Keynesian stimulus would help the economy recover by boosting demand in Ireland and in Europe. Claims that the late 1980s were a success because of drastic cuts to government spending are simply myths. Even Colm McCarthy, a strong supporter of fiscal consolidation who has been directly involved in outlining potential public sector cuts both in the 1980s and today, wrote that 'Parallels with the first Irish fiscal crisis in the 1980s are of limited value given the quite different circumstances', and that the '"slash and burn" stories about 1987, references to the finance minister Mac the Knife, decimation of public services and so forth are just journalistic invention. It never happened'.[18]

Advocates of austerity have also pointed to the cases of Latvia and other so-called REBLL states (Romania, Estonia, Bulgaria, Lithuania and Latvia) as proof that fiscal adjustment does work. In June 2012, Christine Lagarde, the IMF managing director, praised Latvia for its 'success' and 'real achievement' in handling its recession and said the country could serve as 'an inspiration for European leaders grappling with the euro crisis'.[19]

In 2008, Latvia, Estonia and Lithuania implemented deep fiscal consolidation programmes and kept their currencies pegged to the euro while an internal devaluation reduced domestic prices and wages, and Romania and Bulgaria followed on the same path in 2009. By 2011, most of them witnessed higher growth rates than the rest of Europe, and in particular, Southern Europe. The troika seized the opportunity to celebrate the apparent success of the Baltic states and use them as models for other debtor countries to emulate.

In the years before the beginning of the crisis in 2008, the REBLLs had developed a model of economic growth based on significant foreign investment and massive foreign borrowing. They were thus highly vulnerable to external shocks due to their dependence on transnational capital flows, combined with weak export performance and a tendency to develop current account deficits. This state of affairs was partly the result of extensive deindustrialization in the 1990s following the collapse of communism. It forced the emigration of between 10 and 30 per cent of the active part of their labour force to Western Europe. Compounding the situation was a weak capacity to develop infrastructure, and instead a concentration of investment in real estate and finance as opposed to manufacturing. This resulted in a weak export sector, which meant difficulties to earn the foreign exchange necessary to pay for imports.[20]

Nevertheless, those economies grew at a rapid pace in the 2000s due to the abundance of credit to finance consumption. However, the banks providing the credit were mostly foreign. In the early 2000s, encouraged by the prospect of EU membership by the REBLLs, Swedish, Austrian, French, German and even Greek banks went on a 'shopping spree' to buy Eastern European banks. REBLL banking sectors 'became between 80 percent and nearly 100 percent foreign owned in short order'. Those banks did not direct their investments toward industry partly because there were not so many profitable opportunities there in the first place. Instead, they supplied large amounts of credit to consumers and real estate speculators. The latter were thus encouraged to accumulate foreign currency loans, 'building time bombs into their balance sheets set to explode the minute exchange rates moved against them'. This 'transnational credit pump' inflated asset bubbles waiting to burst. In short, the REBLLs' development model encompassed 'the worst features of Ireland, Spain, and Greece combined', making any claim that their policies should be followed to be approached cautiously.[21]

The 2008 crisis came as a combination of a credit crunch, the bursting of inflated assets, and large current account deficits. Foreign banks operating in the REBLLs tightened credit in the face of worldwide financial uncertainty, leading to economic collapse and an EU and IMF intervention to bail out the Eastern and Central European financial systems. In 2009, long before the Irish, Greek and Portuguese bailouts, an agreement was struck between the troika, Western banks, and Romania, Hungary and Latvia. Banks committed to keep their funds in their Eastern European branches in exchange for these governments implementing austerity programmes. So, 'it was all about saving the banks' and the price to pay, 'in the form of austerity, high interest rates, unemployment, and the rest, was dumped once again on the public-sector balance sheets of the states concerned'.[22]

The case of Latvia has been the most discussed and showcased by proponents of austerity as an alleged confirmation of the effectiveness of their doctrine. This small country of 2 million people saw its GDP increase by almost 90 per cent between 2000 and 2007, followed by a sharp drop of 25 per cent from late 2007 to 2009, and a recovery, as of 2013, of 18 per cent. Unemployment surged from 6 per cent in 2007 to 21 per cent in 2010, and decreased to 11.4 per cent in 2013.[23] Latvia implemented a strict programme of internal devaluation, the peg between the euro and the lat (the Latvian currency) was preserved, and a front-loaded fiscal consolidation that emphasized government spending cuts over tax hikes was implemented, supported by the EU, the ECB, the Nordic countries and the IMF. Public sector wages were cut by 20 per cent, pensions were slashed (in a move later ruled to be unconstitutional), and personal income tax allowances were reduced. Fiscal adjustment in 2009 is estimated at about 8 per cent of GDP, with further adjustments of 5.4 per cent of GDP in 2010 and 2.3 per cent in 2011.[24]

However, can we conclude that Latvia's austerity strategy led to economic recovery and expansion, and that it is therefore a lesson applicable to other debtor countries? The short answer is no on both counts. First, the current GDP growth is relatively high because the economic collapse between 2007 and 2009 was so deep in the first place, but GDP is still well below the pre-crisis 2007 peak. As Matt Yglesias observed, if you start with $100 and then drop 25 per cent to $75 and then get 18 per cent growth, you're still only at $88.50. The point is that if the initial drop could have been reduced by better policies, today's GDP would probably be higher.[25]

Second, as noted by Mark Weisbrot, any claim that the internal devaluation strategy was a success implies that there was no better alternative. The main other option, which a number of economists advocated, was to devalue the currency and proceed with an expansionary macroeconomic policy (fiscal and monetary stimulus) instead of the austerity package. Of course, now that this option has been rejected, going back in time to see how it would have fared is not possible, but a good approximation can be obtained by considering the experience of a number of countries that did face a similar crisis to Latvia but chose the alternative path.

This is what a Center for Economic and Policy Research study did by examining the main cases of large, crisis-driven devaluation over the past two decades (there are about a dozen cases). It found that the average loss for countries in crisis situations that did devalue their currency was 5.9 per cent of GDP. The worst performers were Indonesia and Thailand in the late 1990s, which lost 13.4 per cent and 14.2 per cent of GDP, respectively. In contrast, Latvia, which stuck with its peg, lost 25 per cent of GDP, as stated above. Furthermore, looking at GDP three years after the large devaluations, most countries were considerably above their pre-devaluation level of GDP, by an average of 5.7 per cent of GDP; in other words, they had more than recovered. The worst performers were again Indonesia and Thailand, which were still below their pre-devaluation GDP by 7.9 per cent and 4.7 per cent, respectively. In contrast, Latvia, three years after the crisis began, was down by about 21 per cent of GDP. In short, no country that chose devaluation and macroeconomic expansion 'suffered the scale of losses that Latvia has suffered under its "internal devaluation" strategy, and all of them recovered much more quickly'. If the historical evidence favoured a devaluation and not internal devaluation, why did European and Latvian authorities still prefer the latter? One important reason was surely that breaking the peg would have caused Swedish and other European banks to lose billions of euros, since many of the loans they had made to Latvia in euros would not have been fully repaid.[26]

Moreover, the costs of Latvia's internal devaluation go beyond losses of GDP. The official unemployment rate rose to 21 per cent in 2010 and remained relatively high as of 2013 at over 11 per cent, but the situation is actually worse: when those involuntarily working part time and those who have given up looking for a job are considered, the unemployment/underemployment rate reached some 30 per cent in 2010 and 21 per cent in 2011. Also, if not for the substantial emigration that took place because of the crisis, which amounts to 10 per cent of the labour force, unemployment would be higher still by a few percentage points.

Furthermore, the evidence suggests that a significant portion of the growth since 2010 is unrelated to its austerity policies. A telling passage in a recent IMF report on Latvia's 'substantial fiscal consolidation' states that 'Determining with any certainty its effects on output is impossible'. In fact, 'surely, it is unwise to argue, as some have done, that the return to growth from 2009:4 [fourth quarter of 2009] on was due to the expansionary effects of fiscal consolidation. Many other factors were at play'. For example, it 'is likely that, as uncertainty decreased, the economy would have recovered, independently of the path of fiscal policy'. The internal devaluation did not work following the textbook process that would be expected. For example, although public wages were cut significantly, this had limited effects on private wages. The decreases in unit labour costs that are supposed to raise competitiveness thus came not so much from wage cuts as from increases in productivity. Indeed, the 20 per cent cut in public wages 'was of no direct relevance for competitiveness', while wages 'in manufacturing barely fell initially, and then increased'.[27]

Also, it is dubious that Latvia's experience provides any prescription for other European debtor countries. Even the IMF concluded that 'great caution' should be applied in extending the lessons of the Latvian case to other countries, because the evidence from adjustment in the European periphery shows that front-loaded consolidation 'has been associated with negative growth' and internal devaluations have been associated with 'decreases rather than increases in productivity'. The foreign demand that led to increased exports in Latvia and the other Baltic states is not necessarily available to other countries. Their main trading partners, such as Germany, Sweden, Finland and Russia, cannot provide demand for all other countries unless Germany proceeds with a large domestic stimulus programme. In short, as Alf Vanags, director of the Baltic International Center for Economic Policy Studies in Latvia, said, 'The idea of a Latvian "success story" is ridiculous. Latvia is not a model for anybody'. He argued that a better and fairer way out of the crisis would have been to devalue the currency, as outlined above. Morten Hansen, head of the economics department at the Stockholm School of Economics in Riga, Latvia, said that the 'lesson of what Latvia has done is that there is no lesson'. Commenting on Latvia's drastic squeeze on wages and harsh fiscal adjustment, he noted that 'You can only do this in a country that is willing to take serious pain for some time and has a dramatic flexibility in the labor market' – in other words, in a country where the government is authoritarian enough to push unpalatable reforms onto a relatively weak or poorly organized population.[28]

Ireland's austerity programme

Ireland is a poster child for austerity. For example, a pension levy and pay cut amounting to a 14 per cent decrease in take-home pay were imposed on public sector employees, while staff numbers were reduced by about 15,000 between 2008 and 2010. A pay freeze was put in place as part of the Public Service Agreements (also known as the Croke Park Agreements), which have included a number of reforms designed to make labour cheaper and more 'flexible', through geographical redeployment, longer working hours, closer performance monitoring, and suspension of recruitment and promotion. The public sector pay bill was thus reduced by about €1.5 billion between 2010 and 2012. In the private sector, workers have faced redundancies and their number has been reduced by 18 per cent since 2008. The government has also moved towards the (partial) privatization of public assets, in line with the troika's recommendations. This offers investors profitable opportunities in sectors that include utilities, public transportation, the national airline and harvesting rights in forests.[29]

It has been shown that austerity budgets between 2009 and 2014 have hit most harshly those in the bottom income decile (except for those in the top decile, but the fact remains that a smaller income loss is still more difficult to absorb for the poor than a larger loss for the rich). As a result, there has been a noticeable increase in inequality and poverty since 2008. From 2008 to 2011 (the latest data available), Ireland's deprivation rate increased from 13.8 per cent to 24.5 per cent, while the consistent poverty rate rose from 4.2 per cent to 6.9 per cent and the Gini coefficient increased from 30.7 to 31.1. It is difficult to see how the trend has not already worsened as of this writing. Furthermore, labour's share of GDP, after having increased sharply between 2002 and 2008, has decreased equally steeply since 2008. Whereas what researchers refer to as the 'vulnerable class' remained stable over the period 2004–8, when it was about 16.5 per cent, it rose significantly, to 22.6 per cent, in 2009 and sharply again to 29.7 per cent in 2010, so that 'the scale of the economic crisis is reflected in an almost doubling of the level of economic vulnerability'.[30]

Fiscal consolidation has been central to Ireland's austerity strategy. Early on, the government implemented spending cuts in health, education, science, child and social welfare, and capital expenditure, while a public sector pay rise agreed earlier was cancelled. It also increased VAT, introduced an income levy, a public sector levy, a number of tax increases or new taxes such as the motor registration tax, air travel tax, capital gains tax, tax on bank deposits and tax on non-principal residences. With the situation still deteriorating, the government released the *National Recovery Plan 2011–2014*, outlining further adjustments totalling €15 billion (9.7 per cent of GDP) over four years, made up of a €10 billion reduction in expenditures and €5 billion in revenue-raising measures. A worsening fiscal position forced Ireland to agree to the EU-IMF bailout in November 2010, which pursued the same strategy. Most recently, the 2014 budget was criticized by progressive organizations for putting the burden of adjustment on the young and the old. This is even if youth unemployment is currently at 30.4 per cent. The government has cut the rates of jobseeker's allowance from €144 to €100 per week for those between 22 and 24, and from €188 to €144 per week for those aged 25. As Social Justice Ireland noted, this will not create employment and will only force more youth to emigrate. Older people have also been subjected to harsh measures. Spending cuts in services such as home help and community nursing units, the abolition of the Christmas bonus and reductions in the Fuel Allowance, combined with prescription charges hikes and cuts in the Household Benefits Package have affected older people negatively. The average weekly income of the poorest 20 per cent of older people has already dropped by 11.5 per cent between 2009 and 2011, and the new measures will make a bad situation worse.[31]

Significantly, fiscal consolidation has prioritized spending cuts over tax increases, in Ireland and Europe. This, as the Irish think tank TASC noted in a budget analysis, tends to affect the poor more harshly: 'Public expenditure in Ireland provides social welfare and a range of public services that are disproportionately relied on by people on lower incomes. The over-emphasis on cuts over taxes, plus the inclusion of various regressive tax measures, makes the overall effect of Budget 2013 likely to disproportionately hit low income households'. For example, in Budget 2010, the government outlined €760 million in social welfare cuts, including Child Benefit and Disability Allowance, with the latter affecting 96,000 people. Budget 2011 further reduced welfare spending by €873 million, while Budget 2013 added €450 million in cuts to that area.[32]

A number of taxation measures have also favoured higher income groups and the corporate sector. For example, while regressive consumption taxes have been increased, Ireland's low corporation tax remains at 12.5 per cent, as the government stated explicitly in the *National Recovery Plan 2011–2014*: 'While taxation has to play a part in restoring balance to our public finances, this will not apply to our corporation tax rate'. A financial transaction tax could also have been applied to Dublin's International Financial Services Centre (IFSC), which hosts a number of Irish and global financial enterprises. Moreover, although some taxation measures are formally progressive, there is a range of loopholes and breaks which make them more regressive in practice. For example, TASC stated that 'the scale of tax relief enjoyed by high earners for private pensions, pension lump sums, private healthcare and similar outlays indicates that the Exchequer spends significant resources (which could pay for public services benefiting everyone) in order to provide tax breaks that disproportionately benefit higher income groups'. Elsewhere, TASC noted that 'the [2012] Budget largely protects high earners' and that 'the Government's revenue-raising decisions are largely regressive in nature'.[33]

Alternatives to austerity

As will be seen below, the media have strongly supported austerity since 2008, ignoring or dismissing alternative strategies for recovery. They have also turned a blind eye to the Keynesian stimulus packages deployed elsewhere in Europe in 2008/9. However, there are a number of alternatives to austerity, at both the European and domestic levels, which could have been given more space in the press. Although they would sometimes require a few changes in legislation, this would be possible if the political will was there.

First, the ECB could buy peripheral government bonds directly or in secondary markets to allow states in difficulty to conduct Keynesian deficit spending programmes. This would provide renewed demand for the bonds and thus allow governments to borrow at affordable rates. In effect, the ECB would be playing the role central banks usually play when their government needs to borrow to finance expenditures. Proposals for the ECB to monetize deficits and debts have given rise to concerns that 'helicopter drops' of money to buy large amounts of government debt could lead to inflation in the euro-zone. However, inflation is so low at the moment that this should not be too worrying. Moreover, the ECB could always sterilize its interventions after economies have recovered. Also, if governments act counter-cyclically in good times and raise taxes or cut spending when the economy returns to normal, this will reduce the potentially negative effects of the monetization.[34]

Furthermore, as discussed previously, the ECB could simply relax or abandon its directives to peripheral countries to stick to austerity and support stimulus spending programmes. The ECB could also target a higher level of inflation, which would alleviate debtor countries' repayment burden. Issuing eurobonds to raise funds for countries in distress at affordable interest rates with the backing of core eurozone countries would also help. Finally, ulti-mately, if the ECB is unwilling to act in the ways just mentioned, Ireland could leave the eurozone and its newly independent Central Bank could buy Irish government bonds by printing money (monetization). Ireland would thus regain its sovereignty over its fiscal and monetary policy (see Chapter 7).

Of course, critics of those options argue that they are politically impossible because the ECB will not agree to them. It is true that the ECB is unlikely to 'agree' to them, and it would need to be forced to do so, but this is difficult when the media rarely explore or debate those possibilities. Since 2008, the alternatives just mentioned have rarely been discussed anywhere in the media, and when they have been, they have usually been quickly dismissed. Moderate strategies are often not even mentioned. For example, a coalition of periph-eral countries could be formed to negotiate with Germany, which would be more effective than the current approach whereby all debtor countries remain isolated from one another. Moreover, popular referendums could be orga-nized in peripheral countries in order to obtain public support for easing austerity, which would put further political and symbolic pressure on the German government and European authorities.

There is also a range of policies other than austerity that Ireland could implement domestically, as advanced by a number of trade unions and pro-gressive organizations. At a minimum, a milder form of austerity could be deployed. For example, the Irish Congress of Trade Unions (ICTU) argued for an 'alternative fiscal consolidation' that would be less harsh than the government's plans for Budget 2014. Whereas the latter proposed an adjust-ment of €3.1 billion in 2014, two-thirds of which was accounted for by spending cuts, ICTU wanted to reduce the deficit through tax increases on the wealthy and minimize cuts in government spending and target an overall adjustment of €2 billion. Setting a minimum effective tax rate for all cor-porations could also raise more revenue. Ireland's overall tax take is equal to 31.3 per cent of GDP, which is significantly lower than the European average of 35.6 per cent, and there is thus room to tax higher income groups and the business sector. ICTU also called for a capital investment stimulus package of €4.5 billion over two years, funded commercially and drawing on public, private and European investment sources. If the Irish government proceeds with its planned cuts to public spending, by 2018, Ireland will have the second lowest level of primary spending (i.e., after debt interest payments) as a percentage of GDP in the European Union. Only Latvia will spend less on its public services. Similarly, TASC proposed for Budget 2014 an adjustment 'lower than €3.1 billion' which 'should not exceed €2.7 billion'. It should also be 'off-set by increased investment' while 'all adjustments should be made on the revenue side'.[35]

Other proposals go further, such as that made by the union Unite, which opposed fiscal consolidation by arguing that Budget 2014 should not see any adjustment. It suggested instead not to cut government spending at all, to raise taxes on the better off and corporations, and to use the extra revenues generated for useful public spending. Further, the Ireland Strategic Investment Fund (ISIF) should be used to finance a stimulus programme (the ISIF was recently announced by the government and is to be funded by using €6.4 billion from the National Pension Reserve Fund), and the national minimum wage should be raised while protection measures for workers should be implemented.

Unite also put into context the entire austerity strategy by noting that no matter what fiscal adjustments are made, Ireland's fundamental problem is that it lacks a strong indigenous industrial base, the 'elephant in the room'. This has been a historical problem and today the indigenous sector is one of the weakest in Europe. Compared to other small open economies, Ireland 'would need to increase indigenous manufacturing employment by over 100,000 just to reach their average, while non-construction indigenous business would have to grow their value-added by over 40 percent'. Therefore, even if the budget deficit were eliminated, labour made more 'flexible' and a low-tax environment maintained, deeper economic woes would not vanish. It is true that foreign capital can contribute to employment, but its potential appears limited – only 4,700 jobs per year have been created in the past two years by MNCs in the traded sector. For this reason, rolling out a national industrial strategy is crucial, preferably as part of a Keynesian stimulus package.[36]

Supporters of austerity often claim that 'Ireland is broke' so even 'if we want one, we can hardly afford or fund a stimulus package', or that 'the Irish government's funding is dependent on the troika' and that the troika will not let Ireland have a stimulus.[37] It is true that the troika is pressurizing Ireland to implement austerity policies and that membership in the eurozone poses clear obstacles to deficit spending. However, one problem is that Irish elites are perfectly in agreement with that strategy, and therefore, negotiating with the troika seriously about abandoning austerity has never been undertaken. Threatening not to repay Ireland's EU/IMF loans or defaulting on government bonds, preferably in alliance with other peripheral countries, would certainly force the troika to become more flexible on austerity. Making moves toward leaving the eurozone would also have the same effect, but such tactics have remained entirely outside the government's agenda.

In any case, it is not true that there is no money anywhere to fund a stimulus plan. There are some sources of money available, and they do not involve any government borrowing. As part of a stimulus, such spending could be used to increase investment in Ireland significantly, which has fallen from about 25 per cent of GDP in 2007 to 10 per cent in 2012. It is now the very lowest in the EU. This 'investment strike' is damaging the economy in both the short and long term. Investment is needed to replace and upgrade existing infrastructure and capital, which increases competitiveness, while generating employment.[38]

The Nevin Economic Research Institute (NERI) outlined a stimulus strategy of €15 billion over five years to begin reversing austerity's negative impacts and which would not add to the government's debt. Similarly, Social Justice Ireland proposed a €7 billion investment programme over a three-year period which would involve no government borrowing, and thus not add to the government deficit. Importantly, such schemes would likely even reduce the deficit due to the higher government revenues they would generate thanks to renewed economic activity and lower welfare payments due to falling unemployment. Available sources of financing include the ISIF, commercial semi-state borrowings, domestic pension fund investment and funds from the European Investment Bank. NERI proposed that €2 billion of the National Pension Reserve Fund be shifted from overseas investment to a fund to lend to domestic infrastructure projects. Commercial semi-state companies like utility companies could borrow €2 billion from domestic savings, international capital markets and the European Investment Bank, perhaps via the issuance of a national recovery solidarity bond to tap the large annual savings of corporations and some households. Such investment projects could be co-funded by the European Investment Bank and the Council of Europe Bank. The latter two could, for example, match a total of €5 billion. Private sources of funding could also be accessed, such as pension funds, the total value of which is about €70 billion. Because the majority of these sums are invested overseas, financial sweeteners could be implemented to direct a portion toward domestic investment projects. The Labour Party also made a proposal to establish a state-backed Strategic Investment Bank which would lend to small and medium-sized enterprises, invest in strategic companies and finance infrastructure projects.[39]

There is no shortage of investment opportunities and needs. ICTU proposed to improve broadband to raise Ireland's competitiveness. Less than 1 per cent of connections are over fibre optic lines in Ireland, compared to an OECD average of 12 per cent. Implementing energy efficiency measures nationally in residential and commercial buildings is also an important area where more investment would be beneficial for the environment and economically. Transportation projects would also be sensible, in road, rail, light rail and bus services. Water and waste water treatment facilities would benefit from upgrading as well, like health and education infrastructure.[40]

There are other creative proposals to stimulate the economy and alleviate the plight of the unemployed. The economist Michael Taft suggested making the state an Employer of Last Resort (ELR). The concept is simple: when private markets cannot employ people who want to work, and unemployment is high, the state should employ people until a recovery generates more jobs. Hiring would be done through the public sector, including local government and community or non-profit organizations working on socially beneficial projects. Taft calculates that the net cost to the state of employing 50,000 people in such a way would be about $450 million, or 0.7 per cent of total government spending. The gross cost would be reduced by the increased taxation generated and the reductions in welfare payments it would entail. It would not be difficult to find the money for this scheme without any government borrowing. Realistic sources include the government accessing a small part of its large cash reserves (which totalled €25 billion in late 2013). Diverting €450 million from this would have only a minimal impact on the government's liquidity buffer, and would not entail any borrowing, taxation or spending cuts. Alternatively, tax measures on the rich and the corporate sector such as a wealth tax or financial transaction tax could be used to raise the necessary funds.[41]

Another reason often invoked against stimulus is that it would be a 'mad' strategy in Ireland because 'much of any immediate benefit would leak out in increased imports'. Of course, if all the additional expenditures were spent on goods produced abroad, that would reduce the impact of the stimulus, but as economist Michael Burke notes, directing investment towards the purchase of goods and services wholly or mainly produced in Ireland would not have that negative effect. This task would be made still easier if the Irish indigenous productive base were larger, as mentioned above. Furthermore, a lot of Ireland's imports are used as inputs into the production of final products that are then exported, and thus have a positive effect on the balance of payments. For example, there are sectors where import content of inputs is low, such as wholesale trade, health services, real estate services and education, motor repair, retail trade and repair of household goods. Investment in those sectors would significantly boost the domestic economy. There are also economic sectors whose export component of output is larger than import inputs (i.e., sectors that export more than they import). Such sectors are dominated by the multinationals, but there are also indigenous ones like food and beverages manufacturing. Investment in these enterprises and in the provision of inputs to the MNC sector would result in a positive impact on the balance of payments, in addition to increasing output and employment. Finally, there are other economic areas where state investment would boost the economy significantly enough through the multiplier effect that concerns about import content should not detract from the benefits. In some cases, the state could have a direct positive return on its investment. These sectors include agriculture, food and beverage manufacturing, water collection and distribution, among others. Also, investment in tourism promotion, even if done entirely abroad, would probably still make sense as it would bring visitors to the country and generate positive effects on the balance of payments.[42]

Other reasons have been voiced to oppose stimulus. Economist Philip Lane penned an article entitled 'To slacken austerity drive would be a big mistake', in which he opined that 'Ireland's fiscal adjustment is ahead of target. We would lose credibility and court disaster by taking a break' and erode the government's 'hard-won reputation for delivering on its promises'. Here, 'losing credibility' on Ireland's capacity to 'deliver on its promises' refers to Ireland's capacity to repay bank bondholders and shrink government spending on which ordinary people depend. Ireland's loss of credibility in improving its health care system, reducing poverty and fostering economic growth does not seem to be a concern.[43]

In any case, the 'confidence fairy' argument has been advanced numerous times by supporters of austerity, in Ireland and elsewhere. They claim that cutting government budgets will make investors and the public more confident in the economy and that this will lead to recovery. However, there is no evidence for such a claim, as a number of analysts have pointed out. For example, Paul Krugman noted that 'faith in the confidence fairy has worked out about as well for modern Europe as it did for Hoover's America. All around Europe's periphery, from Spain to Latvia, austerity policies have produced Depression-level slumps and Depression-level unemployment; the confidence fairy is nowhere to be seen'. Even if Ireland has been hailed as proof that austerity worked more than once, in fact, each time 'the supposed success turned out to be a mirage; three years into its austerity program, Ireland has yet to show any sign of real recovery from a slump that has driven the unemployment rate to almost 15 percent'. It is also questionable how someone made redundant by cutbacks would experience a rise in confidence in the economy.[44]

It is also sometimes stated that 'there is no alternative' to austerity, as in a piece by Donal Donovan, a former IMF official, who says that 'Critics of austerity fail to offer any viable alternative'. However, a number of alternatives have been proposed, as seen above.[45] There are also rhetorical statements that in fact do not provide support for austerity, such as when it is proclaimed that 'If there is one thing the government needs to deliver to try to help the domestic economy in the months ahead, it is some certainty'. However, it is actual policies that matter, not 'certainty'. For example, certainty that austerity will be deepened would be bad news, but certainty that it will be eased would be good news.[46]

Finally, John McHale, established professor of economics at the National University of Ireland and chair of the Irish Fiscal Advisory Council, is still convinced that 'austerity is succeeding' after five years of failure, and he even sees Ireland as 'an emerging success story' validating the strategy. He says that the lack of growth in Ireland is not due to austerity only, but also to the 'continuing overhang from the bubble period' and the 'weak international environment'. However, the reason why the international environment is weak is that austerity is the norm in Europe, and the reason why the consequences of the housing crash are felt so deeply is because austerity worsened an already bad situation. McHale says that judging the success of austerity should be based on 'whether it succeeds in bringing control over unsustainable public finances' and 'restores the borrowing capacity of the State'. However, economic stimulus would take care of those two issues by increasing government revenue through taxation of a growing economy. Growth would also attract investors more than a sluggish economy. McHale believes that the austerity strategy has been vindicated because default has been 'avoided', while another positive is that 'there have been gains in credibility, hard-won through our success in delivering on what was promised'. However, that Irish elites gain credibility with European authorities by demonstrating that they can implement harsh adjustment programmes is hardly proof that austerity works. Neither is avoiding default on socialized private bank debts.[47]

The role of the media

Since 2008, the media have strongly endorsed austerity and accompanying structural reforms. For example, a *Sunday Independent* piece asserts that 'Deep reform of the civil and public sector has to be the starting point', including redundancies, but we must go 'well beyond' public sector wages by privatizing state-owned companies and micro-managing 'every line of spending'. Journalist Daniel McConnell thinks that 'Everything should be up for change: work practices, contracts of employment, working hours, pensions, organisation, leadership, pay and the numbers employed ... Privatisation, forever long-fingered because the trade unions would not consider it, must be rolled out, both to raise money and to breathe life and competitiveness into the economy. December's Budget must be ferocious, painful and seismic ... and no amount of grandstanding from union leaders ... and the soon-to-be-powerless trade unions can be allowed to obscure reality'. The business community agrees. For example, the Irish Chambers of Commerce chief executive, Ian Talbot, called for increased government 'efficiencies' through privatization. He argued that the state should be 'outsourcing non-core activities', which would have the effect of 'reducing the number of public sector employees'.[48]

The aversion to any form of opposition to austerity is explicit, just like the desire to reduce trade unions' influence and the quality of work conditions. A *Sunday Independent* piece entitled 'Why union blackmail must be faced down' argues that the 'selfish, sneaky and reckless actions of the public sector unions show how out of touch they are'. An *Irish Times* editorial entitled 'Strikes will solve nothing' adds that industrial action 'damages the broad national interest' and is, 'invariably, an admission of failure'. Moreover, it postpones the time when union leaders can 'engage in straight talking with their members' to convince them that austerity is the right path to follow. A *Sunday Independent* editorial entitled 'No good can come out of strike' commented on the trade unions' first attempt at a national strike in November 2009 by stating that 'Schools across the country will be closed, inconveniencing tens of thousands of parents and children, while thousands more must suffer deferred operations as hospitals fall back on reduced staffing levels'. The police corps, 'in the most irresponsible advance warning of all, says that it will not bother to police speeding motorists'. In short, the 'strike is folly, a visceral but outdated response to a very modern crisis'. If the strike succeeds in forcing the government to cut less, it will result in 'condemning all of us to a longer, deeper and more painful recession'. On the other hand, 'If it fails – as it must – to change the Government's mind, then all it achieves is deeper enmity between those in the public sector' and the rest of the population. The media's prescription is simple: 'The Government must stand firm, refusing to concede or negotiate while the unions maintain their stance of belligerent opposition to public policy'. The unions 'must be treated with unflinching determination ... There can be no more blinking, no more wavering: it is time to hold firm, no matter how many strikes are called'.[49]

One way in which the media oppose dissent is through scant coverage or disapproval of protests. There has been less popular resistance to austerity in Ireland than in other European countries, but there still have been a number of marches, strikes and civil society actions. Some are organized by a group in the towns of Ballyhea and Charleville that marches every week against the repayment of bank bondholders and austerity. Other organizations include the 'Anglo: Not Our Debt' campaign, which has opposed repayment of Anglo's odious debts, and the People Before Profit Alliance, which has been successful in electing a number of national and local government officials since the crisis began. Finally, as of this writing, the group 'We're Not Leaving' is emerging as a coalition of youth organizations which campaigns to confront issues of forced emigration and unemployment among people under 35 years of age. However, the groups receive little media coverage, with the result that many people either do not know about them or do not feel like joining them. A *Nexis* search revealed that since the beginning of the crisis, the Ballyhea group has only been covered in three short articles in the *Irish Times*, in one 300-word article in the *Sunday Business Post*, and has been mentioned in one *Irish Independent* piece and in a few more in the *Sunday Independent*, almost exclusively from one columnist (Gene Kerrigan). The *Sunday Times* has not published anything on the group. The organization 'Anglo: Not Our Debt' has received even less coverage. The *Irish Times* had one 95-word article on it, but the other media outlets just mentioned have virtually ignored it.

In order to evaluate in more detail the media's stance on austerity, the remainder of this chapter examines fiscal consolidation. Using the *Nexis* database, all opinion articles and editorials discussing Irish government budgets between 2008 and 2013 in the five main Irish newspapers were considered.[50] Focusing on the budget ensures that the search was both directly relevant to fiscal consolidation (which is an inherently budgetary exercise) and manageable. The search returned a set of 929 articles. Alternative searches, such as including terms like 'spending cuts', 'taxes', 'austerity' and 'fiscal consolidation', were considered. However, the above search was assessed to be the most appropriate. This is because articles including terms like those just mentioned are already indexed under 'Budget' by *Nexis* if they are indeed related to the budget. Articles that mention, say, 'taxes' or 'spending cuts' without being indexed under 'Budget' usually discuss something different and are not relevant to the present study.

The articles were classified according to the views they expressed on fiscal consolidation. This was a relatively simple task because opinion pieces and editorials, by their nature, usually present a clear point of view. First, articles were categorized into the following three groups to identify their general stance towards consolidation:

- 'In favour of fiscal consolidation': articles asserting that the government's fiscal deficit must be reduced to address the crisis. There is a range of possible views in this category. For example, articles may call for achieving fiscal consolidation goals within a shorter or longer time span; they may present a mix of taxation and spending measures; or they may call for a steep or moderate fiscal adjustment. Articles of a 'progressive' nature calling, for example, for sharp tax increases on the wealthy and no spending cuts on welfare programmes, but accepting the need to reduce the government's deficit, were classified in this category (however, there were few of them).
- 'Opposed to fiscal consolidation': articles opposed to reducing the government's fiscal deficit to address the crisis. There is a range of views in this category, from articles calling for significant deficit spending to those explicitly opposed to the strategy of fiscal consolidation without presenting an alternative. Also included were pieces that oppose government spending cuts in general or a specific cut, even if they often did not state explicitly their position relative to the strategy of consolidation itself. This ensured that the opposition to consolidation would not be underestimated.
- 'Neutral': articles that do not take a clear stand on fiscal consolidation. These were mostly descriptive pieces which reported on political or economic policy without advancing a particular view regarding their desirability.

This categorization was supplemented by a second one based on the actual spending and taxation policies suggested by the articles. This sheds light on the reasons given to support views against or in favour of fiscal consolidation. Moreover, it provides another angle to examine the dominance of pro-austerity viewpoints in the press. The following six policies were identified (three for expenditures and three for taxation measures). More than one policy per article could be recorded.

- 'In favour of spending cuts': articles that preferred spending cuts over other policies (e.g., tax hikes).
- 'Opposed to cuts': articles that opposed cuts in general, or specific ones.
- 'In favour of increased government spending': articles that suggested the government should increase spending in general or in particular areas (e.g., infrastructure, welfare).

- 'In favour of tax hikes': articles that preferred tax hikes over other policies (e.g., spending cuts). This includes taxes on consumption, income, etc.
- 'In favour of tax hikes on the wealthy': articles that suggested taxes on the better off or corporations should be increased in priority.
- 'In favour of tax cuts': articles that suggested taxes should be cut, in general or for certain institutions or income levels.

The results are shown in Tables 6.1 and 6.2. Table 6.1 shows the views of the press on fiscal consolidation. Table 6.2 rearranges some of the data to highlight how articles in favour of consolidation, against it, or neutral justify their views. What follows discusses the main themes that emerge from the dataset.

Significant support for fiscal consolidation

Significant support for fiscal consolidation is clear. Among the total of 929 articles, 535 (58 per cent) are in favour of fiscal consolidation, 102 (11 per cent) against it, and 292 (31 per cent) neutral. No time pattern could be detected in the evolution of views on fiscal consolidation, apart from the fact that a larger number of articles appear towards the end of years (in the months of November and December) because this is the time at which the budget is discussed. No significant differences were observed between different types of articles, namely editorials, articles written by journalists and those authored by outside writers.

At the outset of the crisis, the media immediately called for a campaign to 'educate' the public about the need for fiscal consolidation. The *Irish Times* editors lamented the fact that 'Members of the general public still do not

Table 6.1 Number of newspaper articles by stance on fiscal consolidation, 2008–13, n=929

	Pro FC	Vs FC	Neutral	Pro cuts	Vs cuts	Pro government spending	Pro tax	Pro tax on wealthy	Pro tax cuts
Total (n=929)	535	102	292	290	66	22	86	41	36
Irish Times (n=411)	235	61	115	115	48	13	43	34	7
Irish Independent (n=158)	57	13	88	24	10	5	7	2	5
Sunday Independent (n=143)	87	14	42	66	5	2	10	1	16
Sunday Business Post (n=149)	114	8	27	70	3	1	24	3	6
Sunday Times (n=68)	42	5	21	15	0	1	2	1	2

Notes: Pro FC: in favour of fiscal consolidation; Vs FC: opposed to fiscal consolidation; Pro cuts: in favour of spending cuts; Vs cuts: opposed to spending cuts; Pro government spending: in favour of increased government spending; Pro tax: in favour of tax hikes; Pro tax on wealthy: in favour of prioritizing tax hikes on higher income groups and/or corporations; Pro tax cuts: in favour of tax cuts.

Table 6.2 Number of newspaper articles by stance on fiscal consolidation (rearranged subset), 2008–13

	Pro cuts	Vs cuts	Pro government spending	Pro tax	Pro tax on wealthy	Pro tax cuts
Pro FC	282	7	3	86	16	14
Vs FC	2	53	17	0	19	15
Neutral	6	6	2	0	6	7

Notes: Pro FC: in favour of fiscal consolidation; Vs FC: opposed to fiscal consolidation; Pro cuts: in favour of spending cuts; Vs cuts: opposed to spending cuts; Pro government spending: in favour of increased government spending; Pro tax: in favour of tax hikes; Pro tax on wealthy: in favour of prioritizing tax hikes on higher income groups and/or corporations; Pro tax cuts: in favour of tax cuts.

appreciate the possible extent of the economic downturn', given that two-thirds of respondents in a national poll thought the budget was too tough and only 10 per cent believed it was not tough enough. The editors thus concluded that 'the Government will have a major job to do in educating public opinion about unpalatable economic realities and the need for civic discipline'. Throughout the crisis, the media have indeed cultivated the belief that relaxing austerity measures would lead to disaster. The *Irish Independent* was explicit about it when it observed that the 'budgetary danger for the Government this year may be that people will come to think the danger has passed' and begin to question cutbacks and tax hikes. The government and media will have to make sure people still believe that there is 'No room for complacency as we're still on a knife-edge'.[51]

Therefore, the media often advise the government on how best to implement austerity, giving up any pretence of keeping governmental power in check. One main figure in this respect is Stephen Collins, the *Irish Times*' political editor, who is often indistinguishable from a government public relations agent. As the budget was about to be presented in early 2009, he wrote a piece entitled 'Government must get this budget right and not waver', in which he stated that the 'public will have to be convinced of the need for further sacrifice and that the approach is fair'. Noting that 'the budget on Tuesday will represent a huge test of political skill and courage on the part of the Government', he added that 'it will also be a test of whether our democracy is capable of responding in a spirit of solidarity to the worst economic crisis since the 1930s, or whether sectional interest will prevail over the common good'. 'Solidarity' here means that the population must accept the government's austerity plans without protest. Collins continued that Minister for Finance Brian Lenihan 'will have to convince the public of the necessity for further sacrifice, while showing them that the approach is fair'. In short, the 'important thing on Tuesday is that the Government has a clear, coherent plan, and that it holds the line against inevitable attacks from all quarters. There is no room for any further mistakes'.[52]

The business community agrees and throughout the crisis, corporate views have been essentially the same as those expressed in the media. The Irish Chambers of Commerce chief executive, Ian Talbot, wrote in late 2011 – at a time when the 'education campaign' called for by the media had seemingly succeeded in convincing Irish people of the need for austerity – that the 'government should be commended for the manner in which it has delivered yet another austerity budget with the minimum of dissension from the general public. Clearly, messages about our circumstances are now well understood and accepted by the general public'. He stated his preference for cuts over tax increases, although he also supported the latter, stating that the 'broadening of the tax base is also vital to ensure a sustainable recovery in government tax revenues. However, our deficit is still far too high, as we all know, and the sooner this gets resolved, the better. There are now few avenues left and the balance of cuts and tax increases in the budget was too light on cuts'. There are many possibilities to weaken labour: 'there have to be vast levels of efficiencies that could be driven via reform of rostering, clamping down on sick leave and modifying bad work practices and rosters that no longer make sense for our society'. There is no wish to consult with unions or the population: 'The fact is that we do not have the time or the luxury to wait for interminable con-sultation and negotiations when what is needed are rapid sustained cuts in the cost of government'.[53]

A *Sunday Independent* editorial set the tone for the media's viewpoint and outlined the opinions on austerity that would be circulated repeatedly in the press over the next five years. Entitled 'State spending must be slashed', it reiterated the myth that government profligacy caused the crisis and that there is therefore no other solution to the crisis than reducing spending, and in particular, cutting down to size the public sector: 'Government spending, which ran riot during the boom years of the Celtic Tiger, has to be slashed, not trimmed. Those cuts will be painful, but they cannot be avoided, and they cannot happen in the absence of public sector reform'. The state should not focus on providing its citizens with the necessary social safety net and welfare, and it should privatize public assets in order for Ireland to regain its compe-titive edge: 'We must hope that the Government manages to free itself from the ideological shackles of social partnership and has the wit to embark on an orderly sale of state-owned assets. Privatisation of companies will increase competition in the economy and help to drive down prices, helping Ireland to reclaim its competitive edge, as well as raising money to pay down our debt'. Indeed, enthusiasm for austerity is ubiquitous. A *Sunday Independent* article commented approvingly on the 'most brutal Budget in Irish history', men-tioning that Minister of Finance Brian Lenihan 'carried out the butchery with brio and bravery. Blood on the shirt is the sure sign of a serious politician'.[54]

The media often absolve business and political leaders of responsibility for the crisis, blaming instead ordinary people, either for their alleged rush to buy expensive houses or simply to 'live beyond their means'. As such, the *Irish Times* made an 'urgent' call 'for more financial education in schools to equip school leavers with basic financial literacy skills' because Irish adults are not well informed on those matters. The editors asked: 'Could greater financial literacy have checked some of the worst excesses in the Irish property market? And how well-informed were home buyers of the different mortgage options and the hazards in making their investment decisions?'[55]

Concern for equity and the plight of lower income groups, the unemployed and the marginalized is usually absent from press coverage – it is the interests of the better off and the business sector that are catered to. This is reflected in an article entitled 'If the primary goal of a society is the eradication of poverty, then you will get only more poverty' – implying that we should not worry about deprivation. Elsewhere, an opinion piece complains that we hear a lot about injustice in relation to the vulnerable, but never in relation to the wealthy, claiming that 'the issue of fairness is never raised when the discussion turns to targeting those on middle or higher incomes even though these are among the most hardpressed people in the country in financial terms'. There are many other examples, such as an *Irish Times* opinion piece by three ESRI researchers entitled 'Budgetary adjustments to crisis have hit richest hardest'. Assertions that the wealthiest are the most 'hardpressed' go unnoticed and uncriticized in the media.[56]

The authorship of the articles is revealing. Of the 929 pieces, 223 are by outside writers (i.e., not journalists). Of these, 65 (29 per cent) are mainstream economists (academic or independent), 62 (28 per cent) are working in the financial or corporate sector (including three in law), and 44 (20 per cent) are political officials in the three main political parties in power during the crisis (Fine Gael, Fianna Fáil, Labour), but of these, only four are from the Labour Party, so that the bulk is from the two dominant right-wing parties. In short, the overwhelming majority of writers (77 per cent) come from elite political or economic elite institutions. The remainder of authors is composed of 19 (9 per cent) academics (excluding mainstream economists), 15 (7 per cent) members of progressive organizations such as the Society of St Vincent de Paul, and only seven (3 per cent) trade union officials (11 writers were classified as 'other'). It is thus a conservative cast of writers who express their views and interests in the media.

Some might say that there is nothing surprising in the fact that the majority of writers on the economic crisis turn out to be economists and those who work in the corporate and financial sector, because they are the specialists. They have dedicated their careers to understanding the complexities and technicalities of the financial industry and thus it is only natural that their voices will be predominant in the media. However, this is wrong for several reasons. First, economists and so-called 'experts' have turned out to be repeatedly wrong on the economy, as this book documents. Second, there are progressive individuals and institutions that are well qualified to comment on the economy, as shown by their numerous publications outside the media, some of which have been mentioned above. Third, incomplete knowledge of complex financial terminology does not prevent one from knowing about important aspects of the crisis, which can often be more revealing than what mainstream economists have to say.

To illustrate, consider well-respected individuals like economist Colm McCarthy and former Prime Minister Garret FitzGerald, who have been given much space in the press to make the point that the public sector must be reduced in size and that austerity is the way forward for Ireland, contrary to all evidence. Progressive analysts like Michael Taft, Kieran Allen and those from the TASC network have been more right about the economy at almost every level, yet they appear only rarely in the media. Even voices from non-specialists are often more illuminating than those of experts from elite institutions. For example, Tom Curran was a carer for his terminally ill wife, Marie Fleming, before she passed away in late 2013. He wrote an article denouncing the government's cuts to carers' allowances and a range of related measures.[57] He described how his wife, in the final stages of multiple sclerosis, was 'in constant pain', had 'no use of her arms or her legs, and no bladder control' and was thus completely dependent. He was her full-time carer and gave up his job and career to be with her 24 hours a day. He wrote: 'I love Marie and would do anything for her. It is my honour to be looking after her daily as I do. But as two people who worked hard and paid our taxes over the years, it is devastating that in our time of need the State is failing us – and thousands and thousands of others who are in a similar situation around the country'. In Ireland, there are over 40,000 full-time carers who provide more than 2.5 million hours of care each week. There are also 160,000 part-time or family carers who provide 3.7 million hours of care each week. That saves the state €4 billion a year. The Carers' Association estimates that if only 10 per cent of carers stopped working, it would cost the state €165 million per year.

Yet, the government does not see carers or those who are cared for as a priority. When Tom Curran was still employed as an IT consultant, he was able to charge more in one day than what he now gets from the state in one month to be a carer 24 hours a day, seven days a week. In the 2013 Budget, the respite grant for carers was cut by nearly 20 per cent, from €1,700 to €1,375, on top of reductions in the mobility allowance grant and home-help services. The 2014 Budget increased prescription charges, which 'will impact hugely', because virtually everybody who has a carer is on medication. Also, removing the telephone allowance for old-age pensioners will add further problems because most people who are cared for depend on the telephone to alert their carer if something is wrong when the carer is outside the house.

On the other hand, the press gives ample space to the leaders of the three establishment political parties to express their views, which inevitably support austerity. For instance, Brian Cowen (prime minister in 2008–11) explained how 'the Government is firmly committed to making the necessary tough choices' and Willie O'Dea (minister for defence in 2004–10) wrote that we 'need to stop living in denial and cut costs even further'. Garret FitzGerald, former prime minister and often regarded as a progressive among establishment figures, is keen on Ireland raising its competitiveness through internal devaluation, writing that 'the only possible way out of the mess' is 'cutting the level of pay in the private sector'. Elsewhere, he reiterates the myth that fiscal profligacy caused the crisis and proposes to entrench belt tightening in the constitution, writing that 'Given our economic collapses from fiscal indiscipline, we need tight budgetary rules ... Ireland needs a tight budgetary discipline, possibly in constitutional form'. Government leaders are praised when they are tough on spending. For example, *Irish Times* columnist Stephen Collins had good words for Prime Minister Enda Kenny, writing that 'the real test of leadership is performance and on that front he has done well'. The prime minister's 'energy and optimism' are even alleged to help foster economic growth: 'Probably his important asset as Taoiseach [prime minister] is an unrelenting energy and optimism. Those qualities have played a significant part in helping to dispel the pall of gloom that hung over the country when he took office. While serious problems will remain there is a growing realisation that the country can recover'.[58]

Even after more than five years of government cutbacks and tax hikes, the media are relentless in their support for fiscal consolidation. Editorials still appear with titles such as 'We should continue to toe the troika line', claim that it would be 'wrong to budge on budget cuts', and that in fact, there 'is a serious case to be made for going beyond the €3.1bn' in planned adjustment. Indeed, 'to suggest that the job of correcting our public finances is nearly over is misleading and potentially dangerous'. If there had not been 'radical surgery' in government spending, 'we would have ended up in a much worse place than we are'. Stephen Collins tries to show that things 'are not nearly as bad as they are often portrayed' after five years of austerity. The weakness of his reasoning demonstrates how difficult it has become for proponents of fiscal consolidation to make their case. He argues that the 'fact that 90 per cent of home owners have signed up to pay their property tax obligations is hardly a sign of a society buckling under the stress of "austerity". On the contrary, it reflects the fact that most people are still doing remarkably well by historical standards'. Therefore, because people continue paying the taxes they are forced to pay, all is well; because people live relatively better than generations ago when the country was impoverished under British colonialism, all is well too. Collins argues that 'according to a range of international yardsticks, we are one of the most prosperous and fairest countries on the planet' and that Ireland is 'one of the best places in the world in which to live'. One supposes this can be readily observed by looking at Ireland's high unemployment rate and defective health care system, among other indicators.[59]

Expenditure cuts first, tax hikes second

The media prefer public sector cuts over tax increases, reflecting the elite consensus and the guidelines of the EU-IMF bailout package. Overall, 290 articles favour expenditure reduction, whereas 127 argue for the necessity of raising taxes. When only articles supporting fiscal consolidation are considered, which allows for a more explicit examination of how this policy preference is justified, a similar pattern is revealed: 282 pieces call for spending cuts, whereas 102 prefer tax increases.

However, the case for fiscal consolidation and the prioritization of spending cuts is often made on questionable grounds. For example, *Irish Times* economics editor Dan O'Brien, in an article entitled 'Government will have to cut old-age pension', says that the government must cut and that there is no time for considerations of social equity during a crisis, because 'History says cut when the economy is weak' is 'the best way out of recession' – whereas in fact, the historical and contemporary evidence shows the opposite. Following the standard case for fiscal consolidation, O'Brien argues that spending cuts should be prioritized over tax hikes, although 'if there is scope for higher taxes anywhere it is on consumption', a regressive measure. O'Brien's first priority is to cut pensions, even though it 'may appear heartless to seek to reduce the incomes of the aged'. The article's caption shows an image of five pairs of scissors to reinforce the point that welfare cuts are 'unavoidable'. Elsewhere, he reiterates his views on fiscal policy when he states that there is no need to worry about belt tightening because 'cuts will not prolong the slump or hinder future growth'. Headlines making the same point abound, such as one stating that 'Cuts have averted national bankruptcy'. Thankfully, economist David McWilliams sees more clearly when he criticizes the consensus in favour of fiscal consolidation by asking bluntly: 'What economic theory tells us that, in the face of a meltdown in the economy, the best thing to do is to reduce expenditure and raise taxes? There is none. The lunatics have taken over the asylum'.[60]

Moreover, IMF research has shown that spending cuts are no more expansionary than tax increases. The reason they are preferred by elites is that they negatively affect lower income groups more significantly. Also, when the state withdraws from certain economic sectors as government expenditures are scaled back, those become subject to privatization, to the benefit of investors. Finally, taxation opens the possibility of capturing a share of income from the wealthy and the corporate sector, which are obvious large sources of taxation revenues.[61] As such, a number of articles have opposed taxing the rich and the business sector and even called to cut their taxes, such as a piece entitled 'Let's slash corporation tax to boost our economy', or one entitled 'It won't pay to tax the rich harder' which claims that 'Squeezing the wealthy is not the solution to the budget deficit'. Several pretexts have been advanced to explain why such taxes would supposedly stifle economic growth. For example, a piece argued that one lesson learned from past experience is that 'constantly increasing the top rate of taxation was not just self-defeating from a revenue-raising standpoint, but it strangled enterprise, wealth creation and recovery. It would be lunacy to forget that lesson for the purpose of political expediency or keeping the trade unions happy'. Another claimed that 'it is a fallacy to say that vast extra sums are there waiting to be collected from "the better off"' and further 'increases would return us to the 1980s, a period devoid of entrepreneurship where many well-off people spent time evading tax'. It also repeated the point made in a number of articles, that 'income tax is a tax on jobs'.[62]

However, in fact, Ireland's low corporate tax rate provides an excellent example of how low taxes do not automatically translate into a strong economy. Compared to other European countries, Ireland's corporate tax regime is one of the lowest, as shown in Figure 6.1 (the precise numbers vary with methodology).[63]

It can be seen that a number of relatively strong, core economies uphold high corporate tax rates (Sweden, Denmark, France, Belgium) while Spain and Ireland, both low-tax jurisdictions, are in crisis. One claim often heard is that high tax rates strangle businesses and lower investment. However, Ireland is at the very bottom of the scale in Europe for investment levels, with the lowest investment as a percentage of GDP in the EU, at 10 per cent. Other countries with higher corporate tax rates witness significantly higher rates of investment, such as Austria (21 per cent), Belgium (21 per cent), France (20 per cent), Sweden (19 per cent) and others.[64]

Returning to Tables 6.1 and 6.2, it is interesting to note that as many as 32 per cent of articles that call for tax hikes specifically argue for raising them in priority or exclusively on high-income earners. Moreover, among the pieces that oppose consolidation, all articles discussing taxes asserted that they should be raised in priority on business or the wealthy but none believed that this should apply to lower income levels. Those numbers show that the media do present viewpoints that diverge from government policies, but that such opinions remain a minority.

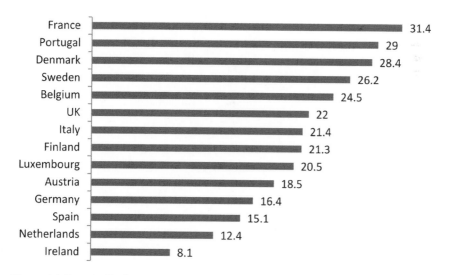

Figure 6.1 Broad effective corporate tax rate, 2011
Source: M. Taft, Unite's Notes on the Front, 27 May 2013, notesonthefront.typepad. com

A *Sunday Independent* editorial illustrates the position most often presented in the press on the relative importance of tax hikes and spending cuts. It argues that economic recovery 'will not come from sharp increases in income tax, or from a range of new indirect taxes disguised as "green" taxes. In fact, the Government risks real and lasting damage to this economy if it believes that it can tax it back to health. It cannot. Before it raises a single tax, it must demonstrate a determination to cut its spending and embrace reform of the public sector'. There are some pieces that go further in their opposition to tax hikes, asserting that the government must consolidate its budget, but that this should be achieved through tax cuts and larger expenditure reductions to make up for them. For example, it is asserted that 'some bad old taxes have to be abolished or reformed, and this will create a further gap in the public finances. The way to fill that gap is not to pile more taxes on workers and consumers, but to begin the task of public sector reform'. However, there are also many articles that favour increasing taxation regardless of income level, and even to target lower income levels in particular. For example, economist Philip Lane writes that because of 'the current low level of net direct taxes paid by typical middle and low income households ... it is inevitable that the burden of higher taxation must fall on these groups'.[65]

The dominant media theme is that government spending cuts are needed. Articles argue that such cuts should be applied to a number of areas, but the overwhelming preference is to reduce the pay and numbers of public sector employees, which is in line with neoliberal principles that seek to privatize public assets. For example, articles abound with titles such as 'Padded public sector is in need of reality check' and 'Bloated public sector a luxury we can no longer afford'. There are a number of other themes: 'Commitment and stamina are required for fiscal consolidation', 'New Budget will prove tough but necessary', 'Only sustained cuts can now keep Ireland afloat', 'We must suffer the pain now – or else we will blight future generations', 'Bill is tough but necessary', 'Tough budget would restore confidence', 'Supplementary budget can begin urgent task of restoring depleted tax revenues', 'Hospitals need emergency surgery on their finances', 'Budget may cut wages and raise taxes to restore competitiveness', '[Austerity] budget will restore confidence and hasten economic recovery', and 'This is not the time to row back on crucial cuts'.[66]

Economist Colm McCarthy made a number of contributions. He was chair of *An Bord Snip Nua* (Special Group on Public Service Numbers and Expenditure Programmes), an advisory committee set up by the government in 2008 to recommend cuts in public expenditures. His committee outlined €5.3 billion in spending cuts, including 17,300 public sector job cuts and a reduction of 5 per cent in social welfare. Not surprisingly, McCarthy, in an article entitled 'The myth that we have lots of options about our debt', claims that there 'is no policy option available that is not deflationary' to deal with Ireland's debt. In another article entitled 'Austerity vital to maintain our economic sovereignty', he outlines succinctly his recommendations about

Ireland's budgetary strategy, which 'will need to include current expenditure cuts, tax increases, a broadening of the revenue base and further cuts in the (still pretty large) capital programme'. Another economist, Alan Ahearne, who was adviser to Minister for Finance Brian Lenihan in 2009–11 when the austerity package was rolled out, writes that the 'inescapable fact is that ongoing fiscal consolidation is necessary in countries with large fiscal deficits, especially in countries with sizeable structural deficits like Ireland'. Similarly, economist Philip Lane says: 'Tough budget needed to stave off grimmer future'.[67]

However, claims that the public sector must be cut down to size so that the economy can recover do not hold water. First, of course, there are some public sector employees who should take pay cuts in the interest of fairness and redistribution of income, like medical consultants, but this applies only to the highest paid public servants. There are also many in the private sector who are overpaid, but the media pay less attention to them. The trade union Impact observed that about 111,000 people in Ireland earn over €100,000 a year, but only 6 per cent of those work in the public service (and half of these are medical consultants). Further, nearly 40 per cent of public sector workers are paid less than €40,000 a year and 75 per cent are on less than €60,000. On the other hand, it was recently revealed that top Irish bankers were paid an average of €1.4 million each in 2012, and in particular, 17 bankers earned an average of over €1.2 million each. They were part of 3,529 bankers in Europe who made €1 million or more in the same year.[68]

Second, cutting public sector wages or reducing the number of public sector employees does not necessarily lead to a reduction in government debt; in fact, it can even increase it. This is because reducing salaries and employment shrinks aggregate demand in the economy and brings down government revenues, in addition to increasing welfare and unemployment expenditures. The ESRI estimated that if €1 billion was saved in 2013 by cutting public sector employment by 18,000, this would increase government debt by 0.6 per cent of GDP in 2013, 0.5 per cent of GDP in 2014, 0.4 per cent of GDP in 2015, and 0.02 per cent of GDP in 2016: the debt position would therefore get worse, not better.[69] Third, Irish public sector labour costs are in fact below the European average, and when poorer Southern European countries are included, they are even lower. Of course, measurements and rankings vary with methodology, but most calculations show similar trends.[70]

Weak opposition to fiscal consolidation

Overall, only 11 per cent of articles (102 out of 929) oppose fiscal consolidation. This is perhaps the strongest piece of evidence to support the claim that the media mostly present elite viewpoints, and this percentage may still overestimate the degree of opposition to austerity found in the press. First, a large majority of articles were classified in this category due to their disagreement with a specific cut or cuts in a particular government sector, even if they did not explicitly argue against fiscal consolidation as a policy. Only a minority of pieces explicitly reject consolidation itself by calling for a fundamentally different strategy, such as Keynesian economic stimulus. This can be seen in the fact that among all articles, 7 per cent (66 pieces) opposed cuts and only 2 per cent (22 pieces) stated a preference for increasing government spending. When only the 102 articles opposed to fiscal consolidation are considered, a similar pattern is found: 52 per cent (53 pieces) of them disagree with specific expenditure cuts while 17 per cent (17 pieces) suggest that public spending should be increased. The nature of the opposition to fiscal consolidation is therefore based mostly on disagreement with particular cuts rather than with the principle of consolidation itself.

This suggests that public discussion is framed around the ways in which fiscal consolidation should be implemented, as opposed to comparing and contrasting it with other strategies. In fact, this was stated explicitly by the *Sunday Business Post* editors during the debate on the €3.5 billion fiscal adjustment for Budget 2013. They wrote that 'all serious participants in the debate – even Sinn Féin – accept the need for a €3.5 billion adjustment'. In fact, 'Acceptance of the €3.5 billion figure is more or less the price for entry to the debate – not because it's right but because it's reality. The fact is that Ireland's deficit cannot be ignored, nor wished away by the economics of magical thinking'. There are nuances and minor differences of opinion within elite circles, but the principle of austerity is virtually never challenged. For example, IBEC, the employers' group, argued that Budget 2014 should ease up slightly on fiscal consolidation 'to rebuild consumer and business confidence and to boost growth'. It favoured an adjustment of €2.6 billion instead of the planned €3.1 billion agreed with the troika – the easing of €500 million would come by abandoning planned tax hikes for 2014. However, IBEC still accepts the need for consolidation. Its chief executive, Danny McCoy, said recently that in 'the broad sweep austerity has worked' and that we 'now have choices and if we had not done the austerity, we would not have this choice'.[71]

A representative example of an article opposing cuts but not addressing the broader question of economic stimulus is one criticizing public libraries' budget reductions. The author says that while rising numbers of unemployed people can be found in public spaces, libraries become less available as areas in which they can spend time, which is deplorable because they provide 'imaginative freedom and safe spaces to explore emotion' and thus, local politicians 'need to grasp that for many of their constituents, libraries are the last truly democratic spaces. Cutbacks to library budgets are a false economy'. However, the article does not propose an alternative economic policy to fiscal consolidation. The economic debate therefore remains focused on what should be cut and what should not. Other examples of such articles include opposition to budgetary cuts in education, Protestant schools' budget, the Equality Authority, a state watchdog, government programmes against racism, the arts and heritage.[72]

Only a handful of pieces oppose austerity directly, for instance by making a clear case for economic stimulus. For example, Richard Boyd Barrett, a member of the People Before Profit Alliance, calls for stopping the bank bailouts and using the billions instead to 'invest in the economy to create jobs, stimulate real enterprise and develop strategic, sustainable industry'. Likewise, Mary Lou McDonald, an MEP and member of the Sinn Féin party, argues that the government should 'stimulate immediate employment by investing in schools, rail infrastructure, green technology and the agri-food sector', in addition to making the tax system more progressive.[73]

Finally, some pieces oppose fiscal consolidation, but are best seen as rhetorical statements by politicians wishing to capture votes. For example, Enda Kenny, the current prime minister who is now implementing Ireland's austerity programme, earlier wrote an article rejecting such measures when he was leader of the parliamentary opposition. He then denounced the 'full frontal attack on workers, on education, on healthcare and on older people'. However, he later wrote another article in which he announced that he had now accepted the need for fiscal consolidation, explaining how his party's 'tough budget would restore confidence'. He stated that some 'will say that further spending cuts and tax increases will only further damage the economy at this delicate time. I was also once of this view, but now believe that the opposite is the case'.[74]

In sum, the media have provided extensive support for economic and political elites' strategy of austerity. This does not mean that such messages are always absorbed uncritically by the population, but nevertheless, they contribute to frame the debate in a way favourable to the government and corporate sector. The relative absence of discussion of cases other than Ireland where Keynesian stimulus has been used to revive economies in a downturn is particularly striking, reinforcing the view that 'there is no alternative'. A similar pattern is apparent in debate over the fate of the euro, discussed in the next chapter.

Notes

1 'We Should Continue to Toe the Troika Line', *ST*, 28 July 2013.

2 D. O'Brien, 'Long, Painful Road to Recovery', *SBP*, 8 February 2009.

3 M. Cooper, 'Add some Creative Ideas to the Debate', *ST*, 10 October 2010.

4 O'Brien, 'Long, Painful Road to Recovery'; R. Peet, 'Inequality, Crisis and Austerity in Finance Capitalism', *Cambridge Journal of Regions, Economy and Society*, 2011, vol. 4, pp. 383–99; H.-J. Chang, 'Britain: A Nation in Decay', *The Guardian*, 8 March 2013, www.guardian.co.uk/commentisfree/2013/mar/08/britain-economy-long-term-fix (accessed 4 May 2013); A. Fraser *et al.*, 'Deepening Neoliberalism via Austerity and "Reform": The Case of Ireland', *Human Geography*, 2013, vol. 6, no. 2, pp. 38–53.

5 D. Scally, 'Nobel Economist Criticises Irish Bondholder Payments', *IT*, 27 January 2012.

6 A. Mody, 'Time for Euro Zone to Revisit Debt Default Option', *IT*, 14 November 2012.

7 M. Karanikolos *et al.*, 'Financial Crisis, Austerity, and Health in Europe', *The Lancet*, 13 April 2013, vol. 381, no. 9874, pp. 1323–31, www.thelancet.com/jour

nals/lancet/article/PIIS0140-6736%2813%2960102-6/abstract (accessed 6 December 2013).

8 D. Grimshaw and J. Rubery, 'Reinforcing Neoliberalism: Crisis and Austerity in the UK', in S. Lehndorff (ed.) *A Triumph of Failed Ideas: European Models of Capitalism in the Crisis*, Brussels: European Trade Union Institute, 2012, pp. 41–58, www.etui.org/Publications2/Books/A-triumph-of-failed-ideas-European-models-of-capitalism-in-the-crisis (accessed 8 December 2013).

9 See the useful survey presented in S. Lehndorff (ed.), *A Triumph of Failed Ideas*.

10 M. Blyth, *Austerity: The History of a Dangerous Idea*, Oxford: Oxford University Press, 2013, p. 60; J.-C. Trichet, 'Stimulate No More – It is Now Time for All to Tighten', *FT*, 22 July 2010.

11 D. Gros and R. Maurer, 'Can Austerity be Self-defeating?' *Intereconomics*, 2012, vol. 47, no. 3, pp. 176–84; W. Schäuble, 'Maligned Germany is Right to Cut Spending', *FT*, 24 June 2010, www.ft.com/intl/cms/s/0/9edd8434-37f33-11df-84a3-00144feabdc0.html#axzz2IJr18l7R (accessed 18 January 2013); B. Broadbent and K. Daly, 'Limiting the Fall-out from Fiscal Adjustments', Goldman Sachs Global Economics, Global Economics Paper 195, 2010, www.irisheconomy.ie/GSGEP195.pdf (accessed 8 December 2013); King *et al.*, 'Making the Same Mistake Again – or is This Time Different?' *Cambridge Journal of Economics*, 2012, vol. 36, no. 1, pp. 1–15; R. Peet, 'Inequality, Crisis and Austerity in Finance Capitalism'; J. Crotty, 'The Great Austerity War: What Caused the US Deficit Crisis and Who Should Pay to Fix it?' *Cambridge Journal of Economics*, 2012, vol. 36, no. 1, pp. 79–104; A. Callinicos, 'Commentary: Contradictions of Austerity', *Cambridge Journal of Economics*, 2012, vol. 36, no. 1, pp. 65–77; D. Grimshaw and J. Rubery, 'The End of the UK's Liberal Collectivist Social Model? The Implications of the Coalition Government's Policy during the Austerity Crisis', *Cambridge Journal of Economics*, 2012, vol. 36, no. 1, pp. 105–26.

12 C. Reinhart and K. Rogoff, 'Growth in a Time of Debt', *American Economic Review*, 2010, vol. 100, no. 2, pp. 573–788; *This Time is Different: Eight Centuries of Financial Folly*, Princeton, NJ: Princeton University Press, 2009; A. Alesina and S. Ardagna, 'Large Changes in Fiscal Policy: Taxes versus Spending', *Tax Policy and the Economy*, 2010, vol. 24, pp. 35–68; A. Alesina and R. Perotti, 'Fiscal Expansions and Adjustments in OECD Countries', *Economic Policy*, 1995, vol. 21, pp. 207–47; A. Alesina *et al.*, 'The Political Economy of Fiscal Adjustments', *Brookings Papers on Economic Activity*, 1998, vol. 1, pp. 197–266, www.brookings.edu/~/media/Projects/BPEA/1998%201/1998a_bpea_alesina_perotti_tavares_obstfeld_eichengreen.PDF (accessed 8 December 2013).

13 L. King *et al.*, 'Making the Same Mistake Again – or is This Time Different?'; R. Pollin, 'US Government Deficits and Debt Amid the Great Recession: What the Evidence Shows', *Cambridge Journal of Economics*, 2012, vol. 36, no. 1, pp. 161–87; M. Sawyer, 'The Tragedy of UK Fiscal Policy in the Aftermath of the Financial Crisis', *Cambridge Journal of Economics*, 2012, vol. 36, no. 1, pp. 205–21.

14 M. Weisbrot, 'Why has Europe's Economy Done Worse than the US?' *The Guardian*, 16 January 2014, www.theguardian.com/commentisfree/2014/jan/16/why-the-european-economy-is-worse (accessed 18 January 2014); D. Baker, *False Profits: Recovering from the Bubble Economy*, Sausalito, CA: PoliPointPress, 2010; L. Taylor *et al.*, 'Fiscal Deficits, Economic Growth and Government Debt in the USA', *Cambridge Journal of Economics*, 2012, vol. 36, no. 1, pp. 189–204.

15 J. Guajardo *et al.*, 'Expansionary Austerity: New International Evidence', IMF Working Paper WP/11/158, July 2011, www.imf.org/external/pubs/ft/wp/2011/wp11158.pdf (accessed 8 December 2013); IMF, 'Will it Hurt? Macroeconomic Effects of Fiscal Consolidation', *World Economic Outlook*, October 2010, p. 95, www.imf.org/external/pubs/ft/weo/2010/02/pdf/c3.pdf (accessed 8 December 2013); O. Blanchard and D. Leigh, 'Growth Forecast Errors and Fiscal Multipliers', IMF

Working Paper WP/13/1, January 2013, p. 1, www.imf.org/external/pubs/ft/wp/2013/wp1301.pdf (accessed 8 December 2013).

16 A. Jayadev and M. Konczal, 'The Boom Not the Slump: The Right Time for Austerity', Roosevelt Institute, 2010, www.rooseveltinstitute.org/sites/all/files/not_the_time_for_austerity.pdf (accessed 15 January 2013); for a similar analysis, see D. Baker, 'The Myth of Expansionary Fiscal Austerity', Centre for Economic and Policy Research, October 2010, www.cepr.net/documents/publications/austerity-myth-2010-10.pdf (accessed 8 December 2013); R. Perotti, 'The "Austerity Myth": Gain without Pain?' BIS Working Papers No. 362, 2011, p. 1, www.bis.org/publ/work362.pdf (accessed 8 December 2013).

17 M. Taft, 'Fiscal Reductionism and the Disconnected Debate: Developing a New Fiscal Platform', in S. Kinsella and A. Leddin (eds) *Understanding Ireland's Economic Crisis: Prospects for Recovery*, Blackrock: Blackhall Publishing, 2010, ch. 6; J. Considine and D. Duffy, 'Tales of Expansionary Fiscal Contractions in Two European Countries: Hindsight and Foresight', Working Paper 0120, Department of Economics, National University of Ireland, Galway, July 2007, aran.library.nuigalway.ie/xmlui/bitstream/handle/10379/1012/paper_0120.pdf?sequence=1 (accessed 15 December 2013).

18 C. McCarthy, 'Fiscal Consolidation in Ireland: Lessons from the First Time', in Kinsella and Leddin (eds) *Understanding Ireland's Economic Crisis*, Kindle edn locations 1979, 2024; see also S. Kinsella, 'Is Ireland Really the Role Model for Austerity?' *Cambridge Journal of Economics*, 2012, vol. 36, no. 1, pp. 223–35.

19 G. Peach, 'IMF Chief Praises Latvia for Handling Crisis', *Business Week*, 5 June 2012, www.businessweek.com/ap/2012-06/D9V743LO1.htm (accessed 12 October 2013).

20 Blyth, *Austerity*, p. 219.

21 Blyth, *Austerity*, pp. 219–20, 222.

22 Blyth, *Austerity*, p. 221; R. de Haas *et al.*, 'Foreign Banks and the Vienna Initiative: Turning Sinners into Saints?' IMF Working Paper WP/12/117, 2012, www.imf.org/external/pubs/ft/wp/2012/wp12117.pdf (accessed 8 December 2013).

23 O. Blanchard *et al.*, 'Boom, Bust, Recovery: Forensics of the Latvia Crisis', Brookings Economic Studies, September 2013, p. 1, www.brookings.edu/~/media/Projects/BPEA/Fall%202013/2013b%20blanchard%20latvia%20crisis.pdf (accessed 10 September 2013).

24 Blanchard *et al.*, 'Boom, Bust, Recovery', p. 18.

25 M. Yglesias, 'Latvia's Sad Strange "Success"', Slate, 2 January 2013, www.slate.com/blogs/moneybox/2013/01/02/latvian_austerity_a_terrifying_success_story.html (accessed 8 November 2013).

26 M. Weisbrot and R. Ray, 'Latvia's Internal Devaluation: A Success Story?' (revised and updated), CEPR, December 2011, p. 7 and table 1, www.cepr.net/documents/publications/latvia-2011-12.pdf (accessed 8 December 2013).

27 Blanchard *et al.*, 'Boom, Bust, Recovery', pp. 20, 22. For a concise discussion, see P. Krugman, 'Latvian Adventures', *NYT*, 19 September 2013, krugman.blogs.nytimes.com/2013/09/19/latvian-adventures/ (accessed 8 November 2013).

28 Blanchard *et al.*, 'Boom, Bust, Recovery', p. 34; On Latvia's exports, see A. Vanags, 'Latvia's Exports: The Real "Success Story"', BICEPS research report, 2013, biceps.org/assets/docs/izpetes-zinojumi/Latvias_exports (accessed 13 October 2013); A. Higgins, 'Used to Hardship, Latvia Accepts Austerity, and its Pain Eases', *NYT*, 2 January 2013.

29 Labour Relations Commission, 'Draft Public Service Agreement 2013–16', 2013, per.gov.ie/wp-content/uploads/LRC-Proposals-printed.pdf (accessed 3 July 2013); IMF, 'Ireland: Selected Issues', IMF Country Report No. 12/265, Washington, DC: IMF, 2012, p. 63, www.imf.org/external/pubs/ft/scr/2012/cr12265.pdf (accessed 8 December 2013); K. Allen and B. O'Boyle, *Austerity Ireland: The Failure of Irish Capitalism*, London: Pluto, 2013.

30 T. Callan *et al.*, 'Distributional Impact of Tax, Welfare and Public Sector Pay Policies: Budget 2014 and Budgets 2009–14', Dublin: Economic and Social Research Institute, 2013, www.esri.ie/UserFiles/publications/QEC2013Win_SA_ Callan.pdf (accessed 29 January 2013); Central Statistics Office, 'Survey on Income and Living Conditions', Dublin: CSO, 13 February 2013, www.cso.ie/en/media/ csoie/releasespublications/documents/silc/2011/silc_2011.pdf (accessed 8 December 2013); B. Nolan *et al.*, 'Inequality and Poverty in Boom and Bust: Ireland as a Case Study', Gini discussion paper 70, Amsterdam: Amsterdam Institute for Advanced Labour Studies, 2012, p. 31, www.uva-aias.net/uploaded_files/publica tions/DP70-Nolan_Maitre_Voitchovsky_Whelan.pdf (accessed 8 December 2013).
31 For details, see P.J. Drudy and M.L. Collins, 'Ireland: From Boom to Austerity', *Cambridge Journal of Regions, Economy and Society*, 2011, vol. 4, pp. 339–54; Government of Ireland, *National Recovery Plan 2011–2014*, Dublin: Stationery Office, 2011, www.budget.gov.ie/The%20National%20Recovery%20Plan%202011– 14.pdf (accessed 8 December 2013); IMF, 'Ireland: Request for an Extended Arrangement – Staff Report; Staff Supplement; Staff Statement; and Press Release on the Executive Board Discussion', Country Report No. 10/366', December 2010, pp. 1, 4, www.imf.org/external/pubs/ft/scr/2010/cr10366.pdf (accessed 8 December 2013); Social Justice Ireland, 'Budget 2014: Analysis & Critique', October 2013, www.socialjustice.ie/sites/default/files/file/Budget/ 2013-10-16%20-%20Budget%20Analysis%202014%20FINALFINAL.pdf (accessed 8 December 2013).
32 S. Theodoropoulou and A. Watt, 'Withdrawal Symptoms: An Assessment of the Austerity Packages in Europe', working paper 2011.02, Brussels: European Trade Union Institute, 2011, www.etui.org/Publications2/Working-Papers/Withdrawal-symptoms-an-assessment-of-the-austerity-packages-in-Europe (accessed 8 December 2013); TASC, 'Lost Opportunities: TASC's Independent Equality and Economic Analysis of Budget 2013', December 2012, p. 3, www.tascnet.ie/upload/file/ TASC%20Response%20to%20Budget%202013.pdf (accessed 23 January 2013).
33 Government of Ireland, *National Recovery Plan 2011–2014*, p. 100; TASC, 'Tax Injustice: Following the Tax Trail', September 2012, p. 11, www.tascnet. ie/upload/file/TASC%20Tax%20Injustice.pdf (accessed 23 January 2013); 'Road-map to Greater Inequality: TASC's Response to Budget 2012', December 2011, pp. 1, 4, www.tascnet.ie/upload/file/Roadmap%20to%20Greater%20Inequality_final.pdf (accessed 23 January 2013).
34 W. Buiter, 'Monetise Public Debt and Deficits', *FT*, 22 November 2008, blogs.ft.com/maverecon/2008/11/monetise-public-debt-and-deficits/#ixzz2ja SmLXjD (accessed 10 July 2013).
35 ICTU, 'Pre-Budget Submission: A Different Fiscal Adjustment is Possible', Autumn 2013, www.ictu.ie/download/pdf/jit16_prebudget_submission_fiscaladjust ment_web.pdf (accessed 10 October 2013); TASC, 'Budget 2014: Choosing and Equitable Route to Recovery', September 2013, pp. 2–3, www.tascnet.ie/upload/file/ TASC_Budget2014%281%29.pdf (accessed 8 December 2013); see also M. Taft, 'The Urgent Priorities', Progressive-economy@TASC, 21 June 2010, www. progressive-economy.ie/2010/06/urgent-priorities.html (accessed 10 July 2013).
36 Unite, 'Beyond Austerity: Proposals for a Thriving Economy, pre-Budget Submis-sion 2014', September 2013, p. 13, unitetheunionireland.files.wordpress.com/2013/ 09/beyond-austerity-final-upload2.pdf (accessed 13 October 2013).
37 'Ibec and Unions Fooling Themselves on Austerity', *SBP*, 14 July 2013.
38 Social Justice Ireland, 'Investing for Growth, Jobs & Recovery', Policy Briefing, September 2013, p.3, table 1, www.socialjustice.ie/sites/default/files/file/ SJI%20Briefing%20Docs/2013-09-02%20-%20Policy%20Briefing%20-%20Investme nt%20-%20jobs%20-%20growth.pdf (accessed 13 July 2013).

39 NERI, *Quarterly Economic Observer*, Dublin: Nevin Economic Research Institute, Spring 2012, www.nerinstitute.net/download/pdf/qeo_spring_2012.pdf (accessed 8 December 2013); Social Justice Ireland, 'Investing for Growth, Jobs & Recovery'; see also V. Duggan, 'Ireland's Investment Crisis: Diagnosis and Prescription', NERI Working Paper 2013/03, June 2013, www.nerinstitute.net/download/pdf/neri_wp201303.pdf (accessed 14 September 2013); Labour Party, 'Strategic Investment Bank: Financing Ireland's Investment Economy', 2010, www.labour.ie/download/pdf/investinginfuture.pdf (accessed 12 September 2013).

40 ICTU, 'Delivering Growth & Jobs: Funding a Major New Investment Programme for Ireland', 2012, www.ictu.ie/download/pdf/delivering_growth_jobs_funding_a_major_new_investment_programme_for_ireland_may_2012.pdf (accessed 22 September 2013).

41 M. Taft, 'The Unemployment Crisis: A Modest 0.7% Response', Unite's Notes on the Front, 26 November 2012, www.notesonthefront.typepad.com/politicaleconomy/2012/11/even-the-government-admits-their-policies-are-having-little-effect-on-job-creation-they-expect-unemployment-to-remain-at-1-1.html (accessed 22 September 2013); G. Steinhauser, 'As Ireland Exits Bailout, a Life Vest or Just Lifeguard?', *WSJ*, 12 November 2012, online.wsj.com/news/articles/SB10001424052702303460004579194030883286454 (accessed 6 December 2013); T. McDonnell, 'Wealth Tax: Options for its Implementation in the Republic of Ireland', NERI Working Paper 2013/No. 6, September 2013, www.nerinstitute.net/download/pdf/neri_wp_no_6_2013_mcdonnell_wealth_tax.pdf (accessed 20 October 2013).

42 C. Taylor, 'Confidence Must be Restored', *SBP*, 7 December 2008; M. Burke, 'The ESRI Quarterly and "the Small Open Economy"', Progressive-economy@TASC, 20 June 2012, www.progressive-economy.ie/2012/06/esri-quarterly-and-small-open-economy.html (accessed 12 September 2013); 'Leakage, and Hot Air', Progressive-economy@TASC, 13 September 2010, www.progressive-economy.ie/2010/09/leakage-and-hot-air.html (accessed 12 September 2013).

43 P. Lane, 'To Slacken Austerity Drive would be a Big Mistake', *IT*, 25 June 2013.

44 P. Krugman, 'Death of a Fairy Tale', *NYT*, 26 April 2012, www.nytimes.com/2012/04/27/opinion/krugman-death-of-a-fairy-tale.html?_r=0 (accessed 8 December 2013).

45 D. Donovan, 'Critics of Austerity Fail to Offer any Viable Alternative', *IT*, 9 May 2013. See also D. Donovan and A. Murphy, *The Fall of the Celtic Tiger: Ireland and the Euro Debt Crisis*, Oxford: Oxford University Press, 2013.

46 C. Taylor, 'We Need Clarity, Not Kite-flying', *SBP*, 12 May 2013.

47 J. McHale, 'People have Endured Pain but Austerity is Succeeding', *IT*, 15 October 2013.

48 A. Ruddock, 'Wall Street is Not to Blame for Our Recession', *SI*, 28 September 2008; D. McConnell, 'Lenihan's Last Chance to Save Us', *SI*, 7 November 2010; I. Talbot, 'Croke Park must Deliver more for Public Finances', *IT*, 4 September 2012.

49 E. Delaney, 'Why Union Blackmail must be Faced Down', *SI*, 21 March 2010; 'Strikes will Solve Nothing', *IT*, 2 November 2009; 'No Good Can Come Out of Strike', *SI*, 22 November 2009.

50 The exact *Nexis* search was: HLEAD(budget!) AND SECTION(comment! OR editorial! OR opinion! OR analysis) AND SUBJECT(budget!), for the *Sunday Business Post, Irish Times, Sunday Times, Irish Independent* and *Sunday Independent*. 'HLEAD' selects articles containing the word 'budget' in their headline or lead paragraph. The search covered the period between 1 January 2008 and 24 October 2013. Only those pieces for which 'Budget!' reached a level of relevance of 85 per cent or more in the indexing were kept to ensure greater relevance (the index and percentage levels are automatically compiled and computed by *Nexis*). A few articles that were judged not to be about the subject at hand were also rejected (for example, an article about the Greek government budget).

51 'Public Attitudes to the Budget', *IT*, 18 November 2008; B. Keenan, 'No Room for Complacency as we're Still on a Knife-edge', *II*, 6 January 2010.

52 S. Collins, 'Government Must get this Budget Right and Not Waver', *IT*, 4 April 2009.

53 I. Talbot, 'Croke Park Agreement is Designed to Underachieve', *SBP*, 11 December 2011.

54 'State Spending must be Slashed', *SI*, 5 April 2009; E. Harris, 'Padded Public Sector is in Need of Reality Check', *SI*, 12 April 2009.

55 'Understanding Money', *IT*, 4 February 2013.

56 K. Myers, 'If the Primary Goal of a Society is the Eradication of Poverty, then you will get Only More Poverty', *II*, 9 December 2010; M. Cooper, 'Add some Creative Ideas to the Debate', *ST*, 10 October 2010; T. Callan, C. Keane and J. Walsh, 'Budgetary Adjustments to Crisis have Hit Richest Hardest', *IT*, 9 December 2010.

57 T. Curran, 'Carers have been Treated Shamefully by this Government, we Deserve a Break', *II*, 17 October 2013.

58 B. Cowen, 'Burden must be Shared by All at Time of Greatest National Need', *IT*, 16 October 2008; W. O'Dea, 'We Need to Stop Living in Denial and Cut Costs Even Further', *SI*, 18 October 2009; G. FitzGerald, 'Ireland Moving to a Level Playing Field in Labour Costs', *IT*, 18 July 2009; G. FitzGerald, 'Different Opposition Views on Bailout "Renegotiation" Unhelpful', *IT*, 5 February 2011; S. Collins, 'Kenny's Optimism Helps Dispel the Pall of Gloom', *IT*, 22 December 2012.

59 'We Should Continue to Toe the Troika Line', *ST*, 28 July 2013; 'Wrong to Budge on Budget Cuts or Tourism Tax', *ST*, 6 October 2013; 'The Job is Not Yet Done on Our Deficit', *SBP*, 28 April 2013; S. Collins, 'Things are Not Nearly as Bad as they are Often Portrayed', *IT*, 1 June 2013.

60 D. O'Brien, 'Government will have to Cut Old-age Pension', *IT*, 15 July 2010; D. O'Brien, 'Government makes Best Use of Meagre Resources', *IT*, 11 November 2011; 'Cuts have Averted National Bankruptcy', *SBP*, 13 December 2009; D. McWilliams, 'Who Will Take the Blame for the Great Depression of 2010?' *SBP*, 8 March 2009.

61 Guajardo *et al.*, 'Expansionary Austerity'; R. Peet, 'Inequality, Crisis and Austerity in Finance Capitalism'.

62 'Let's Slash Corporation Tax to Boost Our Economy', *SI*, 11 April 2010; B. Burgess, 'It Won't Pay to Tax the Rich Harder', *ST*, 30 September 2012; 'More must Pay their Share of Income Tax', *SBP*, 8 November 2009; 'Learning the Lessons from Property Reliefs', *SBP*, 23 January 2011.

63 See also S. Coffey, who reaches similar conclusions in 'Corporate Tax Revenues', Economic Incentives, 30 April 2013, www.economic-incentives.blogspot.ie/2013/04/corporate-tax-revenues.html (accessed 7 December 2013).

64 M. Taft, 'Be Glad You're Not Living in One of those Terrible High-tax Countries', Unite's Notes on the Front, 8 January 2013, notesonthefront.typepad.com/poli ticaleconomy/2013/01/be-glad-youre-not-living-in-one-of-the-those-terrible-high-tax -countries.html (accessed 7 December 2013); Social Justice Ireland, 'Investing for Growth, Jobs & Recovery', p. 3, table 1.

65 'State Spending must be Slashed', *SI*, 5 April 2009; M. Coleman, 'The Rules of the Game are Changing', *SI*, 2 November 2008; P. Lane, 'Excessive Tax Increases Run Risk of Deepening the Recession', *IT*, 7 October 2008.

66 E. Harris, 'Padded Public Sector is in Need of Reality Check', *SI*, 12 April 2009; D. McConnell, 'Bloated Public Sector a Luxury we can no Longer Afford', *SI*, 29 August 2010; A. Ahearne, 'Commitment and Stamina are Required for Fiscal Consolidation', *IT*, 6 September 2008; W. O'Dea, 'New Budget will Prove Tough but Necessary', *SI*, 28 September 2008; A. Beesley, 'Only Sustained Cuts can Now Keep Ireland Afloat', *IT*, 30 September 2010; W. O'Dea, 'We must Suffer the Pain Now – or Else we will Blight Future Generations', *SI*, 19 October 2008; 'Bill is

Tough but Necessary', *IT*, 22 January 2011; E. Kenny, 'Tough Budget would Restore Confidence', *IT*, 27 February 2009; G. FitzGerald, 'Supplementary Budget Can Begin Urgent Task of Restoring Depleted Tax Revenues', *IT*, 28 February 2009; E. Donnellan, 'Hospitals Need Emergency Surgery on their Finances', *IT*, 29 June 2011; C. Keena, 'Budget May Cut Wages and Raise Taxes to Restore Competitiveness', *IT*, 7 April 2009; B. Cowen, 'Budget will Restore Confidence and Hasten Economic Recovery', *IT*, 10 April 2009; B. Keenan, 'This is Not the Time to Row Back on Crucial Cuts', *II*, 3 July 2009.

67 Special Group on Public Service Numbers and Expenditure Programmes, 'Report', July 2009, www.finance.gov.ie/viewdoc.asp?DocID=5861 (accessed 31 October 2013); C. McCarthy, 'The Myth that we have Lots of Options about Our Debt', *SI*, 24 October 2010; 'Austerity Vital to Maintain Our Economic Sovereignty', *IT*, 11 October 2010; A. Ahearne, 'Targeted Area Investment is Palatable Idea', *SI*, 22 April 2012; P. Lane, 'Tough Budget Needed to Stave Off Grimmer Future', *IT*, 4 November 2009.

68 B. Harbor, 'Calling Time on Croke Park Deal would be a Foolish Move', *IT*, 11 September 2012; P. Newenham, 'Top Bankers were Paid Average of €1.4m Last Year', *IT*, 30 November 2013.

69 M. Taft, 'Stop the Presses! Cutting Public Sector Employment Actually Increases the Debt', Unite's Notes on the Front, 27 August 2013, notesonthefront.typepad. com/politicaleconomy/2013/08/stop-the-presses-cutting-public-sector-employment-a ctually-increases-the-debt.html (accessed 8 December 2013); 'Cutting Public Sector Pay and Jobs – the High Cost of Irrelevance. The Recession Diaries – March 11', Unite's Notes on the Front, 11 March 2010, notesonthefront.typepad.com/poli ticaleconomy/2010/03/in-a-previous-post-we-saw-that-public-sector-labour-costs-are -below-average-by-eu-15-standards-the-argument-that-irish-publ.html (accessed 8 December 2013); 'Memo to IBEC', Progressive-economy Blog, 30 January 2010, www.progressive-economy.ie/2010/01/memo-to-ibec.html (accessed 8 December 2013); T. Healy and R. O'Farrell, 'Impact on the Government Deficit of a Reduction in the Public Sector Pay Bill', NERI Research in Brief, May 2013, www.ner institute.net/download/pdf/inbrief_public_sector_pay_may_2013.pdf (accessed 8 December 2013).

70 M. Taft, 'Revisiting Headlines – Public Sector Labour Costs. The Recession Diaries – March 2nd', Unite's Notes on the Front, 2 March 2010, notesonthefront. typepad.com/politicaleconomy/2010/03/with-industrial-action-in-the-public-sector-r amping-up-a-couple-of-notches-it-is-worth-revisiting-a-couple-of-issues-in-rela.html (accessed 8 December 2013).

71 'Private Sector Growth must be Priority in Budget 2013', *SBP*, 2 December 2012; 'Strategies for Growth', *IT*, 9 July 2013.

72 D. Bolger, 'The Last Truly Democratic Space, where Nobody Moves You Along', *IT*, 26 May 2012; 'Targeting the Little Ones', *IT*, 21 October 2008; 'Budget Cuts and Protestant Schools', *IT*, 25 April 2009; C. Coulter, 'Budget Cuts will Severely Limit Effectiveness of State Watchdogs', *IT*, 11 November 2008; P. Watt, 'Budget Cutbacks Weaken State's Capacity to Combat Racism', *IT*, 19 November 2008; 'Challenges for Arts Policy', *IT*, 29 December 2011; P. Cox, 'Investment in Heritage Key to Luring the Cultural Tourist', 4 January 2012.

73 R. Boyd Barrett, 'We will Not Find Solutions in Failed Neoliberal Mantras', *IT*, 28 October 2010; M.L. McDonald, 'SF Wants to Forge a New Alliance and Offer Egalitarian Alternative', *IT*, 13 May 2009.

74 E. Kenny, 'Medical Card Decision a Breach of Public Trust', *IT*, 20 October 2008; 'A Fine Gael Tough Budget would Restore Confidence', 27 February 2009.

7   Beyond the eurozone?

Ireland leaving the euro would 'quickly drift back to real poverty, on the scale of the 1950s'.
(Stephen Collins, *Irish Times*, 3 December 2011[1])

Euro exit could cost €45,000 for each family.
(Nick Webb, *Sunday Independent*, 11 September 2011[2])

When examining the problems of Ireland and the European periphery, it is useful to look beyond the eurozone at countries which once faced similar conditions but adopted different policies that turned out to be relatively successful. This chapter discusses the cases of Argentina and Iceland to illustrate the potentially positive outcomes associated with a country having its own currency and that forces creditors to absorb losses during a financial crisis. The European and Irish media have covered negatively such successful cases that invalidate the strategy of internal devaluation, or have ignored them. In particular, the option of leaving the euro is not a black and white issue, and reasonable arguments could have been made for or against it during the crisis. However, the chapter makes the point that the media have only presented one side of the picture on this subject.

Leaving the euro?

As seen in Chapter 2, the common currency provides a number of advantages for European elites. However, since the beginning of the crisis, there has been some discussion of the possibility for peripheral countries to leave the euro and re-establish their own currency. As of this writing, the issue has subsided along with the financial turbulence in the eurozone, but it remains important and could come back to prominence in the not too distant future. In any case, the ECB and European authorities have been opposed to the strategy, as they believe that the political and symbolic ramifications of a country leaving the eurozone would affect the value of the euro negatively. They point to the numerous complications that would arise from a euro break-up, including producing and distributing a new currency throughout a national territory, repaying debts denominated in euro, redrawing contracts written in euros, and so on. There is no point denying that those problems are real in economic and logistical terms. However, it is important to state that analysts favourable to peripheral countries leaving the euro have often conceived of this strategy not as an ideal path to recovery, but as a possibly second-best option when the ECB and European governments refuse to implement other policies that would be more effective and easier to deploy.

There is a range of simpler options for the eurozone which would not involve any members leaving it.[3] To elaborate on the previous chapter, the ECB could abandon its austerity strategy. This could involve guaranteeing peripheral governments' sovereign debt, permitting more deficit spending, and sustaining a higher level of inflation in Germany and other core countries. The latter would allow peripheral countries to regain competitiveness while suffering less of the pain inflicted by austerity. For example, if the ECB increased its inflation target to 3–4 per cent instead of 2 per cent, this would alleviate the burden of debt by eroding its real value, benefiting both heavily indebted governments and individuals having to pay large mortgages. Even the IMF's chief economist, Olivier Blanchard, suggested that this strategy could be beneficial.[4] If the ECB bought an additional €3 trillion of member countries' debt to pump reserves into the banking system, the ECB could choose to hold this debt indefinitely. The advantage of doing so is that the interest paid to the ECB would be refunded to member countries, thereby reducing the interest burden they face. Once the economy recovered, the ECB could raise its reserve requirement in order to prevent inflation from rising excessively.[5]

A number of analysts have advocated that the ECB should buy more public debt from peripheral governments and create money in doing so, which would put to rest speculation against their sovereign debt. The OECD has recently endorsed this view, in a 'direct call' to engage in 'quantitative easing', as done by the US Federal Reserve.[6] The ECB pumped €1 trillion of liquidity into European banks starting in December 2011 to keep them afloat and persuade them to lend to governments in difficulty. However, the banks did not buy enough government debt, and in any case the strategy is a very indirect way of supporting governments' borrowing. Instead, the ECB should be a direct lender of last resort and buy large amounts of sovereign debt itself and 'put a floor' on the bond prices to calm the markets. Some have objected that doing so could expose it to losses if governments eventually default. However, if the goal is to preserve the integrity of the eurozone, this is an incidental consequence. Also, the ECB, as a central bank, could always simply print money to make up on its losses. Inflation could theoretically rise if vast quantities of money are created, but given the relatively small size of peripheral economies, this should not be a problem. Moreover, as seen above, more inflation would most likely be a good thing. In summer 2012, the ECB moved toward a more interventionist stance when its head, Mario Draghi, announced that it would do 'whatever it takes' to preserve the euro. This was followed by the announcement of an 'Outright Monetary Transactions' (OMT) programme through which the ECB could potentially buy unlimited amounts of sovereign bonds from peripheral governments. Even if no such purchases had yet been made as of this writing, its announcement put an end to the threat of financial meltdown by lowering the interest rates on sovereign bonds in the periphery. Likewise, the threat of a euro break-up has receded.[7]

A number of analysts also argue that eurobonds would alleviate the crisis. Although the details vary from one proposal to another, the plan essentially consists in a single authority, for example the ECB, issuing bonds and thus borrowing on behalf of the union, and transferring the funds raised to member countries that need them. The bonds would be guaranteed jointly and severally by all eurozone governments, doing away with the principle of individual country responsibility. A limited version of this is the EFSF itself, but it could be expanded. Eurobonds would allow peripheral countries to borrow at lower interest rates thanks to the backing of stronger members, but there has been opposition to the scheme from Germany and other core countries because it would expose them to losses.[8]

Another alternative would be to establish fiscal federalism and a full fiscal union. This would create a European federal state that could raise its own taxes and operate its own budget for all member states. It could also issue federal bonds (eurobonds), borrow and spend to recapitalize banks, undertake investment projects across the eurozone, or for any other priority it may set for itself. Although interesting, this proposal is in practice still far from acceptance. However, its value has been explained by Paul Krugman by comparing Ireland and Nevada, 'two economies that, scenery aside, look quite similar at the moment': both had huge property bubbles that burst; both fell into deep recessions that led to soaring unemployment; and both have faced many defaults or risk of defaults on home mortgages. However, in Nevada, 'these shocks are buffered, to an important extent, by the federal government'. Nevada is now paying less in taxes to Washington but its older residents still get their Social Security cheques and Medicare is still disbursing funds to pay for the medical bills. In other words, Nevada is receiving a lot of aid, while the deposits in its banks are still guaranteed by the FDIC, a federal agency, and some of the losses from mortgage defaults are being absorbed by Fannie and Freddie, institutions which are backed by the federal government. Ireland, by contrast, 'is mostly on its own, having to bail out its own banks, having to pay for retirement and health care out of its own greatly diminished revenue'. Therefore, although times are difficult in both places, Nevada is doing better.[9]

If such alternatives are not deployed to any significant extent – and so far, they have indeed been limited, with the important exception of OMT – the option of abandoning the euro becomes more attractive. This is why a number of economists have voiced support for peripheral countries to explore this possibility, such as Paul Krugman, Costas Lapavitsas, Dean Baker and Mark Weisbrot, and in Ireland, Terrence McDonough and David McWilliams.[10]

Of course, leaving the eurozone is a path fraught with obstacles of a political, economic and legal nature.[11] For example, creating a new currency would be more difficult than de-pegging it from another one, as was done in Argentina, which still had its own peso pegged to the US dollar, compared to European countries which have lost their national currency. Distributing new coins and notes to the country's businesses and ATMs could take a few weeks, and sorting out the conversion of debts and contracts in euros into the new national denomination would be tedious. Yet, even if peripheral countries achieved only half of, say, Argentina's growth after it abandoned its peg, it would still be impressive and much better than what they have achieved by staying in the eurozone since the crisis began. Also, the transition could be effected much faster if the government produced IOUs or debit cards that could be distributed to the population and businesses rapidly in order to meet liquidity needs nationwide until physical notes and coins are in circulation. Moreover, as was done in Cyprus, capital controls would almost certainly need to be imposed to prevent depositors from taking their money out of the country, if they learned that a devaluation was imminent. In this respect, a bank run could be averted by announcing the decision to abandon the euro by surprise on a Friday afternoon and declaring a bank holiday of a few days to give time to implement such controls. However, this is difficult to do without leaks of information.

If peripheral countries were to leave the euro and return to a new domestic currency, the latter would almost certainly initially depreciate significantly relative to the euro, a fact that has been emphasized by opponents of the scheme. However, this is not necessarily a negative outcome, as long as the drop in value is well managed and monitored. Indeed, many studies have examined the effects of the real exchange rate on growth based on the experience of a large number of countries over the last few decades.[12] What is reassuring is that a 'systematic finding appears common to almost all': maintaining a competitive (i.e., undervalued) exchange rate has positive effects on economic growth, while overvaluation tends to slow down growth. A competitive exchange rate can, among other things, improve the trade balance and stimulate the export sector, while an overvalued currency may lead to rising imports and a deteriorating balance of payments. One recent survey concludes that an overvalued real exchange rate 'can lead to disastrous outcomes affecting short and medium term growth'. In particular, 'fixed and semi-fixed exchange rate regimes' focused on lowering inflation instead of fostering growth and employment can lead to currency 'appreciation and balance of payment and financial crises'. Therefore, the aim should be to target and preserve a stable and competitive exchange rate.[13]

Similar conclusions may be drawn for the case of large devaluations, or currency collapses, which have been shown to have potentially positive effects on growth (although some studies have emphasized their contractionary impacts[14]). For example, in a recent comprehensive survey of 108 countries for the period 1960–2006, ECB and IMF researchers conclude that large devaluations 'tend to have a positive effect on output', that 'the likelihood of a positive growth rate in the year of the collapse is over two times more likely than a contraction', and that 'positive growth rates in the years that follow such episodes [devaluations] are the norm'. They note that while it is true that currency collapses are associated with significant losses in GDP, countries tend to suffer those losses before their currency collapses, not after. Thus, it is not the currency devaluation that causes the loss of GDP, but other economic factors.[15]

In short, although analysts may reasonably differ on the desirability of leaving the euro, it must be acknowledged that there is substantial evidence that the strategy should not be seen as ominously as it has often been depicted. It is also worth noting that many of the commentators strongly opposed to Ireland leaving the euro are the same individuals who never could identify the housing bubble when it was growing, who strongly agreed with using tax-payers' money to save the banks, and who have enthusiastically supported austerity and government cutbacks that affect the poor disproportionately. Their claims should thus not be accepted automatically.

Elites and the media have strongly supported the common currency. A *Sunday Independent* poll among the chief executives of Ireland's top 200 companies reveals that the vast majority of them, nearly 82 per cent, believe that Ireland should stick to the euro, while not even 5 per cent feel that the country should leave the eurozone (the remainder is undecided).[16] Minister for Finance Brian Lenihan said that abandoning it would be a 'disaster' and would lead to 'a collapse of the banking system'. Peter Sutherland, a promi-nent Irish banker and chairman of Goldman Sachs International, thinks that the failure of the single currency would have 'calamitous effects'. Others describe the idea of leaving the euro as 'fantasy-land', 'economic suicide', and a move that would be 'catastrophic to the nation's financial health'. The 'nuclear option of a euro exit combined with sovereign default may make for good theatre, but it's an awfully dumb solution'. It would allegedly be impractical and 'would pose serious technical challenges', such as repro-gramming ATMs and cash machines, while capital flight would result in large flows of money out of the country. Further, the pressure on the banking system would be such that 'economic recession would prove inevitable' while 'a dire employment situation would deteriorate'. The currency would depreciate drastically and the 'outstanding stock of euro-denominated debt would prove unbearable'. Others argue that leaving the euro is inadvisable because it would trigger inflation and Ireland would have to establish a new currency from scratch, which would be complicated. In fact, peripheral countries should fear any nation exiting the euro, which could 'lead to a tidal wave of market pressure, with one weakling after another forced from the union as markets question their capacity to survive'.[17]

The situation is alleged to be so dangerous that the *Irish Times*' Stephen Collins asserts that 'Whatever price we pay to keep euro is worth it' and the decision 'should be a no-brainer'. Ditching the euro would mean 'an uncer-tain future that could so easily descend into economic and political chaos'.

We would 'quickly drift back to real poverty, on the scale of the 1950s'. Also, an article entitled 'Euro exit could cost €45,000 for each family' mentions a UBS report which 'slammed' the option of leaving the euro and setting up a new currency and wonders 'Why on earth would a country go through this much trauma'. Leaving the euro and devaluing is unlikely to regain competitiveness and furthermore, 'Europe would impose massive tariffs against the exports of the seceding country'.[18]

The *Irish Times* warns that a euro break-up would cause a 'euro zone catastrophe'. If the euro sank in value, 'Europe's banks would collapse', people 'would lose their savings', a lot of 'wealth would disappear', bank shares and bonds would become 'worthless' and governments would default. This would have 'massive knock-on effects' for pension funds which massive defaults could 'destroy'. In short, a collapse of the euro would be a 'cataclysm' and 'the most destructive event in Europe since the Second World War'. Other articles surmise that an exit from the euro 'would be a disaster' and declare bluntly that 'Leaving the eurozone is simply not an option for Ireland'. If it happened, the 'money supply, trade and economic growth would crumble'. Any euro exit could 'trigger the dreaded domino effect', which would lead to the 'armageddon of disorderly collapse' in which 'the public services would collapse for want of funds'.[19]

Some also play on fears that leaving the eurozone 'would run the risk of Ireland being expelled from the EU' by turning facts on their head and stating that 'the evidence (from Iceland and elsewhere) strongly suggests membership of the euro zone has afforded Ireland a priceless measure of protection' during the crisis. Likewise, economists like Trinity College Dublin Professor Philip Lane have claimed that the EMU framework 'is not responsible for the financial crisis' and only 'entertaining thoughts of leaving the euro area' would lead Ireland to be 'hammered by capital flight and steep increases in risk premia'. Another analyst opines that if Ireland left the eurozone, 'Households' savings would evaporate, businesses would collapse, banks would impose capital controls, there would be months of turmoil. And at the end of it all, we would be poorer for the move'. However, the evidence suggests that leaving the euro is an option that is worth exploring.[20]

Iceland

There are many similarities between the rise and fall of Iceland and Ireland. Before the crisis, Iceland's neoliberal politicians and civil servants pushed through privatization and deregulation in the 1990s and 2000s. This, combined with cronyism among the elites, 'enabled a small group of financiers to leverage government-guaranteed deposits into a vast wave of mergers and acquisitions abroad, and redistribute enough of the profits back home to make the economy boom'. Much of the same happened in the United States, Britain and Ireland, but it has been argued that Iceland stands out 'as a more transparent illustration of how "masters of the universe" confidence, sophistic ideology, mercenary gain, mendacity and sheer ignorance combined to drive the boom and bust'.[21]

Iceland was one of the poorest countries in Western Europe at the end of World War II. In the post-war period, its economy and political system have been dominated by a group of 14 families known locally as the 'Octopus'. The economy has been based on fishing, supplying a North Atlantic Treaty Organization (NATO) base, domestic banking and insurance, importing and distributing of oil, as well as transport. Starting in the 1970s, neoliberal ideas spread among the country's leadership. From 1991 to 2004, Prime Minister David Oddsson focused on privatizing and deregulating the economy by invoking Thatcher's and Reagan's ideas as models. In 1998–2002, the government privatized the two main state-owned banks and supported the creation of a third one through mergers of smaller banks. The banks' new owners set up private equity companies and a cycle of borrowing and lending soon emerged. The bank owners took major loans from the banks, using their shares as collateral; they in turn made loans to the private equity companies; those loans were used to buy assets, which became collateral for more gigantic loans, with which more assets could be bought. By 2006, Iceland's three major banks became part of the biggest 300 globally. Iceland's elites cheered their banks' owners and managers as 'our go-getting Vikings' and the government adjusted the tax burden from the top to the bottom half of the income scale, claiming that this would strengthen 'incentives for risk taking'.[22]

Even when signs surfaced of impending problems about financial institutions' growing balance sheets and stability risks, public relations campaigns gave a positive spin to those developments. For example, in 2006, American monetary economist Frederic Mishkin penned a report commissioned by Iceland's Chamber of Commerce which claimed that the banking system was stable. The chamber paid Mishkin US$135,000 for the 30-page report. The following year, Professor Richard Portes of the London Business School was paid £58,000 to produce a second report which reached similar conclusions. Further, a number of individuals were invited to Iceland 'to preach the gospel of neoliberal economics', such as Arthur Laffer, a supply-side economist of the Reagan years, who stated in late 2007 that the country 'should be a model to the world'.[23]

However, large imbalances developed and it became ever more difficult for the banks to remain sustainable. The current account deficit reached 24 per cent of GDP in 2006, almost the biggest in the world, and the stock market increased by nine times between 2001 and 2007. The assets of the country's three main banks rose from 1.7 times GDP in 2003 to nearly 9.0 times GDP in late 2007, second only to Switzerland. The Central Bank did not have the capacity to back them up as lender of last resort, given that many of their assets were of questionable quality and in foreign currencies. To raise more funds to pay for more asset purchases and reimburse debt coming to maturity, Landsbanki decided to raise retail deposits by establishing online branches called Icesave in Britain and the Netherlands, which offered high interest to attract savers.[24]

In September 2008, the crisis hit, coming on the heels of the Lehman failure and seizure of the money markets. The krona, Iceland's currency, sank from 90 to the euro in early 2008 to 190 in November 2008, the stock market collapsed by about 98 per cent during the year, and unemployment surged from an average of 1.6 per cent in 2008 to an average of 8.1 per cent in 2010. The IMF arrived in Iceland, the first time it had been called in to organize a rescue of a developed country since Britain in 1976.

It has been noted that Iceland has fared better during the crisis than countries that have followed EU-IMF dictates closely, like Ireland. First, whereas in 2008, the unemployment rate was 4.8 percentage points higher in Ireland than Iceland, in late 2013 it was 8.7 points higher in Ireland (see Figure 7.1). Moreover, Ireland's poor performance is compounded by the fact that it has seen massive emigration, without which its unemployment rate would be even higher.

Second, Iceland has been much better at keeping government debt from accumulating. In 2007, the two countries' net general government debt-to-GDP ratios were almost identical at about 10 per cent of GDP, but by 2013, Ireland's net debt had surged to 105 per cent of GDP while Iceland's had reached only 64 per cent. Third, as economists like Paul Krugman and Constantin Gurdgiev have argued, Iceland has performed better than Ireland in terms of GDP growth and trade since the crisis began.

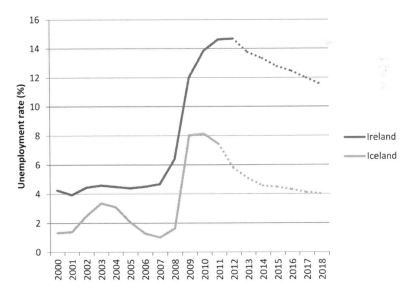

Figure 7.1 Unemployment rate in Ireland and Iceland (% of total labour force, dotted lines are estimates)
Source: IMF World Economic Outlook database, October 2013, www.imf.org

Overall, the point is not that Iceland has performed better than Ireland at all levels. None of the two economies can be considered a stellar success and both have significant problems. Nevertheless, perhaps Krugman summarizes the situation well when he writes that 'Ireland did everything it was supposed to; nobody would describe it as "healing". Iceland broke all the rules, and things are not too bad'.[25]

What rules did Iceland break? The IMF organized a conference on the subject in 2011, gathering some well-known economists like Krugman and Joseph Stiglitz. The conference's key message was that unorthodox policies can work better than conventional ones and appear to have been relatively successful in putting Iceland back on the road to recovery. For example, the austerity implemented was softer than that usually prescribed by the IMF, as the big cuts in public spending were postponed into 2010–11. Moreover, capital controls, which are usually rejected by the IMF, did prevent massive capital outflows. Stiglitz endorsed Iceland's policy response and said that 'What Iceland did was right. It would have been wrong to burden future generations with the mistakes of the financial system'. Likewise for Krugman, who noted that 'Iceland zigged when all the conventional wisdom was that it should zag'. He stated that the 'idea that there would be a huge reputational penalty for allowing private sector parties to go bust and default on their external obligations has not turned out to be true'.[26]

Perhaps the most significant difference between Iceland and eurozone countries is that it kept its own currency, which enabled a more flexible response to the crisis. In this respect, Dean Baker noted that the people of Iceland should be 'thanking the god of small currencies every day for the fact that the country had its own currency, as opposed to, say, being part of the eurozone at the time that its financial system imploded'. When the crisis struck, Iceland was able to let its currency decline relative to its trading partners. This made imports more expensive and they dropped sharply. Conversely, exports were made cheaper, resulting in an export surge. One important effect was that Iceland's very large trade deficits, which reached more than 28 per cent of GDP in 2008, reversed over the next several years and contributed to restoring economic growth while bringing unemployment down. By early 2012, the unemployment rate in Iceland was 6.2 per cent, which compared favourably to 13.6 per cent in Portugal, 14.5 per cent in Ireland, 19.2 per cent in Greece and 22.9 per cent in Spain. Of course, Iceland never joined the eurozone, and therefore did not face the logistical problems that Ireland would face if it chose to exit the euro and re-establish a national currency. Nevertheless, Iceland's advantages are real.[27]

Two other advantages of being outside the eurozone can be noted. First, it allows countries not to follow the ECB's strict policy of keeping inflation low. Letting inflation rise alleviates the burden of debtors, but this strategy has not been available to eurozone countries. In contrast, inflation in Iceland reached 12 per cent in 2008 and 2009. Second, eurozone countries have been subject to European Commission and ECB pressure to adopt strict austerity programmes. In Iceland, a number of analysts have noted that austerity has been more flexible, as mentioned above.[28]

The Icesave dispute provides an important illustration of democratic input and resistance to policy making. As a result of the crisis, Landsbanki's depositors at branches in the Netherlands and Britain lost access to their deposits in October 2008. The question was then to determine who would assume payment for their deposits. Because Iceland was unable to pay the British and Dutch governments did assume the payments, and it was decided that they would be repaid through the liquidation of Landsbanki. During the resolution process, the Icelandic government came under pressure to repay the deposits. In particular, the parliament passed two acts that allowed the state to conclude agreements with Britain and the Netherlands. The first one determined that €5.5 billion, equivalent to 50 per cent of Iceland's GDP, would be repaid to Britain and the Netherlands between 2016 and 2023. However, in early 2010, a referendum was held and the deal was rejected by 93 per cent of voters. Then, a second deal, more favourable to Iceland, was submitted to a referendum in April 2011, but was also rejected by 66 per cent of voters. In short, through the Icesave referendums, the population prevented their government from socializing private bank debts.[29]

Another lesson is that creditors and bondholders were burned and absorbed a share of financial institutions' losses through a debt-for-equity swap. The government created three new banks to hold the domestic assets and liabilities of the old (failed) banks, while the banks' foreign assets and liabilities were dealt with through negotiations with the creditors. The new banks were recapitalized by the government at a substantial cost, amounting to 14 per cent of GDP. However, the state should recoup the funds invested in recapitalization once the economy and the new banks recover. Moreover, a substantial part of the recapitalization was accomplished through the swap with the foreign creditors, limiting the necessary government outlays. In short, whereas Ireland bailed out its banks, Iceland bailed them in. It is difficult to calculate precisely what would have happened if Iceland had followed Ireland's path and guaranteed all liabilities of domestic banks instead of letting them fail and then contributing to their recapitalization, but one study estimated that the impact on the country would have been clearly more negative.[30]

The Irish media have not publicized the case of Iceland to a great extent since 2008. Few articles have presented a positive view of this approach to the crisis, although David McWilliams has been an exception. It is interesting that the case has not been more debated in the media, because the policies Iceland adopted, although diverging from orthodoxy, nevertheless remained within the realm of mainstream opinion. As seen above, the IMF even organized a conference in 2011 praising its achievements and the use of heterodox methods.[31]

Articles have sometimes explicitly rejected the Icelandic model as a possibility for Ireland. A piece in the *Irish Times* criticized 'negative commentary which relies on spurious examples and the selective use of data to prove a point', such as those who think 'that the Irish Government should follow Iceland's example and default'. It claimed that the 'truth of the matter is that the Icelandic economy remains mired in deep recession' and that the alleged improvement in unemployment figures 'is a mirage'. In short, 'the idea that we follow Iceland's example is simply ludicrous'. In the same paper, Dan O'Brien downplayed the advantages of Iceland having its own currency, claiming that the 'Benefits for Ireland of being in euro have been greater than benefits for Iceland of having its own currency'. References made explicitly or in passing to the alleged superiority of the euro over an Irish domestic currency have been many. When commenting on Iceland's predicament in late 2008, the *Irish Times* stated plainly that the euro afforded protection to Ireland in time of financial crisis. Icelandic politicians now say that 'it is essential for a small state to have the protection of euro membership for a highly open economy … The lessons for Ireland, had we not been in the euro during these same weeks, are plain to see'.[32]

Also, the relevance of the two Icesave referenda has been almost completely ignored. An *Irish Times* editorial opined that parliamentary negotiation with bondholders is a better path than popular referendums: in other words, political elites should decide for the population, which should not participate in such decisions. Commenting on Iceland's second referendum, it stated that while 'Those pressing for a referendum on Ireland's bank bailout agreements with the European Union and the International Monetary Fund will gain heart from this result … Both Fine Gael and Labour [the two political parties in power] sought a mandate from voters to ensure bank bondholders share the costs of the bailout, within an EU-IMF framework. This remains the best route to achieving the objective over the several years it will necessarily take to secure it'. Also, the issue has often simply been left unaddressed. An article in the *Irish Times* entitled 'Should Ireland's citizens refuse to bail out the banks?' noted that whereas in Ireland the government has maintained that banks cannot fail, in Iceland the population had the opportunity to vote on some bank debts. Yet, the question contained in the title was not answered. The piece simply ended by posing the same question again: 'Should Ireland follow the Iceland example and refuse to bail out Anglo? What are the consequences when the voices of civic society become louder in a country's economic affairs?' This is not a very strong endorsement of democracy.[33]

Argentina

Left-of-centre Latin American governments that have come to power over the last decade and a half have challenged neoliberal orthodoxy and seen improvements in their economic growth rates. For example, Argentina addressed its debt crisis in 2001 by defaulting on some of its creditors and adopting strategies that enabled the economy to recover strongly over a relatively short period of time, growing at about 9 per cent annually in real terms until the 2008 global crisis (Figure 7.2). Buenos Aires essentially did the opposite of what the ECB and IMF are pressurizing Ireland and peripheral countries to do, and predictably, Argentina's experience has not been publicized by the European and Irish media.[34]

Although what follows emphasizes the positive aspects of the Argentine recovery after 2001, this is not to say that the Kirchner administrations have been flawless. They have been criticized for failing to extend redistributive reforms further in a number of socio-economic areas, with the result that multiple problems still remain. Moreover, since 2007, economic and social statistics have been manipulated by the government, and it is thus difficult to obtain reliable data. Nevertheless, that political and economic mistakes have been made and that policy could have been more progressive should not obscure the fact that the default and devaluation were positive for economic growth.[35]

The 2001 default was the outcome of a development model characterized by the accumulation of debt since the 1970s. When a military regime came to power in 1976, public debt amounted to about $8 billion, but when it left seven years later, it had surged to $45 billion. In the 1990s, President Carlos Menem implemented neoliberal policies inspired by the 'Washington Consensus' under the Convertibility Plan, the main components of which included a liberalization of trade and financial and capital accounts, the

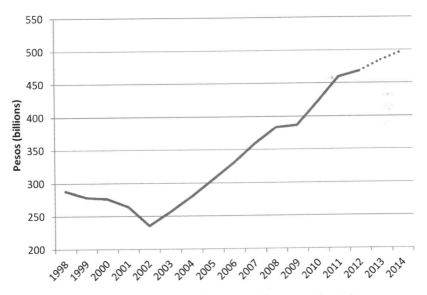

Figure 7.2 Argentina's GDP (constant prices, dotted lines are estimates)
Source: IMF World Economic Outlook database, October 2013, www.imf.org
Note: IMF data are based on officially reported data. However, since 2008, alternative data sources have shown significantly lower real growth than the official data.

privatization of state-owned enterprises, and the pegging of the peso to the US dollar on a one-to-one exchange rate. The hope was that foreign capital would flow into the country and lead to prosperity thanks to a 'trickle-down' effect. The Convertibility Plan did lead to a significant reduction in inflation, but it also exacerbated economic problems. External interest rate shocks, the privatization of social security (leading to a loss of government revenues) and capital flight all contributed to the debt build-up. As the crisis reached boiling point, the IMF's recessionary policies of fiscal consolidation made the situation worse, until the default in December 2001 and abandonment of the peg a few weeks later.[36]

The default led to a sharp, but short, economic contraction during which GDP dropped by 5 per cent in the first quarter of 2002. However, the recovery began immediately thereafter and real GDP reached its pre-recession level in three years, thanks to real annual growth of 8 to 9 per cent. The expansion continued until 2009, when it slowed down considerably due to domestic factors and the global recession, but picked up in 2010 and 2011.[37]

This performance challenges common perceptions of the consequences of default. What is interesting is that it was achieved despite the debt restructuring, little foreign direct investment and a relative isolation from global financial markets, factors which are often perceived as crucial to generate growth. Furthermore, social indicators improved. Poverty was reduced from about half the population in 2002 to approximately 30 per cent of the population today, while extreme poverty followed the same downward trend. Income inequality also dropped: people in the 95th percentile enjoyed incomes 32 times larger than those in the fifth percentile in 2001, but by 2010, this figure had decreased to 17, largely due to rising incomes among those at the bottom of the ladder. Moreover, unemployment fell by about half to settle at 8.0 per cent by 2010, while employment reached a record high of 55.7 per cent. It is true that those statistics have been somewhat unreliable since 2007, but whatever lack of improvement in social indicators there is should be blamed more on bad social policy than the default and devaluation.[38]

The recovery and rapid growth may be attributed to three main sets of policies discussed in more detail below. First, the default itself freed the country from an unsustainable debt burden and interest payments and permitted the enactment of policies geared towards economic recovery instead of debt repayment and IMF-style fiscal consolidation. Second, eliminating the peso-dollar peg and targeting a stable and competitive exchange rate made prices more predictable, which is important for investment and consumption decisions. It also led to an improvement of the trade balance by boosting exports and reducing imports. Third, the government intervened in the economy to redistribute income and adopted a more flexible fiscal approach than IMF-inspired austerity programmes would have entailed.[39] What follows describes the main themes in mainstream media coverage of Argentina's economic strategy. The latter invalidates so many of the troika's principles that it provoked a clearly negative reaction from the European media. Articles

published since 2008 discussing economic conditions in Argentina were identified using the *Nexis* database and individual newspapers' databases if they
were not included in *Nexis*. Nearly 1,000 articles in the main Irish, German,
French and British newspapers were considered.[40]

Representing the default's consequences as catastrophic and ignoring its benefits

The literature on default states clearly that sovereigns that do not repay their
debts in their entirety do not usually suffer significant long-term consequences, and Argentina confirms this. Nevertheless, the media have depicted
the country's default as catastrophic while its positive consequences have been
mentioned only in passing, if at all.

The Irish media have reported little on Argentina's default and subsequent
growth, and when they did, painted a misleading picture of the reality, giving
the impression that debt cancellation led to negative consequences up to this
day. For example, an *Irish Times* article entitled 'Ourselves alone: what happens if Ireland defaults?' describes the situation in Argentina in 2002 just after
it defaulted, thus, in a passage worth quoting at length:

> Word races though the city slums that there is food on the freeway and
> it's still alive. A cattle truck has overturned, spilling 22 head of prime
> Angus beef across the road. Within minutes 600 hungry residents mob
> the area, wielding machetes and carving knives. 'Kill the cows! Take what
> you can', they shout to each other. Live cattle are sloppily killed and
> diced. Fights break out for bits of flesh in bloody tugs of war.

The article continues:

> After the default came the meltdown: a 70 per cent devaluation of the
> peso in six months, a rapidly shrinking economy, an avalanche of poverty
> and unemployment. Millions of middle managers, salaried factory work-
> ers and state employees lost their jobs in the sell-off of state-run industries
> and the collapse of local companies.

The piece relies on so-called experts affiliated with financial institutions. It asks
if a default would turn the Irish into 'international pariahs' and says that economists 'rarely agree on anything, but the consensus on the last is that, yes, we
would be pariahs'. It quotes Fergal O'Brien, IBEC's chief economist, as saying
that a default could result in a situation where 'you don't have commerce, so
there's nothing on the shelves, nothing is being bought or sold', a situation so
bad that 'With no functioning bank system there's no guarantee that the
ATMs would continue to work'.[41]

An *Irish Times* series entitled 'Argentina 10 years after default' provides
more negative stories. One quotes an Argentine as saying: 'I lost my job

and ... my wife left me taking our son ... the crash cost me my family. Eventually, I ended up on the streets, sometimes eating in soup kitchens. There was no work and no money circulating. It was terrible but at least you did not feel alone. In my neighbourhood many people were in the same situation'. Another piece gives the impression that Argentina never really recovered. Entitled 'Still haunted by legacy of the crash', it asserts that a 'widespread lack of economic confidence remains' in the country. An *Irish Independent* article entitled 'The middle classes were begging for food in the street' reports approvingly on Irish Finance Minister Michael Noonan's assertion that Ireland will suffer like Argentina if it does not repay its debts. Noonan said that after 2001, Argentines 'were searching the rubbish bins to try and feed their kids. People who never had a poor day in their lives were in penury and they got totally wiped out'. In short, 'Bond markets have long memories – ask Argentina'.[42]

An article in the Irish edition of the London *Times* entitled 'Rioting, looting, bartering, killing: what happened when Argentina defaulted' squarely states that 'Default means upheaval', while describing how in December 2001 'Shops were looted, buildings set on fire, streets were paved with broken and abandoned goods, shopfronts were smashed and in the clashes with police, more than 30 people were killed within sight of the presidential balcony'. However, the article does not tell the story of the subsequent recovery, and is factually incorrect: the rioting, looting and killing happened before the default, not after. Bartering was well developed before the default and continued for a while after. Similarly, a *Financial Times* editorial asserts that the country has 'been mired in relative stagnation ... South America badly needs good regional leadership, but Argentina can barely lead itself. Until this improves, it continues to be a land of squandered opportunities'.[43]

Some commentators are more accurate, like David McWilliams, who in an article entitled 'There is life after default, take a look at Argentina', reports that 'Argentina has experienced 10 straight years of solid economic growth since it defaulted and abandoned its currency link with the US dollar'. This led to 'a burst of entrepreneurial activity', exports 'took off and from having a perennial trade deficit, importing all sorts of finery with other people's money, Argentina began running a trade surplus'.[44]

The media have sometimes made analogies between Argentina and the European periphery and concluded that the latter should not follow the former's path. For example, an article in *Le Monde* entitled 'The Argentine miracle was a sham' argues that 'Buenos Aires has not finished paying for his 2001 bankruptcy. Greece would be well advised not to follow this precedent'. The piece states that today the country is still 'classified "D", the worst grade' and 'considered a "risky" country' by credit insurance companies. Moreover, the 'miracle' is due mostly to the booming prices of primary commodities, but now that prices are decreasing, 'the Argentine model is becoming shaky'. Therefore, Greece should not follow Argentina because today, it would not benefit from booming commodity prices.[45]

An article in the *Süddeutsche Zeitung* makes a similar point, asking: 'What happens when a country goes bust? A sovereign default is often followed by a banking crash and credit crunch. Then the economy crashes. Poverty and riots are the result'. Athens should thus not follow Buenos Aires' path, because 'like Argentina, Greece would be cut off from the financial market for an indefinite timeframe. Without new loans it could hardly finance its current expenditure ... The people would take to the barricades, perhaps even loot shops. Poverty and rioting would be the consequence, as once in Argentina'. Thus, one of the important 'lessons from Argentina' is that 'those who alienate investors suffer in the long term'. In short, 'a default à la Argentina in 2001 would have monstrous effects ... A Greek default would be the worst solution'. An article entitled 'Nightmare Argentina' sums it up: 'Until today, the country has not recovered from the 2001 economic crisis'.[46]

One recurring theme is to interpret economic conditions from the perspective of investors and the corporate sector. This is why many references are made to the 'uneasiness', 'fears' and 'disappointments' of investors facing this or that decision by the Argentine government. However, the fact is that Argentina was able to recover with little input from international finance. The expansion was driven largely by domestic demand: for example, FDI was only 1.4 per cent of GDP for the years 2003 to 2007. Nevertheless, the press has emphasized how worrying developments restraining global investors' freedom have been to them.[47]

The main benefit of default (and the elimination of the peg) is the autonomy and flexibility it provided to Argentina's government over its macroeconomic policy, which ultimately accounted for the recovery. It made possible a policy shift away from debt repayment and toward the fulfilment of domestic needs. Lengthy negotiations with creditors led to a favourable debt swap that cancelled $62.3 billion of debt and replaced it with $35.3 billion in new debt – a haircut of 43.4 per cent. Moreover, the maturity of the new bonds was considerably longer and their interest rate lower, while 44 per cent of them were denominated in pesos instead of foreign currency, protecting Argentina from the risks of exchange rate fluctuations. Last, the debt swap substantially reduced the country's debt-to-GDP ratio from 113 per cent in December 2001 to 72 per cent.[48] Debt cancelation helped the recovery by redressing government finances. Indeed, the public sector account shifted from a deficit of 5.6 per cent of GDP in 2001 to a surplus of 1.9 per cent in 2005, a total improvement of 7.6 per cent of GDP in four years, for which there are several reasons. One is an increase in tax collection, itself aided by the recovery, but the reduction of interest payments on the debt, essentially resulting from the default, also played a not insignificant role: it accounted for 1.4 percentage points of the total 7.6 per cent improvement. Whereas interest payments on the public debt represented nearly 4.0 per cent of GDP in 2001, they dropped to 2.4 per cent in 2005.[49]

Explaining growth through a lucky 'commodity boom' but neglecting domestic policy

Mainstream commentary's primary explanation for Argentina's success is that the expansion materialized thanks to a global commodity boom that boosted exports – in particular, agricultural ones. The implication of such an analysis is that Argentina's post-default recovery was not due to policy decisions that other countries can emulate but to favourable global conditions which would not be present at other times and places. An *Irish Times* article refers to the Kirchner government as 'an aggressive presidency' which is 'financed by a boom in commodities'. It says that the 'commodities boom is like giving the government a Marshall Plan every year with no questions asked, and this commodity cycle has been exceptionally long. Populism always works when there is money. But when you eventually have to pay the price it is already too late'. A piece in *Le Monde* entitled 'Raw materials have ensured the Kirchner's success in Argentina' states that the post-default years are just the latest example of the fact that in Argentina's history, 'economic performance has rarely reflected whether or not policies were judicious'. It concludes that 'success is sometimes only a matter of luck'. Another article says that Greece should not follow Argentina's example because future global prices will not be as favourable to its exports: Greece's 'soil is not as rich as Argentina's ... Greece's only raw material is its sunny climate'.[50]

While it is true that exports made a contribution to the economic expansion, it has been overstated by the media while the role of policy making and domestic factors has been neglected. First, the importance of exports relative to the size of the total economy has actually decreased during the recovery. Indeed, in 2002, exports accounted for 24.9 per cent of GDP, but this figure dropped steadily over the years, to reach 18.4 per cent in 2010. In particular, exports of primary products (mining, agriculture, fishing, forestry) and related manufacturing goods (food, beverages, tobacco products) have seen their share of GDP decrease from 14.7 per cent in 2002 to 10.7 per cent in 2010.[51]

Second, it is domestic demand that drove the expansion and as such the Argentine experience was characterized by the World Bank as a 'demand led recovery'. This can be seen from the relative contribution of various national income components to growth. Ministry of Economy data show that between 2003 and 2010, real GDP grew between 8.5 per cent to 9.3 per cent every year (except for 2008/9, when growth was lower). However, exports only accounted for between 0.8 and 1.8 percentage points annually. The bulk of the growth was accounted for by the increases in consumption and investment, which each contributed between 2.9 and 7.1 percentage points annually. The boom in global commodity prices did help Argentina, but its positive effects came mostly in 2006–8, when the expansion was already in full swing.[52] The recovery started in the second quarter of 2002, only three months after the default. It was initially triggered by the devaluation of the peso and the government's stabilization of the foreign exchange market and domestic prices. This made exports more competitive and, more importantly, imports more expensive. The latter thus decreased significantly, which stimulated domestic production of formerly imported goods. From the third quarter of 2002 until the second quarter of 2004, growth was driven by an increase in domestic demand, which grew at a 12.7 per cent annual rate. The private sector was able to take advantage of the stabilization of macroeconomic variables and investment grew at a rate of 40.9 per cent during this second phase. Starting in the third quarter of 2004, exports began to expand more strongly, at an annual rate averaging 11 per cent until mid-2006. Both exports and domestic demand stimulated the expansion. The government's strategy of preserving a competitive exchange rate played an important role in export growth.[53]

Opposing government intervention in the economy

Argentina's default set the stage for its subsequent recovery, but debt cancellation is no guarantee of economic revival. For example, Greece accomplished a large debt restructuring in 2012, but is not on the path to recovery. One significant difference with Argentina is that Greece stuck to austerity policies and the euro (under pressure from the troika), while Argentina did not. A careful study concluded that during Argentina's expansion, employment grew 'very fast', the 'quality of new jobs tended to improve, as formal jobs grew faster than informal ones', 'unemployment and underemployment fell in a sustained way', 'real wages recovered', 'income distribution improved', and 'poverty and extreme poverty declined'. These developments are drastically different from conditions in Europe's peripheral countries.[54]

The benefits of government intervention to preserve a stable and competitive exchange rate were seen above, but social policy also had a positive impact. Inequality decreased thanks to the growth in employment, the rise in wages and the government's incomes policy. The latter involved the enactment of increments and lump-sum increases in the minimum wage, which redistributed income downwards. Also, public social expenditures tripled, increasing from 10.3 to 14.2 per cent of GDP in real terms between 2002 and 2010. For example, cash transfers were provided to unemployed persons with children, a programme that reached 20 per cent of all households in 2003. In 2009, the government launched the 'Universal Allocation per Child', a programme of cash transfers to poor households aimed at children to reduce poverty. Another programme that helped jump start the expansion is the unemployment subsidy scheme 'Plan Jefas y Jefes de Hogar Desocupados' (Programme for the Unemployed Male and Female Heads of Household) launched in 2002, which provided income to some 1.8 million people, about 11 per cent of the active population.[55]

However, the media have derided or neglected to mention those achievements, painting instead a picture of the Kirchner government as power hungry. The *Irish Times* described it as one of South America's 'most confrontational, authoritarian regimes, always seeking to concentrate ever more power in the presidency' at the expense of 'congress, the courts and the economy's private sector'. The French press has referred to Néstor Kirchner as 'Argentina's Strongman' and claimed that the 'Kirchners have pushed to an extreme the hyperpresidentialist logic, in the pure hegemonic tradition of Latin America's caudillos'.[56]

One policy that generated much opposition in the media is the Kirchners' (re)nationalization of strategic economic sectors. For example, oil and gas company YPF, which had been privatized in the 1990s, was nationalized in 2012 (similarly, private pension funds were nationalized in 2008). Spanish oil company Repsol owned 57 per cent of YPF, and therefore the move angered European elites. However, there was nothing extraordinary about the rena-tionalization, as many oil producers in the world also have state-owned com-panies and, in a way, Argentina was simply catching up with its neighbours Bolivia and Ecuador, which have increased their governments' role in their natural resources. However, the German press ran articles entitled 'The return of the caudillos' and stated that 'Argentina's government has become the Kirchners' family business', and that Cristina Kirchner 'has what it takes to become Argentina's first "caudilla"'. Also, she 'is driving Argentina into the abyss' because she 'has an iron and damaging grip on the economy'. The nationalization of oil reflects a 'form of national socialism that characterises the country for more than 70 years' and that 'burdens the whole region'. In short, 'Kirchner's Argentina is a security risk in Latin America that burdens the whole region and impairs European commitments there'. An article decrying 'Argentina's way into the planned economy' sums it up by citing an Argentine doctor who laments that 'you feel almost like a prisoner in your own country'. The *Financial Times* editors asserted that Argentina 'is drifting fast towards an almost certainly ruinous policy of autarky, with the nationa-lisation of the main oil company, YPF, and imposition of currency and import controls'.[57]

Dramatization of the problem of inflation

Inflation is perhaps the issue emphasized the most in media coverage of Argentina. The reporting is invariably alarmist and points to alleged crises caused by the rise in prices. Further, journalists have denounced repeatedly the government's manipulation of inflation figures and used it as a spring-board to attack the Kirchner administration from all angles, from their poli-cies to their perceived personalities. The Irish press referred to a deficit 'largely caused by' the 'lavish and ever-rising social spending and fuel and transport subsidies' enacted by the Kirchner government, which 'has increas-ingly taken to printing money to cover the gaps', which 'has further fed inflation'. Dramatic renderings of the situation are provided by headlines such as 'Thousands of zeros and no value', while another piece states that 'several waves of high inflation have emaciated the country's currency. A peso of 1963 is only worth 0.0000000000001 pesos today. Four currency reforms in forty years have brought devaluations of up to three digits'.[58]

It is true that inflation has been high in Argentina and that it is a problem, especially since 2007/8, when it reached 31 per cent according to independent estimates. For example, if inflation remains high but the currency does not depreciate enough in response, Argentine goods could become less competitive on the world market, just as domestic industries supplying the Argentine market could be outcompeted by cheaper imports. This could lead to rising levels of unemployment and a reduced growth rate. Therefore, containing inflation remains a challenge for the Argentine government. According to Mario Damill and his colleagues, manipulation of inflation data by the government started in January 2007, which has also affected official measurements of poverty because they depend on the cost of baskets of goods. The media have relished pointing out such problems, but have gone further to attack the Kirchners' personalities. For example, Cristina Kirchner is a 'woman obsessed with her physical appearance'. She is referred to as 'Queen Cristina' and said to be 'a glamorous, auburn-haired leftwinger, known for her pugilistic political style' with a 'penchant for elegant fashion', who 'remains defiant' and 'likes to play the victim'. On the other hand, 'Néstor Kirchner may have given up his beloved cigarettes but the former president remains hooked on power'.[59]

However, as Mark Weisbrot argues, sacrificing inflation reduction to boost growth, lower inequality and increase employment has benefited the majority of the population, and the strategy has thus been positive overall. Moreover, historically, other countries have experienced high levels of growth combined with high inflation, such as South Korea in the 1970s and 1980s as it made the transition from poor to higher-income country. Therefore, it is not as if Argentina's inflation problem negates all its other economic accomplishments. In any case, European authorities' obsession with inflation has not led to recovery, and it is thus unclear why that approach would be preferable.[60]

In sum, the experiences of Iceland and Argentina present different strategies to address the crisis and which have been more successful than the troika's austerity policies. This is not to say that the two countries did everything right, but rather that they provide examples of approaches that should be, or should have been, implemented in Ireland and other peripheral countries. This includes democratic participation of citizens in economic decisions, forcing bondholders to absorb all or some of the losses on their investments, considering the option of re-establishing a national currency, and redistributing income downwards.

Notes

1 S. Collins, 'Whatever Price we Pay to Keep Euro is Worth it', *IT*, 3 December 2011.
2 N. Webb, 'Euro Exit Could Cost €45,000 for Each Family', *SI*, 11 September 2011.

3 A useful survey of the options is provided by W. Buiter and E. Rahbari, 'The Future of the Euro Area: Fiscal Union, Break-up or Blundering Towards a "You Break it you Own it Europe"', *Citi Economics, Global Economics View*, 9 September 2011, faculty.london.edu/mjacobides/assets/documents/Citi_Euro_Fu ture_Note_9.9.11.pdf (accessed 9 December 2013); see also J. Stiglitz, 'An Agenda to Save the Euro', Project Syndicate, 4 December 2013, www.project-syndicate.org/ commentary/joseph-e-stiglitz-says-that-the-europe-will-not-recover-unless-and-until -the-eurozone-is-fundamentally-reformed (accessed 9 December 2013).

4 O. Blanchard *et al.*, 'Rethinking Macroeconomic Policy', IMF SPN/10/03, Washington: IMF, 12 February 2010, www.imf.org/external/pubs/ft/spn/2010/ spn1003.pdf (accessed 9 December 2013); see also D. Baker, 'Fighting Back Against the Eurozone Tyrants', *Al Jazeera*, 28 November 2012, www.aljazeera. com/indepth/opinion/2012/11/20121127122035750225.html (accessed 2 October 2013).

5 D. Baker, 'What Makes the IMF Think it's Right About Greece?' *The Guardian*, 20 June 2011, www.theguardian.com/commentisfree/cifamerica/2011/jun/20/imf-economists-greece-crisis?utm_source=feedburner&utm_medium=feed&utm_campa ign=Feed%3A+theguardian%2Fcommentisfree%2Frss+%28Comment+is+free%29 (accessed 10 June 2013); A. Watt, 'The ECB Must Play its Part', *Social Europe Journal*, 21 June 2011, www.social-europe.eu/2011/06/the-ecb-must-play-its-part/ (accessed 20 June 2013); P. Krugman, 'Europe's Economic Suicide', *NYT*, 15 April 2012, www.nytimes.com/2012/04/16/opinion/krugman-europes-economic-suicide. html?_r=0 (accessed 20 June 2013).

6 M. Weisbrot, 'How the ECB came to Control the Fate of the World Economy', *Real-World Economics Review* blog, 3 August 2012, rwer.wordpress. com/2012/08/03/how-the-ecb-came-to-control-the-fate-of-the-world-economy/#mor e-9394 (accessed 12 June 2013); 'Eurozone Austerity Faces Increasing Political Challenges as Economy Worsens', *Real-World Economics Review* blog, 30 April 2012, rwer.wordpress.com/2012/07/31/germany-is-scared-to-throw-greece-out-of-the-euro/ #more-9386 (accessed 20 June 2013); R. Emmott, 'OECD Calls on ECB to Buy Euro Zone Assets A', *Reuters*, 19 November 2013, www.reuters.com/article/2013/11/19/ oecd-economy-eurozone-idUSL5N0J41PU20131119 (accessed 19 November 2013).

7 P. de Grauwe, 'The ECB Still has to become the Lender of Last Resort', *Social Europe Journal*, 9 March 2012, www.social-europe.eu/2012/03/the-ecb-still-has-to-become-a-lender-of-last-resort/ (accessed 10 March 2013); P. de Grauwe, 'Only a More Active ECB Can Solve the Euro Crisis', CEPS Policy Brief No. 250, August 2011, www.ceps.be/book/only-more-active-ecb-can-solve-euro-crisis (accessed 9 December 2013).

8 J. Delpla and J. von Weizsäcker, 'The Blue Bond Proposal', *Bruegel Policy Brief 2010/13*, May 2010, www.bruegel.org/publications/publication-detail/publication/ 403-the-blue-bond-proposal/ (accessed 9 December 2013); J.C. Juncker and G. Tremonti, 'E-bonds would End the Crisis', *FT*, 5 December 2010, www.ft.com/intl/ cms/s/0/540d41c2-009f-11e0-aa29-00144feab49a.html (accessed 9 December 2013); G. Amato and G. Verhofstadt, 'A Plan to Save the Euro and Curb Speculators', *FT*, 3 July 2011, www.ft.com/intl/cms/s/0/1c6c3d0c-a59c-11e0-83b2-00144feabdc0. html (accessed 9 December 2013); T. Palley, 'The European Monetary Union Needs a Government Banker', *Challenge*, 2011, vol. 54, no. 4, pp. 5–21.

9 P. Krugman, *End this Depression Now!*, New York: W.W. Norton, 2012, Kindle edn location 2632.

10 P. Krugman, 'Leaving the Euro May be Greece's Only Feasible Option', *IT*, 10 May 2010; 'Cyprus, Seriously', *NYT* blog, 26 March 2013, krugman.blogs.nytimes. com/2013/03/26/cyprus-seriously/?smid=tw-NytimesKrugman&seid=auto (accessed 9 December 2013); D. Baker, 'The Euro Alternative to Greek Default and the Drachma', *The Guardian*, 7 May 2012, www.theguardian.com/commentisfree/cif

america/2012/may/07/euro-alternative-greek-default-drachma (accessed 8 December 2013); 'Germany is Scared to Throw Greece Out of the Euro', *Real-World Economics Review* blog, 31 July 2012, rwer.wordpress.com/2012/07/31/germany-is-scared-to-throw-greece-out-of-the-euro/#more-9386 (accessed 1 December 2013); C. Lapavitsas, *Crisis in the Eurozone*, London: Verso, 2012; F. Gartland, 'State Should Default on Debt and Leave Euro, Economist Tells Left-wing Forum', *IT*, 27 June 2011; D. McWilliams, 'Ditching the Euro Could Boost Our Failing Economy', *II*, 6 May 2009; *Follow the Money: The Tale of the Merchant of Ennis*, Dublin: Gill and Macmillan, 2009, ch. 19–20.

11 Buiter and Rahbari, 'The Future of the Euro Area'; H. Flassbeck and C. Lapavitsas, 'The Systemic Crisis of the Euro – True Causes and Effective Therapies', *Studien*, Berlin: Rosa-Luxemburg-Stiftung, 2013, www.rosalux.de/fileadmin/rls_up loads/pdfs/Studien/Studien_The_systemic_crisis_web.pdf (accessed 9 December 2013); A. Watt, 'Why Left-wing Advocates of an End to the Single Currency are Wrong', *Social Europe Journal*, 10 July 2013, www.social-europe.eu/2013/07/why-left-wing-advocates-of-an-end-to-the-single-currency-are-wrong/ (accessed 9 December 2013).

12 D. Rodrik, 'The Real Exchange Rate and Economic Growth', *Brookings Papers on Economic Activity*, 2008, pp. 365–412, www.brookings.edu/~/media/projects/bpea/fall%202008/2008b_bpea_rodrik.pdf (accessed 9 December 2013); B. Eichengreen, 'The Real Exchange Rate and Economic Growth', Working Paper No. 4, Commission on Growth and Development, 2008, www.kantakji.com/fiqh/Files/Eco nomics/c361.pdf (accessed 9 December 2013); R. Hausmann *et al.*, 'Growth Accelerations', *Journal of Economic Growth*, 2005, vol. 10, pp. 303–29.

13 M. Rapetti *et al.*, 'The Real Exchange Rate and Economic Growth: Are Developing Countries Different?' Working Paper 2011-07, Department of Economics, University of Massachusetts-Amherst, 2011, p. 2, www.umass.edu/economics/publi cations/2011-07.pdf (accessed 9 December 2013); A. Razmi *et al.*, 'The Real Exchange Rate and Economic Development', Working Paper 2011-08, Department of Economics, University of Massachusetts-Amherst, 2011, scholarworks.umass. edu/econ_workingpaper/116/ (accessed 9 December 2013); R. Frenkel and M. Rapetti, 'A Concise History of Exchange Rate Regimes in Latin America', CEPR, April 2010, p. 5, www.cepr.net/documents/publications/exchange-rates-latin-americ a-2010-04.pdf (accessed 9 December 2013).

14 See for example, S. Morley, 'On the Effect of Devaluation During Stabilization Programs in LDC's', *The Review of Economics and Statistics*, 1992, vol. 74, no. 1, pp. 21–27; P. Gupta *et al.*, 'Behavior of Output During Currency Crises', *Journal of International Economics*, 2007, vol. 72, pp. 428–50.

15 M. Bussière, 'Chronicle of Currency Collapses: Re examining the Effects on Output', *Journal of International Money and finance*, 2012, vol. 31, p. 680; see also M. Weisbrot and R. Ray, 'Latvia's Internal Devaluation: A Success Story?' (revised and updated), CEPR, December 2011, www.cepr.net/documents/publications/latvia-2011-12.pdf (accessed 8 December 2013).

16 'Burn the Bank Bondholders – 45pc of Bosses', *SI*, 10 April 2011. See also L. McBride, 'Owners Want to Keep Euro', *SI*, 7 August 2011; C. Keena, '90% of Exporters Want to Stay in Euro', *IT*, 24 November 2010.

17 'Is it Time to Start Thinking the Unthinkable', *SI*, 9 May 2010; S. Collins, 'Eurozone at Risk of Losing a Member to Default, Warns Sutherland', *II*, 17 January 2012; F. Kennedy, 'Now We Don't Have it, so Let's Turn to Where We Put it', *SI*, 7 November 2010; C. Fell, 'Solo Run on Currency would be Economic Suicide', *IT*, 6 August 2010; A. Beesley, 'Dutch Calls for Greek Exit Option could have Tragic Consequences for Ireland', *IT*, 9 September 2011; C. McCarthy, 'We Need to Stay the Course because there are No Shortcuts to Recovery', *SI*, 2 January 2011.

18 S. Collins, 'Whatever Price We Pay to Keep Euro is Worth it', *IT*, 3 December 2011; N. Webb, 'Euro Exit Could Cost €45,000 for Each Family', *SI*, 11 September 2011.
19 D. O'Brien, 'Time is Running Out to Prevent a Euro Zone Catastrophe', *IT*, 15 June 2012; P. McArdle, 'There's No Escape from the Euro Club', *IT*, 15 January 2010; B. Keenan, 'Leaving the Eurozone is Simply Not an Option for Ireland', *SI*, 18 December 2011.
20 J. O'Leary, 'Abandoning Euro is a Nil Sum Game', *IT*, 23 January 2009; P. Lane, 'Working for Recovery from within the Euro Zone', *IT*, 30 January 2009; S. Kinsella, 'Eurozone's Strength is also at the Heart of its Undoing', *SI*, 17 June 2012.
21 R. Wade and S. Sigurgeirsdottir, 'Iceland's Meltdown: The Rise and Fall of International Banking in the North Atlantic', *Brazilian Journal of Political Economy*, 2011, vol. 31, no. 5 (125), pp. 684–85; R. Wade and S. Sigurgeirsdottir, 'Iceland's Rise, Fall, Stabilisation and Beyond', *Cambridge Journal of Economics*, 2012, vol. 36, no. 1, pp. 127–44.
22 Wade and Sigurgeirsdottir, 'Iceland's Meltdown', p. 687.
23 Wade and Sigurgeirsdottir, 'Iceland's Meltdown', p. 690.
24 Wade and Sigurgeirsdottir, 'Iceland's Meltdown', p. 688.
25 C. Gurdgiev, 'Ireland v Iceland: Full Deck', True Economics, 27 October 2013, trueeconomics.blogspot.ie/2013/10/27102013-ireland-v-iceland-full-deck.html?spref=tw#! (accessed 2 December 2013); P. Krugman, 'The Times Does Iceland', *NYT* blog, 8 July 2012, krugman.blogs.nytimes.com/2012/07/08/the-times-does-iceland/?_r=0 (accessed 15 November 2013).
26 IMF, 'Iceland's Unorthodox Policies Suggest Alternative Way Out of Crisis', 3 November 2011, www.imf.org/external/pubs/ft/survey/so/2011/car110311a.htm (accessed 9 December 2013).
27 D. Baker, 'The Iceland Follies: Loony Currency Schemes', *Al Jazeera*, 6 March 2012, www.aljazeera.com/indepth/opinion/2012/03/20123695537108259.html (accessed 3 December 2013); see also D. Howden, 'The Iceland and Ireland Banking Crises: Lessons for the Future', Working Paper, Mercatus Center, George Mason University, 2012, mercatus.org/publication/iceland-and-ireland-banking-crises-lessons-future (accessed 9 December 2013).
28 Baker, 'Iceland Follies'.
29 For a clear summary, see Iceland's Ministry for Foreign Affairs website, www.mfa.is/tasks/icesave/q-a/ (accessed 9 December 2013); T. Thorgeirsson and P. van den Noord, 'The Icelandic Banking Collapse: Was the Optimal Policy Path Chosen?' Working Paper no. 62, Central Bank of Iceland, March 2013, p. 6, www.sedlabanki.is/library/Skr%C3%A1arsafn-EN/Working-Papers/WP%2062.pdf (accessed 9 December 2013); Wade and Sigurgeirsdottir, 'Iceland's Rise, Fall, Stabilisation and Beyond', p. 139.
30 A. Sighvatsson and G. Gunnarsson, 'Iceland's Financial Disaster and its Fiscal Impact', in J.R. LaBrosse, R. Olivares-Caminal and D. Singh (eds) *Managing Risk in the Financial System*, Aldershot, Edward Elgar Publishing, 2011, p. 145; P. Alexander, 'Icelandic Banks Still Waiting for the Thaw', *The Banker*, 1 August 2011, www.thebanker.com/World/Western-Europe/Iceland/Icelandic-banks-still-waiting-for-the-thaw?ct=true (accessed 30 July 2013); Thorgeirsson and van den Noord, 'The Icelandic Banking Collapse'; see also Howden, 'The Iceland and Ireland Banking Crises'.
31 D. McWilliams, 'Recovery is Going to be Local', *SBP*, 26 September 2010.
32 C. Fell, 'Ireland is No Iceland Despite its Woes', *IT*, 1 October 2010; D. O'Brien, 'Swift Action Can Prevent Bubble from Reoccurring', *IT*, 25 February 2011; 'Iceland and the EU', *IT*, 18 November 2008.
33 'Iceland says No in Payback Vote', *IT*, 12 April 2011; E. Byrne, 'Should Ireland's Citizens Refuse to Bail Out the Banks?' *IT*, 2 March 2010.

34 IMF, *World Economic Outlook Database*, www.imf.org/external/pubs/ft/weo/2013/ 01/weodata/index.aspx (accessed 4 May 2013); D. Baker, 'Ireland Should Do an Argentina', *The Guardian*, 22 November 2010, www.guardian.co.uk/commentis free/cifamerica/2010/nov/22/ecb-ireland-bailout-argentina (accessed 4 May 2013); P. Krugman, 'Exit and Exports', *NYT* blog, 14 May 2012, krugman.blogs.nytimes. com/2012/05/14/exit-and-exports/ (accessed 3 May 2013); 'More on Greek and Argentine Exports', *NYT* blog, 15 May 2012, krugman.blogs.nytimes.com/2012/05/ 15/more-on-greek-and-argentine-exports/?src=tp (accessed 3 May 2013); M. Weisbrot *et al.*, 'The Argentine Success Story and its Implications', CEPR, October 2011, www.cepr.net/documents/publications/argentina-success-2011-10.pdf (accessed 9 December 2013).

35 For example, see Weisbrot *et al.*, 'The Argentine Success Story and its Implications'; A. Cibils and R. Lo Vuolo, 'At Debt's Door: What Can We Learn from Argentina's Recent Debt Crisis and Restructuring?' *Seattle Journal of Social Justice*, 2007, vol. 5, no. 2, pp. 755–95; B. Dangl, *Dancing with Dynamite*, Oakland: AK Press, 2010; C. Wylde, 'State, Society and Markets in Argentina: The Political Economy of *Neodesarrollismo* under Néstor Kirchner, 2003–7', *Bulletin of Latin American Research*, 2011, vol. 30, no. 4, pp. 436–52.

36 Cibils and Lo Vuolo, 'At Debt's Door'; M. Damill *et al.*, 'Argentina: A Decade of Currency Board. An Analysis of Growth, Employment and Income Distribution', Employment Paper 2002/42, Geneva: International Labour Office, 2002, www.ilo.org/wcmsp5/groups/public/-ed_emp/documents/publication/wcms_142375. pdf (accessed 9 December 2013); P. Blustein, *And the Money Kept Rolling In (and Out)*, New York: PublicAffairs, 2005.

37 IMF, *World Economic Outlook Database*.

38 W. Baer *et al.*, 'Argentina's Default and the Lack of Dire Consequences', Discussion Papers series 10/09, Department of Economics, City University London, 2009, www.city.ac.uk/-data/assets/pdf_file/0009/73845/1009.pdf (accessed 9 December 2013); Weisbrot *et al.*, 'The Argentine Success Story and its Implications', pp. 1, 8–9; M. Damill *et al.*, 'Macroeconomic Policy for Full and Productive Employment and Decent Work for All: An Analysis of the Argentine Experience', Employment Working Paper No. 109, Geneva: International Labour Organization, 2011, p. 67, www.ilo.org/wcmsp5/groups/public/-ed_emp/-emp_policy/documents/ publication/wcms_173147.pdf (accessed 9 December 2013).

39 Baer *et al.*, 'Argentina's Default'; Cibils and Lo Vuolo, 'At Debt's Door'; Weisbrot *et al.*, 'The Argentine Success Story and its Implications'; M. Weisbrot and L. Sandoval, 'Argentina's Economic Recovery: Policy Choices and Implications', CEPR, October 2007, www.cepr.net/documents/publications/argentina_recovery_ 2007_10.pdf (accessed 9 December 2013); R. Frenkel and M. Rapetti, 'Argentina's Monetary and Exchange Rate Policies after the Convertibility Regime Collapse', CEPR, April 2007, www.cepr.net/documents/publications/argentina_2007_04.pdf (accessed 9 December 2013).

40 The *Nexis* database classifies articles according to a number of topical categories, one of which is 'economic conditions', which was used here. The database also allows for the specification that only articles making 'strong reference' to the chosen topic be returned, which is the procedure that was followed. A few newspapers, such as the *Frankfurter Allgemeine Zeitung* and the *Süddeutsche Zeitung*, are not included in *Nexis*, and were accessed using their own database, available online for a fee.

41 K. Sheridan, 'Ourselves Alone: What Happens if Ireland Defaults?' *IT*, 14 May 2011.

42 T. Hennigan, 'I Lost My Job and My Wife Left Me Taking Our Son ... the Crash Cost Me My Family', *IT*, 16 May 2011; T. Hennigan, 'Still Haunted by Legacy of the Crash', *IT*, 17 May 2011; C. Palmer, 'The Middle Classes were Begging for

Food in the Street', *II*, 30 July 2011; L. Noonan, 'Bond Markets have Long Memories – Ask Argentina', *II*, 9 October 2010.

43 A. Graham-Yooll, 'Rioting, Looting, Bartering, Killing: What Happened when Argentina Defaulted', *TT*, 19 May 2012; 'In a Tango of Debt: A Land of Opportunities Squandered by Peronism', *FT*, 15 October 2009.

44 D. McWilliams, 'There is Life After Default, Take a Look at Argentina', *II*, 1 June 2011.

45 C. Gatinois and C. Legrand, 'Le miracle argentin était en trompe-l'œil', *LM*, 24 June 2012.

46 C. Hoffmann, 'Was passiert, wenn nein land pleite geht?' *SZ*, 13 September 2011; A. Hagelüken, 'Lehren aus Argentinien', *SZ*, 2 December 2009; A. Hagelüken, 'CONTRA', *SZ*, 18 February 2012; P. Burghardt and S. Boehringer, 'Albtraum Argentinien', *SZ*, 29 April 2010.

47 Weisbrot and Sandoval, 'Argentina's Economic Recovery', p. 14.

48 E. Helleiner, 'The Strange Story of Bush and the Argentine Debt Crisis', *Third World Quarterly*, 2005, vol. 26, no. 6, pp. 951–69; Cibils and Lo Vuolo, 'At Debt's Door', p. 776; M. Damill *et al.*, 'Macroeconomic Policy Changes in Argentina at the Turn of the Century', in M. Novick *et al.* (eds) *In the Wake of the Crisis: Argentina's New Economic and Labour Policy Directions and their Impact*, Geneva: International Labour Organization, 2007, p. 85, www.ilo.org/wcmsp5/groups/public/-dgreports/-inst/documents/publication/wcms_193767.pdf   (accessed   9 December 2013).

49 M. Damill *et al.*, 'Macroeconomic Policy Changes in Argentina at the Turn of the Century', in M. Novick *et al.* (eds) *In the Wake of the Crisis: Argentina's New Economic and Labour Policy Directions and their Impact*, Geneva: International Labour Organization, 2007, pp. 81, 83, www.ilo.org/wcmsp5/groups/public/-dgreports/-inst/documents/publication/wcms_193767.pdf (accessed 9 December 2013); M.A. Cohen, *Argentina's Economic Growth and Recovery*, Milton Park: Routledge, 2012.

50 T. Hennigan, 'Culture of Corruption that Erodes Democracy', *IT*, 18 May 2011; M. Hutchinson, 'Les matières premières ont assuré le succès des Kirchner en Argentine', *LM*, 30 October 2010; C. Gatinois and C. Legrand, 'Le miracle argentin était en trompe-l'œil', *LM*, 24 June 2012.

51 Weisbrot *et al.*, 'The Argentine Success Story and its Implications', p. 7.

52 World Bank, 'Country Assistance Strategy for the Argentine Republic 2006–8', Report No. 34015-AR, May 2006, p. 17, siteresources.worldbank.org/INTAR GENTINA/Resources/1CASAr.pdf (accessed 9 December 2013); INDEC database, Cuentas Nacionales, Producto Interno Bruto (PIB), spreadsheet 'Oferta y demanda globales, en milliones de pesos a precios de 1993', www.indec.mecon.ar/ (accessed 2 May 2013); Weisbrot *et al.*, 'The Argentine Success Story and its Implications', p. 6; Frenkel and Rapetti, 'Argentina's Monetary and Exchange Rate Policies', p. 11.

53 Damill *et al.*, 'Macroeconomic Policy Changes in Argentina'.

54 Damill *et al.*, 'Macroeconomic Policy for Full and Productive Employment', p. 24.

55 J. Grugel and M.P. Riggirozzi, 'The Return of the State in Argentina', *International Affairs*, 2007, vol. 83, no. 1, pp. 87–107; Weisbrot *et al.*, 'The Argentine Success Story and its Implications', pp. 10–11; S. Levitsky and M.V. Murillo, 'Argentina: From Kirchner to Kirchner', *Journal of Democracy*, 2008, vol. 19, no. 2, pp. 16–30; Damill *et al.*, 'Macroeconomic Policy for Full and Productive Employment', p. 27.

56 T. Hennigan, 'Culture of Corruption that Erodes Democracy', *IT*, 18 May 2011; T. Hennigan, 'Kirchner Dynasty Now Under Threat', *IT*, 26 June 2009; P. Damour, 'Décès de Néstor Kirchner, l'homme fort d'Argentine', *LF*, 28 October 2010; P. Damour, 'Cristina Kirchner, veuve à poigne', *LM*, 24 October 2011 (quoting lawyer Daniel Sabsay).

57 M. Weisbrot, 'Argentina's Critics are Wrong Again About Renationalising Oil', *The Guardian*, 18 April 2012, www.guardian.co.uk/commentisfree/cifamerica/2012/apr/18/argentina-critics-oil-nationalise (accessed 4 May 2013); J. Oehrlein, 'Die rückkehr der caudillos', *FAZ*, 2 November 2007; H. Stausberg, 'Wirtschaftsdirigismus: Cristina Kirchner treibt Argentinien in den abgrund', *DW*, 16 October 2012; H. Stausberg, 'Zwei nachbarn, zwei linksregierungen', *DW*, 14 April 2012; H. Stausberg, 'Kirchners Argentinien', *DW*, 19 April 2012; C. Moses, 'Argentiniens weg in die planwirtschaft', *FAZ*, 25 September 2012; 'Poor by Default: Argentina's Stonewalling of Foreign Creditors is Costly', *FT*, 1 November 2012.

58 T. Hennigan, 'Protest in Buenos Aires as Authorities Step Up Action to Stem Capital Flight', *IT*, 7 June 2012; J. Oehrlein, 'Hinter tausend nullen kein wert', *FAZ*, 5 July 2012; C. Moses, 'Argentiniens sparer sind ständig auf der flucht', *FAZ*, 20 August 2009.

59 Weisbrot *et al.*, 'The Argentine Success Story and its Implications'; Damill *et al.*, 'Macroeconomic Policy for Full and Productive Employment', p. 32; P. Damour, 'Cristina Kirchner, veuve à poigne', *LM*, 24 October 2011; 'Queen Cristina: Hubris Awaits the Argentine Leader after Sunday's Election', *FT*, 21 October 2011; H. Strange, 'President's Righteous Anger Casts Shadow of Eva Perón', *TT*, 18 April 2012; 'Poor by Default: Argentina's Stonewalling of Foreign Creditors is Costly', *FT*, 1 November 2012; J. Webber, 'A Profligate President', *FT*, 19 February 2010.

60 Weisbrot *et al.*, 'The Argentine Success Story and its Implications'.

8 Conclusion

This book has argued that the policy response to, and media coverage of, the crisis have reflected the interests and viewpoints of political and economic elites. During the housing bubble years, Irish banks borrowed heavily on international markets, which was facilitated by financial deregulation in Europe and the low interest rates brought about by the introduction of the euro. A significant portion of those funds was lent to the domestic property sector, leading to house price inflation. This development model was unsustainable but was preserved because it benefited the financial sector due to increased lending activity while other economic sectors profited thanks to the general high-pace growth. The political class reaped rewards in the form of taxes and electoral success brought about by popular satisfaction with levels of economic growth never seen before. The media sustained the bubble and rarely adopted a critical perspective. Yet, it would not have been difficult to look across the Irish Sea and consult *The Economist* magazine to obtain a different perspective, or to read David McWilliams and Morgan Kelly in the pages of Irish newspapers. One damning statistic is that between 2000 and 2007, *Prime Time*, a leading current affairs programme shown on RTÉ, the state broadcaster, talked about the housing bubble in only 1 per cent of its 700 shows, and most of those argued that there was no bubble.

When the crisis hit, a few politicians decided to provide banks with a blanket guarantee instead of letting them fail and create one or several 'good banks', which would have been a much fairer strategy. On the contrary, taxpayers were made responsible for some €365 billion of liabilities. The media cheered on this decision, without which they argued the economy would have collapsed. As if this was not enough, they then supported the creation of NAMA, the bad bank that purchased financial institutions' toxic loans, and the funnelling of public funds into the banks to recapitalize them, instead of forcing their creditors to absorb losses. It was recently reported that across Europe, taxpayers have put a total of €473 billion of capital into banks since 2008. It is one clear illustration that under neoliberalism, although free market principles are applied to labour by attacking work conditions and forcing ordinary people to pay for banks, the state provides significant services for the powerful and can shield them from the laws of market competition when they are in difficulty.[1]

Government finances continued to deteriorate, a predictable outcome given that the state had assumed private bank debts and failed to adopt a Keynesian stimulus programme to revive the economy in the wake of the housing bubble collapse. Ireland was thus forced to accept a €67.5 billion EU-IMF bailout in late 2010. Irish ruling circles and the media would have preferred not to have to ask for aid because it implied a loss of sovereignty over their country. However, once it became inevitable, they accepted it because austerity conditions attached to it were very similar to those they had enforced on their own in the previous two years. The events surrounding the bailout shed light on the class-based nature of the state. Ireland did lose some sovereignty over its own affairs due to the close monitoring of economic policy by the EU and the IMF. However, with or without a bailout, the population has not had a significant input into the decisions enacted in response to the crisis. The media debate about the loss of sovereignty implied by an EU-IMF bailout rarely considered popular sovereignty, restricting itself to discussing the pros and cons of Irish versus European leaders directing the country. It reveals that news organizations are concerned with the interests of power holders, while there are clear limits to popular participation in government decisions. The same applies to the regular claims that Ireland will 'lose credibility' if it does not implement harsh austerity measures and reduce government deficits. Such warnings are periodically foregrounded in the news, but there seems to be no concern about Ireland's loss of credibility with respect to ensuring decent public services for its citizens, reducing poverty and hospital waiting lines, as well as stimulating the economy, following the overwhelming historical and contemporary evidence that it is a more effective way to recover from a downturn.

The idea that creditors could have been forced to absorb some of the losses through haircuts has been voiced by a number of commentators, but arguments in favour of a significant default have been difficult to find in the press. This is even if there are a number of potential default points that could have been identified and debated, from government bonds, bank debt and ECB loans to promissory notes. The fact that there have only been a few calls for repudiating the promissory notes in their entirety is particularly revealing of the media's acceptance of elites' agenda. Indeed, defaulting on the notes would have had virtually no practical consequences: no investor would have taken any losses and there would have been no negative effect on eurozone inflation. Inflation, especially in the core countries, would in any case be a good thing from the point of view of debtors as it would allow them to regain competitiveness, and hence would constitute an important step toward resolving the European crisis.

The implementation of austerity policies provides an ongoing confirmation that the media are an important component of the ideological apparatus that serves to legitimize policies that benefit ruling circles. The systematic analysis of all opinion articles on fiscal consolidation in the five main Irish newspapers revealed that only 11 per cent of media coverage opposes austerity, and that this opposition is weak. It usually either consists in rejecting specific spending cuts without proposing an economic alternative to consolidation, or seeks to adjust government plans to make them fairer while accepting the need to reduce the deficit. Furthermore, spending cuts are prioritized over tax hikes because they affect the poor and vulnerable segments of society more directly, whereas the corporate sector and the wealthy are adamant that taxes on their income should not be raised, and should in fact be cut.

The book has compared the Irish case with other examples better to contextualize it. There were, and still are, alternatives that could be adopted and which would likely lead to fairer outcomes. For example, bank creditors could have been dealt with through a debt-for-equity swap to force them to absorb some losses, as Iceland did. Banks could have been nationalized with stricter conditions on their operations, as Scandinavia did in the 1990s. Economic stimulus could have been implemented, as in most European countries for a short period at the beginning of the crisis, and as in numerous historical cases, most notably in the United States during the Great Depression in the 1930s. Moreover, a democratic debt audit could have been organized and formed the basis for defaulting on illegitimate debts, following Ecuador. A sovereign default could also have been orchestrated, as in Argentina, perhaps with an exit from the eurozone to regain monetary sovereignty. It is significant that the Irish and European media have usually dismissed those alternatives, when they were reported.

One issue that the book has not addressed directly is that of the differences between newspapers' coverage in Ireland. Do the general conclusions presented in the previous pages apply equally to all news organizations, or are there some that clearly depart from the consensus? The answer is that there are differences between newspapers, but they are best seen as minor, or tactical, rather than fundamental in nature. The mass media reflect the range of elite opinion and interests, including debates within ruling circles, and this is what we see in newspapers. For example, there is a lot of debate about austerity in the press, but it mostly revolves around how best to implement it, a tactical question, and not about questioning it as a failed strategy. Therefore, although it is interesting to compare news outlets' coverage of the crisis, to do so in an overly detailed way would be to miss the broader, and more significant, point that they all tend to accept the same principles, such as the socialization of private debts, limiting democratic input into policy making, and maintaining or increasing power and wealth inequalities in the country.

To illustrate, differences in coverage between newspapers can be examined briefly for the issue of austerity, discussed in Chapter 6. The preference for fiscal consolidation is significant in all newspapers and varies from 57 per cent of articles in the *Irish Times* to 77 per cent in the *Sunday Business Post*.[2] Conversely, opposition to fiscal consolidation is small in all newspapers, varying from 5 per cent of articles in the *Sunday Business Post* to 15 per cent in the *Irish Times*. Such differences are not very surprising. The media are not monolithic outlets that all print the same pieces by the same authors. Some fairly critical pieces also appear regularly, but they remain a minority. On economic policy, the *Independent* newspapers and *Sunday Business Post* are ideologically to the right of the *Irish Times*, and this explains why some more opposition to conservative economic policies is more likely to appear in the latter than the former. This could be traced, in part, to the fact that the *Irish Times* is governed by a Trust which ensures some level of independence from commercial interests. For example, it does not have beneficial shareholders and cannot pay dividends. Nevertheless, this independence from commercial interests should not be exaggerated, as the newspaper is dependent on advertising revenues and sales, in line with the pattern discussed above in the mainstream media. A number of its board directors also come from establishment institutions. Therefore, in general, the *Irish Times* remains favourable to fiscal consolidation.

Another, broader issue is the extent to which Irish media coverage of the crisis is representative of other European countries' media coverage of the crisis. It is worth stating at the outset that it is not possible to answer this question with full satisfaction without conducting more research into other countries' experience. Because this research has largely not been done yet, what follows is better seen as reflections rather than conclusive statements.

First, there is no reason to expect that media coverage in other European countries is significantly different from Ireland for the bulk of their mass media. Large private news organizations anywhere function essentially according to the same corporate principles as outlined above, while state-owned organizations tend to follow their government's ideology. In theory, there is perhaps more space for dissent in public news outlets, since their management and operations depend indirectly on elected officials, who can be influenced and removed democratically. The extent to which this is effective, in turn, depends on how democratic a country is – namely, whether there are institutional channels that allow citizens' participation and input in decisions related to the media. If the political class is dominated by conservative groups and individuals, as in Ireland, this will usually be reflected in the nature of public media. On the other hand, a more progressive political leadership would be expected to take decisions related to public media that are more conducive to critical views being presented in the news. News organizations are, in a way, products of the society in which they exist. In a conservative society like Ireland, it is thus no surprise that the state broadcaster is relatively conservative and that no left-of-centre private media outlet has emerged. In countries like France, where historically, leftist forces have been able to integrate the mainstream of politics and economics to a greater extent, it would be expected that such viewpoints will be reflected in a larger portion of media coverage.

In this respect, one main difference between Ireland and a number of other European countries should arise in the coverage of the latter's mass media organizations that are distinctly centre-left or left politically. A good example is the *Guardian* in Britain. It contains commentary more critical than the majority of the mass media in Ireland, the United Kingdom and Europe in general. In France, there are also newspapers with a significant readership that provide views more at odds with mainstream thinking, such as *Le Monde Diplomatique, Libération,* or *Le Canard Enchaîné.* The same could be said about some other European countries – but not Ireland. Indeed, the Irish mass media landscape extends from the centre to the right, but no news organization could be described as progressive, left or even centre-left in orientation. Ireland is thus at the conservative end of the spectrum in its media coverage of the crisis in Europe, although the spectrum does not appear to be very broad.

Precisely how Irish media compare to other countries' media would need to be assessed through further research. For example, this author has examined the British media for their views about austerity in the United Kingdom, implemented since 2010 by the coalition government formed by the Conservative Party and the Liberal Democrats. Following the methodology presented in Chapter 6, some 350 opinion pieces published since 2010 were examined in the *Financial Times, The Times,* the *Daily Telegraph* and the *Guardian.* The analysis reveals that the British press has largely supported the views of elites during the crisis. When the *Guardian* is excluded, 56 per cent of articles are in favour of austerity, 13 per cent are opposed to it, and 31 per cent are neutral. Such trends are comparable to the Irish press. However, the *Guardian* is more critical. Only 7 per cent of its articles support austerity, whereas 52 per cent oppose it and 40 per cent are neutral. Nevertheless, even if its overall stance has been critical of the coalition's austerity, this does not mean that its opposition to it has been as fundamental and resolute as might be imagined. Some of its columnists are conservative or not always as critical as they could be of government policy. For example, one wrote that the 'cuts in public spending are sensible and overdue' because the 'state sector under Labour became fat and inefficient, while the consequent budget deficit posed a genuine risk to state borrowing'. Still, it constitutes one difference with the Irish media, and the same would apply to other countries where equivalent news organizations are found.[3]

On the other hand, differences between Irish and European media should not be exaggerated. The latter have also largely supported governments' response to the crisis. Chapter 7 showed that British, German and French newspapers unanimously condemned the Argentine alternative to dealing with a debt crisis in a fairer way, even though it resulted in many positive outcomes. When a left-of-centre government comes to power, when foreign creditors are told that they will have to take losses on their investments, when a common currency is abandoned, and when the state becomes more active in redistributing income downwards, the European media convey a negative picture of those events.

Other examples of the conservative character of the European press are provided by looking at its coverage of the plight of peripheral countries, and in particular Greece. In his study of European and American media coverage of the Greek crisis, George Tzogopoulos concludes that news organizations have presented an 'extremely negative picture' of the country and notes a 'remarkable degree of consensus in criticising the Hellenic Republic for its crisis'. Stories have emphasized corruption, tax evasion, and excessive bureaucracy that stifles entrepreneurship and the entry of foreign capital. For instance, numerous explicit or implicit statements can be found about 'lazy peripheral countries that need to be disciplined by the righteous German-led core'. The German tabloid *Bild's* stereotypical comparison of lazy Greeks and hard-working Germans is revealing when it states that: 'In our country [Germany] petrol stations have cash registers, taxi drivers give receipts and farmers do not swindle EU subsidies with millions of olive trees that do not exist'; 'Here, nobody needs to pay a €1,000 bribe to get a hospital bed in time'; and 'People work until they are 67 here. There is no longer a 14-month salary for civil servants'. Likewise, in Britain, a *Sun* editorial referred to the 'eurozone's wasters like lazy Greece, where many retire on fat pensions in the 50s and tax dodging is a national pastime'. Moreover, the media reflected global investors' interests when they encouraged Greece to sell its national assets, including beaches, utilities, a state lottery and more. A *Bild* headline read 'Bankrupted Greeks, sell your islands ... and the Acropolis along with them!' while others provide their readers with guidelines to purchasing assets without getting submerged in a 'sea of red tape'.[4]

The German press has often complained about sending financial aid to the periphery, as made clear in headlines like 'Even more money for the bankrupt Greeks? Bild says no!' and 'Billion of taxpayers' money for the Greeks' which could be used instead to fix German roads so that there are 'fewer potholes'. *Die Welt* opined that Greece must 'push through reforms that are overdue' to bring the country 'into the modern world', including 'significant shrinkage of the state enterprises': 'Only if Greece turns entrepreneur friendly and open will it attract investments that move the country forward'. There are also some 'golden rules' that should be adopted to deal with peripheral governments, such as 'tougher sanctions', including 'the withdrawal of voting rights for budget sinners' at the European level.[5]

Irish media coverage of the crisis is thus relatively more conservative than in other European countries. In fact, it is probably comparable to US media coverage of the US economic crisis. Like Ireland, the United States does not have any major left-of-centre news outlets. The overwhelming majority of the media are large, private corporations and the views they present vary from centre-right to right politically. As such, during the housing bubble, the media were overwhelmingly supportive of it, or turned a blind eye to its inherently unstable nature. Only a few economists identified it and warned about it early on.[6]

When the crisis hit, the government orchestrated a massive US$700 billion bank bailout through the Troubled Assets Relief Program (TARP). Economist Dean Baker noted how the financial industry was 'able to enlist the media in this effort, turning many reporters into TARP cheerleaders until the bill passed Congress'. A number of prominent economists opposed the TARP, but they were 'portrayed as knuckle-scraping Neandertals'. When the investment banks Bear Stearns and Lehman Brothers collapsed in 2008, the media became filled with warnings of another impending Great Depression and loudly claimed that there was no time to lose in saving the financial system. It was alleged that the economy would quickly grind to a halt because of the heightened level of distrust among banks which would lead to a breakdown of interbank transactions. However, in fact, if the situation had indeed deteriorated to such a point, the Federal Reserve could have taken over the largest banks temporarily until confidence returned. The Fed actually used to have contingency plans for such an eventuality in the 1980s, and they could have been used to avert a worsening of the situation. Moreover, the TARP contained virtually no strings attached to change the nature of banks' management and operations. For example, although a clause was included to restrict 'golden parachutes' – large pay packages for executives leaving a bank – in reality, the legislation was written in a way that made it ineffective. Some of the major media outlets like the *Washington Post* and *Wall Street Journal* did report this fact – but *after* Congress approved the bill.[7]

As the economy continued to deteriorate, in early 2009, newly elected President Obama did what the Irish government has refused to do to this day: implement a stimulus package to revive the economy. It amounted to $700 billion and was composed of funds for infrastructure, unemployment benefits, investment and tax cuts. However, the problem is that it was not large enough to make up for the lost demand in the economy due to the collapse of the housing bubble and ensuing economic downturn. It has been estimated that in net terms, the annual stimulus from the government came to about $150 billion a year in 2009 and 2010, a little over 10 per cent of what was needed to offset the lost annual demand from the deflation of the real estate bubble. Nevertheless, it was better than nothing. Yet, the media and political establishment, and in particular the Republican Party, were very much opposed to any larger stimulus package, preaching the virtues of balanced budgets and fiscal restraint. It is partly because of such media messages that the political will to organize a larger stimulus did not emerge.[8]

In sum, the precise extent to which the mass media reflect elite interests varies from one country to another, just like the amount of dissent that appears in their coverage of current economic events. However, it remains the norm that views that are critical of mainstream thinking and that challenge directly the status quo and unequal distribution of resources in society constitute a small minority. In order to create news organisations that do act like real watchdogs and challenge power, the political economic structure of the existing media landscape should be altered. In particular, as long as news outlets are dominated by corporations driven by the bottom line, there can be little hope to transform them. In fact, what is referred to as the 'alternative media', much of it on the internet, provides an obvious model for a more progressive media. They are run as small businesses, foundations, or institutes not too dependent on advertising. They partly rely on their readers' donations to survive and promote the work of critical investigative journalists. They seek to uncover human stories that do not make it to the front pages of the mainstream newspapers. They work for justice, not profit. This is the kind of media that offers a real alternative to the dominant mainstream news outlets.

Notes

1 A. Barker, 'EU Reaches Landmark Deal on Failed Banks', *FT*, 12 December 2013, www.ft.com/intl/cms/s/0/555f3ade-6303-11e3-a87d-00144feabdc0.html?sitee dition=intl#axzz2nFmPJBto (accessed 12 December 2013).
2 Only 36 per cent of pieces support fiscal consolidation in the *Irish Independent*, but this low percentage is due to the large number of neutral pieces, and is thus misleading – the newspaper is in fact clearly supportive of fiscal consolidation.
3 S. Jenkins, 'Osborne Must Hold VAT Hike to Avert the Double Dip', *The Guardian*, 14 July 2010, www.theguardian.com/commentisfree/2010/jul/13/george-osborne-hold-hike-double-dip (accessed 12 December 2013).
4 G. Tzogopoulos, *The Greek Crisis in the Media: Stereotyping in the International Press*, Farnham: Ashgate, 2013, pp. 102, 104, 113–15; J. Carr, 'Paradise with a Sting in the Tail', *WSJ*, 12 March 2012, online.wsj.com/news/articles/ SB10001424052970203358704577235201695305214 (accessed 14 December 2013); C. Forelle, 'Ailing Greece Tries National Tag Sale', *WSJ*, 28 June 2011, online.wsj. com/news/articles/SB10001424052702304231204576405861389511594 (accessed 14 December 2013).
5 'Noch mehr geld für pleite-Griechen? Bild sagt nein!', *Bild*, 27 February 2012, www.bild.de/politik/inland/griechenland-krise/bild-sagt-nein-teil-2-22851260. bild.html (accessed 23 December 2013); B. Frischemeyer and J.W. Schäfer, 'Milliarden steuergelder für die Griechen. Elterngeld? Schlaglöcher? Flughäfen?' *Bild*, 28 November 2012, www.bild.de/politik/ausland/griechenland-krise/neue-milliarden-hilfe-unsere-gelder-presseschau-27401024.bild.html (accessed 23 December 2013); C. Wergins, 'Lob der Griechen: Athen verabschiedet den sparhaushalt. Nun müssen weitere reformen folgen', *DW*, 24 December 2010; K. Lauk, 'Europas schulden laufen aus dem ruder: Wo bleiben die sanktionen?' *DW*, 19 October 2010.
6 There is no space here to review the US media landscape, but see the notes in Chapter 2 for further reading on the subject; A. Harber, 'When a Watchdog Doesn't Bark', *Rhodes Journalism Review*, 2009, September, pp. 20–21; D. Baker, 'The Run-up in Home Prices: A Bubble', *Challenge*, 2002, vol. 45, no. 5, pp. 93–119.
7 D. Baker, *False Profits: Recovering from the Bubble Economy*, Sausalito, CA: PoliPointPress, 2010.
8 For details, see Baker, *False Profits*, ch. 5.

References

Alesina, A. and Ardagna, S., 'Large Changes in Fiscal Policy: Taxes versus Spending', NBER Working Paper No. 15438, 2009, www.nber.org/papers/w15438.pdf?new_window=1 (accessed 8 December 2013).

——'Large Changes in Fiscal Policy: Taxes versus Spending', *Tax Policy and the Economy*, 2010, vol. 24, pp. 35–68.

Alesina, A. and Perotti, R., 'Fiscal Expansions and Adjustments in OECD Countries', *Economic Policy*, 1995, vol. 21, pp. 207–47.

Alesina, A., Perotti, R. and Tavares, J., 'The Political Economy of Fiscal Adjustments', *Brookings Papers on Economic Activity*, 1998, vol. 1, 197–266, www.brookings.edu/~/media/Projects/BPEA/1998%201/1998a_bpea_alesina_perotti_tavares_obstfeld_eichengreen.PDF (accessed 8 December 2013).

Allen, K., *Ireland's Economic Crash: A Radical Agenda for Change*, Dublin: Liffey Press, 2009.

Allen, K. and O'Boyle, B., *Austerity Ireland: The Failure of Irish Capitalism*, London: Pluto, 2013.

Baer, W., Margot, D. and Montes-Rojas, G., 'Argentina's Default and the Lack of Dire Consequences', Discussion Papers series 10/09, Department of Economics, City University London, 2009, www.city.ac.uk/-data/assets/pdf_file/0009/73845/1009.pdf (accessed 9 December 2013).

Bagdikian, B., *The New Media Monopoly*, Boston: Beacon Press, 2004.

Baker, D., 'The Run-up in Home Prices: A Bubble', *Challenge*, 2002, vol. 45, no. 5, pp. 93–119.

——'The Housing Bubble and the Financial Crisis', *Real-World Economics Review*, 2008, no. 46, pp. 73–81, paecon.net/PAEReview/issue46/Baker46.pdf (accessed 10 December 2013).

——*Plunder and Blunder: The Rise and Fall of the Bubble Economy*, Sausalito, CA: PoliPointPress, 2009.

——*False Profits: Recovering from the Bubble Economy*, Sausalito, CA: PoliPointPress, 2010a.

——'The Myth of Expansionary Fiscal Austerity', Centre for Economic and Policy Research, October 2010b, www.cepr.net/documents/publications/austerity-myth-2010-10.pdf (accessed 8 December 2013).

——*The End of Loser Liberalism: Making Markets Progressive*, Washington, DC: CEPR, 2011.

Barnes, S. and Smyth, D., 'The Government's Balance Sheet after the Crisis: A Comprehensive Perspective', Irish Fiscal Advisory Council, September 2013, www.

fiscalcouncil.ie/wp-content/uploads/2013/09/Balance-Sheet1.pdf (accessed 22 November 2013).

Becerra, M.A. and Mastrini, G., 'Crisis. What Crisis? Argentine Media in View of the 2008 International Financial Crisis', *International Journal of Communication*, 2010, vol. 4, pp. 611–29.

Bello, W., 'The Capitalist Conjuncture: Over-accumulation, Financial Crises, and the Retreat from Globalization', *Third World Quarterly*, 2006, vol. 27, no. 8, pp. 1345–67.

Bibow, J., 'The Euro Debt Crisis and Germany's Euro Trilemma', Working paper no. 721, Levy Economics Institute of Bard College, May 2012, www.levyinstitute.org/pubs/wp_721.pdf (accessed 11 December 2013).

Blanchard, O., Dell'Ariccia, G. and Mauro, P., 'Rethinking Macroeconomic Policy', IMF SPN/10/03, Washington: IMF, 12 February 2010, www.imf.org/external/pubs/ft/spn/2010/spn1003.pdf (accessed 9 December 2013).

Blanchard, O., Griffiths, M. and Gruss, B., 'Boom, Bust, Recovery: Forensics of the Latvia Crisis', Brookings Economic Studies, September 2013, www.brookings.edu/~/media/Projects/BPEA/Fall%202013/2013b%20blanchard%20latvia%20crisis.pdf (accessed 10 September 2013).

Blanchard, O. and Leigh, D., 'Growth Forecast Errors and Fiscal Multipliers', IMF Working Paper WP/13/1, January 2013, www.imf.org/external/pubs/ft/wp/2013/wp1301.pdf (accessed 8 December 2013).

Blustein, P., *And the Money Kept Rolling In (and Out)*, New York: PublicAffairs, 2005.

Blyth, M., *Austerity: The History of a Dangerous Idea*, Oxford: Oxford University Press, 2013.

Bonesmo Fredriksen, K., 'Income Inequality in the European Union', Economics department working papers no. 952, Paris: OECD publishing, 2012, dx.doi.org/10.1787/5k9bdt47q5zt-en (accessed 11 December 2013).

Borensztein, E. and Panizza, U., 'The Costs of Sovereign Default', IMF Staff Papers, vol. 56, no. 4, Washington: International Monetary Fund, 2009, www.imf.org/external/pubs/ft/wp/2008/wp08238.pdf (accessed 5 December 2013).

Bourdieu, P. and Wacquant, L., 'NewLiberalSpeak. Notes on the New Planetary Vulgate', *Radical Philosophy*, 2001, vol. 105, January/February, pp. 2–5.

Boyd-Barrett, O., 'Judith Miller, the *New York Times*, and the Propaganda Model', *Journalism Studies*, 2004, vol. 5, no. 4, pp. 435–49.

Boyer, R., 'The Four Fallacies of Contemporary Austerity Policies: The Lost Keynesian Legacy', *Cambridge Journal of Economics*, 2012, vol. 36, no. 1, pp. 283–312.

Brahm, N.G., Jr, 'Understanding Noam Chomsky: A Reconsideration', *Critical Studies in Media Communication*, 2006, vol. 23, no. 5, pp. 453–61.

Brawn, D., *Ireland's House Party: What the Estate Agents Don't Want You to Know*, Dublin: Gill and Macmillan, 2009.

Brenner, N., Peck, J. and Theodore, N., 'Variegated Neoliberalization: Geographies, Modalities, Path-ways', *Global Networks*, 2010, vol. 10, pp. 182–222.

Brenner, R., *The Economics of Global Turbulence: The Advanced Capitalist Economies from Long Boom to Long Downturn, 1945–2005*, London: Verso, 2006.

Broadbent, B. and Daly, K., 'Limiting the Fall-out from Fiscal Adjustments', Goldman Sachs Global Economics, Global Economics Paper 195, 2010, www.irisheconomy.ie/GSGEP195.pdf (accessed 8 December 2013).

Buiter, W. and Rahbari, E., 'The Future of the Euro Area: Fiscal Union, Break-up or Blundering Towards a "You Break it You Own it Europe"', *Citi Economics, Global*

Economics View, 9 September 2011, faculty.london.edu/mjacobides/assets/document s/Citi_Euro_Future_Note_9.9.11.pdf (accessed 9 December 2013).

Bussière, M., Saxena, S.C. and Tovar, C.E., 'Chronicle of Currency Collapses: Re-examining the Effects on Output', *Journal of International Money and Finance*, 2012, vol. 31, pp. 680–708.

Callan, T., Keane, C., Savage, M. and Walsh, J.R., 'Distributional Impact of Tax, Welfare and Public Sector Pay Policies: Budget 2014 and Budgets 2009–14', Dublin: Economic and Social Research Institute, 2013, www.esri.ie/UserFiles/publications/ QEC2013Win_SA_Callan.pdf (accessed 29 December 2013).

Carroll, W., *The Making of a Transnational Capitalist Class: Corporate Power in the 21st Century*, London: Zed Books, 2010.

Carswell, S., *Anglo Republic: Inside the Bank that Broke Ireland*, London: Penguin, 2011.

Case, K. and Shiller, R., 'Is there a Bubble in the Housing Market?' *Brookings Papers on Economic Activity*, 2003, vol. 2, pp. 301–62.

Central Bank of Ireland, 'Section 2: The Irish Housing Market: Fundamental and Non-fundamental Influences', Financial Stability Report, 2004, pp. 50–73, cb3. weblink.ie/data/FinStaRepFiles/The%20Irish%20Housing%20Market%20-%20Fund amental%20and%20Non-Fundamental%20Influences%20.PDF (accessed 9 December 2013).

Central Statistics Office, 'Survey on Income and Living Conditions', Dublin: CSO, 13 February 2013, www.cso.ie/en/media/csoie/releasespublications/documents/silc/2011/ silc_2011.pdf (accessed 8 December 2013).

Chakravarty, P. and Schiller, D., 'Neoliberal Newspeak and Digital Capitalism in Crisis', *International Journal of Communication*, 2010, vol. 4, pp. 670–92.

Chang, H.-J., *Bad Samaritans: The Myth of Free Trade and the Secret History of Capitalism*, New York: Bloomsbury Press, 2008.

——23 *Things they Don't Tell You about Capitalism*, London: Allen Lane, 2010.

Chuhan, P. and Sturzenegger, F. 'Default Episodes in the 1980s and 1990s: What have we Learned?' in J. Aizenman and B. Pinto (eds) *Managing Economic Volatility and Crises*, Cambridge: Cambridge University Press, 2005, pp. 471–519.

Cibils, A. and Lo Vuolo, R., 'At Debt's Door: What Can We Learn from Argentina's Recent Debt Crisis and Restructuring?' *Seattle Journal of Social Justice*, 2007, vol. 5, no. 2, pp. 755–95.

Clancy, P., O'Connor, N. and Dillon, K., 'Mapping the Golden Circle', Dublin: TASC, 2010, www.tascnet.ie/upload/file/MtGC%20ISSU.pdf (accessed 2 July 2013).

Clark, G.L., Thrift, N. and Tickell, A., 'Performing Finance: The Industry, the Media and its Image', *Review of International Political Economy*, 2004, vol. 11, no. 2, pp. 289–310.

Clinch, P., Convery, F. and Walsh, B., *After the Celtic Tiger: Challenges Ahead*, Dublin: O'Brien Press, 2002.

Coates, D. and Everett, M. 'Profiling the Cross-border Funding of Irish Banking System', Economic Letter Series, vol. 2013, no. 4, Central Bank of Ireland, www. centralbank.ie/publications/Documents/Economic_Letter_2013_V4.pdf (accessed 25 January 2014).

Coffey, S. 'Ireland's Public Debt – Tell me a Story we have not Heard Yet … ', in B. Lucey, C. Larkin and C. Gurdgiev (eds) *What if Ireland Default?* Blackrock: Orpen Press, 2012, chapter 4.

Cohen, J. and Rogers, J., 'Knowledge, Morality and Hope: The Social Thought of Noam Chomsky', *New Left Review*, 1992, vol. 187, pp. 5–27.

Cohen, M.A., *Argentina's Economic Growth and Recovery*, Milton Park: Routledge, 2012.

Coleman, M., *The Best is Yet to Come*, Blackrock: Blackhall, 2007.

Considine, J. and Duffy, D., 'Tales of Expansionary Fiscal Contractions in Two European Countries: Hindsight and Foresight', Working Paper 0120, Department of Economics, National University of Ireland, Galway, July 2007, aran.library.nuigalway.ie/xmlui/bitstream/handle/10379/1012/paper_0120.pdf?sequence=1 (accessed 15 December 2013).

Cooper, M., *How Ireland Really Went Bust*, London: Penguin, 2011.

Corner, J., 'The Model in Question: A Response to Klaehn on Herman and Chomsky', *European Journal of Communication*, 2003, vol. 18, no. 3, pp. 367–75.

Crotty, J., 'The Great Austerity War: What Caused the US Deficit Crisis and Who Should Pay to Fix it?' *Cambridge Journal of Economics*, 2012, vol. 36, no. 1, pp. 79–104.

Damill, M., Frenkel, R. and Maurizio, R., 'Argentina: A Decade of Currency Board. An Analysis of Growth, Employment and Income Distribution', Employment Paper 2002/42, International Labour Office: Geneva, 2002, www.ilo.org/wcmsp5/groups/public/-ed_emp/documents/publication/wcms_142375.pdf (accessed 9 December 2013).

——'Macroeconomic Policy Changes in Argentina at the Turn of the Century', in M. Novick *et al.* (eds) *In the Wake of the Crisis: Argentina's New Economic and Labour Policy Directions and their Impact*, Geneva: International Labour Organization, 2007, pp. 51–129, www.ilo.org/wcmsp5/groups/public/-dgreports/-inst/documents/publication/wcms_193767.pdf (accessed 9 December 2013).

——'Macroeconomic Policy for Full and Productive Employment and Decent Work for all: An Analysis of the Argentine Experience', Employment Working Paper No. 109, Geneva: International Labour Organization, 2011, www.ilo.org/wcmsp5/groups/public/-ed_emp/-emp_policy/documents/publication/wcms_173147.pdf (accessed 9 December 2013).

Dangl, B., *Dancing with Dynamite*, Oakland: AK Press, 2010.

de Grauwe, P., 'Only a More Active ECB Can Solve the Euro Crisis', CEPS Policy Brief No. 250, August 2011, www.ceps.be/book/only-more-active-ecb-can-solve-euro-crisis (accessed 9 December 2013).

de Haas, R., Korniyenki, Y., Loukoianova, E. and Pivovarsky, A., 'Foreign Banks and the Vienna Initiative: Turning Sinners into Saints?' IMF Working Paper WP/12/117, 2012, www.imf.org/external/pubs/ft/wp/2012/wp12117.pdf (accessed 8 December 2013).

Delpla, J. and von Weizsäcker, J., 'The Blue Bond Proposal', *Bruegel Policy Brief 2010/13*, May 2010, www.bruegel.org/publications/publication-detail/publication/403-the-blue-bond-proposal/ (accessed 9 December 2013).

de Paoli, B., Hoggarth, G., Saporta, V. 'Costs of Sovereign Default', Bank of England Financial Stability Paper no. 1, London: Bank of England, July 2006, www.bankofengland.co.uk/publications/Documents/fsr/fs_paper01.pdf (accessed 5 December 2013).

——'Output Costs of Sovereign Crises: Some Empirical Estimates', Working Paper No. 362, London: Bank of England, 2009, www.bankofengland.co.uk/research/Documents/workingpapers/2009/wp362.pdf (accessed 5 December 2013).

Desai, R. 'The Last Empire? From Nation-building Compulsion to Nation-wrecking Futility and Beyond', *Third World Quarterly*, 2007, vol. 28, no. 2, pp. 435–56.

Donovan, D. and Murphy, A., *The Fall of the Celtic Tiger: Ireland and the Euro Debt Crisis*, Oxford: Oxford University Press, 2013.

Drudy, P.J. and Collins, M.L., 'Ireland: From Boom to Austerity', *Cambridge Journal of Regions, Economy and Society*, 2011, vol. 4, pp. 339–54.

Duggan, V., 'Ireland's Investment Crisis: Diagnosis and Prescription', NERI Working Paper 2013/03, June 2013, www.nerinstitute.net/download/pdf/neri_wp201303.pdf (accessed 14 September 2013).

Duménil, G. and Lévy, J., *The Crisis of Neoliberalism*, Cambridge, MA: Harvard University Press, 2011.

Durham, M. and Kellner, D., *Media and Cultural Studies: Keyworks*, 2nd edn, Hoboken, NJ: Wiley-Blackwell, 2012.

Economic and Policy Institute, *The State of Working America*, 12th edn, 2013, www.stateofworkingamerica.org/subjects/overview/?reader (accessed 11 December 2013).

Eichengreen, B., 'The U.S. Capital Market and Foreign Lending, 1920–55', in J. Sachs (ed.) *Developing Country Debt and Economic Performance*, vol. 1, Chicago: University of Chicago Press, 1989, pp. 211–40.

——'The Real Exchange Rate and Economic Growth', Working Paper No 4, Commission on Growth and Development, 2008, www.kantakji.com/fiqh/Files/Economics/c361.pdf (accessed 9 December 2013).

Englund, P., 'The Swedish Banking Crisis: Roots and Consequences', *Oxford Review of Economic Policy*, 1999, vol. 15, no. 3, pp. 80–97.

Englund, P. and Vihriälä, V., 'Financial Crisis in Finland and Sweden: Similar but Not Quite the Same', in L. Jonung, J. Kiander and P. Vartia (eds) *The Great Financial Crisis in Finland and Sweden: The Nordic Experience of Financial Liberalization*, Cheltenham: Edward Elgar, 2009, pp. 71–130.

Euro Area Countries, 'Declaration on a Concerted European Action Plan of the Euro Area Countries', Summit of the Euro Area Countries, 12 October 2008, ec.europa.eu/economy_finance/publications/publication13260_en.pdf (accessed 12 March 2013).

European Central Bank, 'Opinion of the European Central Bank of 31 August 2009 on the Establishment of the National Asset Management Agency', CON/2009/68, 31 August 2009, www.ecb.europa.eu/ecb/legal/pdf/opinion_con_2009_68_f_sign.pdf (accessed 29 May 2013).

European Commission, 'State aid NN 48/2008 – Ireland', Brussels: European Commission, 13 October 2008, ec.europa.eu/eu_law/state_aids/comp-2008/nn048-08.pdf (accessed 4 December 2013).

——'Opinion of the European Central Bank of 3 October 2008 at the Request of the Irish Minister for Finance on a Draft Credit Institutions (Financial Support) Bill 2008', CON/2008/44, 3 October 2008, www.ecb.europa.eu/ecb/legal/pdf/en_con_2008_44.pdf (accessed 12 October 2013).

——'Communication from the Commission on the Treatment of Impaired Assets in the Community Banking Sector', Brussels: European Commission, 2009, ec.europa.eu/competition/state_aid/legislation/impaired_assets.pdf (accessed 4 April 2013).

Fahy, D., O'Brien, M. and Poti, V., 'Combative Critics or Captured Collaborators? Irish Financial Journalism and the End of the Celtic Tiger', *Irish Communications Review*, 2010, vol. 12, pp. 5–20.

Finn, D., 'Ireland on the Turn? Political and Economic Consequences of the Crash', *New Left Review*, 2011, vol. 67, pp. 5–39.

FitzGerald, J. and Kearney, I., 'Irish Government Debt and Implied Debt Dynamics: 2011–15', ESRI research article, Dublin: Economic and Social Research Institute, 2011, www.esri.ie/UserFiles/publications/QEC2011Aut_SA_FitzGerald.pdf (accessed 5 December 2013)

FitzGerald, J., Kearney, I. and Žnuderl, N., 'Irish Government Debt and Implied Debt Dynamics: 2012–15', Dublin: Economic and Social Research Institute, 2012, www. euroframe.org/fileadmin/user_upload/euroframe/docs/2012/EUROF12_FitzGerald_ Kearney_Znurdel.pdf (accessed 13 February 2013).

Flassbeck, H. and Lapavitsas, C. 'The Systemic Crisis of the Euro – True Causes and Effective Therapies', *Studien*, Berlin: Rosa-Luxemburg-Stiftung, 2013, www.rosalux. de/fileadmin/rls_uploads/pdfs/Studien/Studien_The_systemic_crisis_web.pdf (accessed 9 December 2013).

Fraser, A., Murphy, E. and Kelly, S., 'Deepening Neoliberalism via Austerity and "Reform": The Case of Ireland', *Human Geography*, 2013, vol. 6, no. 2, pp. 38–53.

Fraser, M., 'Five Reasons for Crash Blindness', *British Journalism Review*, 2009, vol. 20, pp. 78–83.

Frenkel, R. and Rapetti, M., 'Argentina's Monetary and Exchange Rate Policies after the Convertibility Regime Collapse', CEPR, April 2007, www.cepr.net/documents/ publications/argentina_2007_04.pdf (accessed 9 December 2013).

——'A Concise History of Exchange Rate Regimes in Latin America', CEPR, April 2010, www.cepr.net/documents/publications/exchange-rates-latin-america-2010-04.pdf (accessed 9 December 2013).

Fuentes, M. and Saravia, D., 'Sovereign Defaulters: Do International Capital Markets Punish Them?' *Journal of Development Economics*, 2010, vol. 91, pp. 336–47.

Gelos, R.G., Sahay, R. and Sandleris, G., 'Sovereign Borrowing by Developing Countries: What Determines Market Access?' IMF Working Paper WP/04/221, November, Washington: International Monetary Fund, 2004, www.imf.org/external/ pubs/ft/wp/2004/wp04221.pdf (accessed 5 December 2013).

——'Sovereign Borrowing by Developing Countries: What Determines Market Access?' *Journal of International Economics*, 2011, vol. 83, pp. 243–54.

Government of Ireland, *National Recovery Plan 2011–2014*, Dublin: Stationery Office, 2011, www.budget.gov.ie/The%20National%20Recovery%20Plan%202011-14.pdf (accessed 8 December 2013).

Gramsci, A., *Selections from the Prison Notebooks*, trans. Q. Hoare and G. Nowell Smith, London: Lawrence & Wishart, 1971.

Grimshaw, D. and Rubery, J., 'The End of the UK's Liberal Collectivist Social Model? The Implications of the Coalition Government's Policy During the Austerity Crisis', *Cambridge Journal of Economics*, 2012a, vol. 36, no. 1, pp. 105–26.

——'Reinforcing Neoliberalism: Crisis and Austerity in the UK', in S. Lehndorff (ed.) *A Triumph of Failed Ideas: European Models of Capitalism in the Crisis*, Brussels: European Trade Union Institute, 2012b, pp. 41–58, www.etui.org/Publications2/ Books/A-triumph-of-failed-ideas-European-models-of-capitalism-in-the-crisis (accessed 8 December 2013).

Gros, D. and Maurer, R., 'Can Austerity be Self-defeating?' *Intereconomics*, 2012, vol. 47, no. 3, pp. 176–84.

Grugel, J. and Riggirozzi, M.P., 'The Return of the State in Argentina', *International Affairs*, 2007, vol. 83, no. 1, pp. 87–107.

Guajardo, J., Leigh, D. and Pescatori, A., 'Expansionary Austerity: New International Evidence', IMF Working Paper WP/11/158, July 2011, www.imf.org/external/pubs/ ft/wp/2011/wp11158.pdf (accessed 8 December 2013).

Guinnane, T., 'Financial Vergangenheitsbewaeltigung: The 1953 London Debt Agreement', Discussion Paper No. 880, Economic Growth Center, Yale University, 2004, papers.ssrn. com/sol3/papers.cfm?abstract_id=493802 (accessed 29 June 2013).

Gupta, P., Mishra, D. and Sahay, R., 'Behavior of Output During Currency Crises', *Journal of International Economics*, 2007, vol. 72, pp. 428–50.

Gurdgiev, C., 'Debt Restructuring in Ireland: Orderly, Selective and Unavoidable', in B. Lucey, C. Larkin and C. Gurdgiev (eds) *What if Ireland Default?* Blackrock: Orpen Press, 2012, chapter 3.

Harber, A., 'When a Watchdog Doesn't Bark', *Rhodes Journalism Review*, 2009, September, pp. 20–21.

Hardt, M. and Negri, A., *Empire*, Cambridge, MA: Harvard University Press, 2000.

Harvey, D., *A Brief History of Neoliberalism*, Oxford: Oxford University Press, 2005.

——*The Enigma of Capital and the Crises of Capitalism*, London: Profile Books, 2010.

Hausmann, R., Pritchett, L. and Rodrik, D., 'Growth Accelerations', *Journal of Economic Growth*, 2005, vol. 10, pp. 303–29.

Healy, T., 'Private Bank Debts and Public Finances: Some Options for Ireland', NERI Working Paper 2013/01, February 2013, www.nerinstitute.net/download/pdf/ner i_wp20131_private_bank_debt_public_finances_.pdf (accessed 4 December 2013).

Healy, T. and O'Farrell, R., 'Impact on the Government Deficit of a Reduction in the Public Sector Pay Bill', NERI Research in Brief, May 2013, www.nerinstitute.net/download/pdf/inbrief_public_sector_pay_may_2013.pdf (accessed 8 December 2013).

Helleiner, E., 'The Strange Story of Bush and the Argentine Debt Crisis', *Third World Quarterly*, 2005, vol. 26, no. 6, pp. 951–69.

Herman, E., 'The Propaganda Model: A Retrospective', *Journalism Studies*, 2000, vol. 1, no. 1, pp. 101–12.

Herman, E.S. and Chomsky, N., *Manufacturing Consent: The Political Economy of the Mass Media*, New York: Pantheon, 2002.

Herring, E. and Robinson, P., 'Too Polemical or Too Critical? Chomsky on the Study of the News Media and US Foreign Policy', *Review of International Studies*, 2003, vol. 29, pp. 553–68.

Honohan, P., 'The Irish Banking Crisis: Regulatory and Financial Stability Policy 2003–8. A Report to the Minister for Finance by the Governor of the Central Bank', 2010, www.bankinginquiry.gov.ie/ (accessed 27 December 2012).

Honohan, P. and Walsh, B., 'Catching-up with the Leaders: The Irish Hare', *Brookings Papers on Economic Activity*, 2002, vol. 1, pp. 1–79, researchrepository.ucd.ie/bitstream/handle/10197/1596/walshb_article_pub_012.pdf?sequence=3 (accessed 10 December 2013).

Howden, D., 'The Iceland and Ireland Banking Crises: Lessons for the Future', Working Paper, Mercatus Center, George Mason University, 2012, mercatus.org/publication/iceland-and-ireland-banking-crises-lessons-future (accessed 9 December 2013).

Howse, R. 'The Concept of Odious Debt in Public International Law', UNCTAD Discussion Papers No. 185, Geneva: United Nations Conference on Trade and Development, 2007, unctad.org/en/docs/osgdp20074_en.pdf (accessed 5 December 2013).

ICTU (Irish Congress of Trade Unions), 'Delivering Growth & Jobs: Funding a Major New Investment Programme for Ireland', 2012, www.ictu.ie/download/pdf/delivering_growth_jobs_funding_a_major_new_investment_programme_for_ireland_may_2012.pdf (accessed 22 September 2013).

——'Pre-Budget Submission: A Different Fiscal Adjustment is Possible', Autumn 2013, www.ictu.ie/download/pdf/jit16_prebudget_submission_fiscaladjustment_web.pdf (accessed 10 October 2013).

Internal Auditing Commission for Public Credit of Ecuador, 'Final Report of the Integral Auditing of the Ecuadorian Debt. Executive Summary', Quito: Internal Auditing Commission, 2008, www.jubileeusa.org/fileadmin/user_upload/ Ecuador/Internal_Auditing_Commission_for_Public_Credit_of_Ecuador_Commissi on.pdf (accessed 5 December 2013).

International Monetary Fund, 'Ireland: 2009 Article IV Consultation – Staff Report', IMF Country Report No. 09/195, June 2009, pp. 15–16, www.imf.org/external/pubs/ ft/scr/2009/cr09195.pdf (accessed 20 June 2013).

——'Ireland: 2010 Article IV Consultation – Staff Report', IMF Country Report No. 10/209, July 2010a, pp. 1, 3, www.imf.org/external/pubs/ft/scr/2010/cr10209.pdf (accessed 12 July 2013).

——'Will it Hurt? Macroeconomic Effects of Fiscal Consolidation', *World Economic Outlook*, October 2010b, pp. 93–123, www.imf.org/external/pubs/ft/weo/2010/02/pdf/ c3.pdf (accessed 8 December 2013).

——'Ireland: Request for an Extended Arrangement-staff Report; Staff Supplement; Staff Statement; and Press Release on the Executive Board Discussion', Country Report No. 10/366, December 2010c, www.imf.org/external/pubs/ft/scr/2010/ cr10366.pdf (accessed 8 December 2013).

——'Iceland's Unorthodox Policies Suggest Alternative Way Out of Crisis', 3 November 2011, www.imf.org/external/pubs/ft/survey/so/2011/car110311a.htm (accessed 9 December 2013).

——'Ireland: Selected Issues', IMF Country Report No. 12/265, Washington DC: IMF, 2012, www.imf.org/external/pubs/ft/scr/2012/cr12265.pdf (accessed 8 December 2013).

——'Ireland: Tenth Review Under the Extended Arrangement', Country Report 13/ 163, Washington, DC: IMF, June 2013, p. 11, www.imf.org/external/pubs/ft/scr/ 2013/cr13163.pdf (accessed 5 December 2013).

Jayadev, A. and Konczal, M., 'The Boom Not the Slump: The Right Time for Austerity', Roosevelt Institute, 2010, www.rooseveltinstitute.org/sites/all/files/not_ the_time_for_austerity.pdf (accessed 15 January 2013).

Jonung, L., 'The Swedish Model for Resolving the Banking Crisis of 1991–93. Seven Reasons Why it was Successful', Economic Paper 360, Brussels: European Commission, 2009, ec.europa.eu/economy_finance/publications/publication14098_en.pdf (accessed 13 November 2013).

——'Lessons from the Nordic Financial Crisis', Report for the American Economic Association meeting of January 2011, www.aeaweb.org/aea/2011conference/pro gram/retrieve.php?pdfid=413 (accessed 10 October 2013).

Jorgensen, E. and Sachs, J., 'Default and Renegotiation of Latin American Foreign Bonds in the Interwar Period', in B. Eichengreen and P. Lindert (eds) *The International Debt Crisis in Historical Perspective*, Cambridge, MA: MIT Press, 1989, pp. 48–85.

Kamalodin, S., 'To Default, or Not to Default: What are the Economic and Political Costs of Sovereign Default?' Utrecht: Rabobank Economic Research Department, April 2011, economics.rabobank.com/PageFiles/7288/SP1102ska%20To%20default% 20or%20not%20to%20default_tcm64-138583.pdf (accessed 5 December 2013).

Karanikolos, M., 'Financial Crisis, Austerity, and Health in Europe', *The Lancet*, 13 April 2013, vol. 381, no. 9874, pp. 1323–31, www.thelancet.com/journals/lancet/ article/PIIS0140-6736%2813%2960102-6/abstract (accessed 6 December 2013).

Kellner, D., *Media Culture: Cultural Studies, Identity and Politics between the Modern and the Post-modern*, London: Routledge, 1995.

Kelly, M., 'On the Likely Extent of Falls in Irish House Prices', UCD Centre of Economic Research Working Paper series, WP07/01, February 2007, www.ucd.ie/economics/research/papers/2007/WP07.01.pdf (accessed 9 December 2013).

——'Whatever Happened to Ireland?' Discussion Paper No. 7811, London: Centre for Economic Policy Research, May 2010.

Kerrigan, G., *The Big Lie: Who Profits from Ireland's Austerity?* London: Transworld Ireland, 2012.

Killian, S., Garvey, J. and Shaw, F., 'Au Audit of Irish Debt', University of Limerick, September 2011, www.debtireland.org/download/pdf/audit_of_irish_debt6.pdf (accessed 5 December 2013).

King, L., Kitson, M., Konzelmann, S. and Wilkinson, F., 'Making the Same Mistake Again – Or is this Time Different?' *Cambridge Journal of Economics*, 2012, vol. 36, no. 1, pp. 1–15.

Kinsella, S., 'Is Ireland Really the Role Model for Austerity?' *Cambridge Journal of Economics*, 2012a, vol. 36, no. 1, pp. 223–35.

——'A Very Irish Default, or When a Default is Not a Default?' in B. Lucey, C. Larkin and C. Gurdgiev (eds) *What if Ireland Default?* Blackrock: Orpen Press, 2012b, chapter 5.

Kirby, P., *The Celtic Tiger in Distress: Growth with Inequality in Ireland*, Basingstoke: Palgrave, 2002a.

——'Contested Pedigrees of the Celtic Tiger', in P. Kirby, L. Gibbons and M. Cronin (eds) *Reinventing Ireland: Culture, Society and the Global Economy*, London: Pluto, 2002b, pp. 21–37.

——*Celtic Tiger in Collapse: Explaining the Weaknesses of the Irish Model*, Basingstoke: Palgrave Macmillan, 2010.

Kirby, P., Gibbons, L. and Cronin, M., 'Introduction: The Reinvention of Ireland: A Critical Perspective', in P. Kirby, L. Gibbons and M. Cronin (eds) *Reinventing Ireland: Culture, Society and the Global Economy*, London: Pluto, 2002, pp. 1–20.

Kirby, P. and Murphy, M. 'Ireland as a "Competition State"', in M. Adshead, P. Kirby and M. Millar (eds) *Contesting the State: Lessons from the Irish Case*, Manchester: Manchester University Press, 2008, pp. 120–42.

——'Globalisation and Models of State: Debates and Evidence from Ireland', *New Political Economy*, 2011, vol. 16, no. 1, pp. 19–39.

Kitchin, R. and Bartley, B., 'Ireland in the Twenty First Century', in B. Bartley and R. Kitchin (eds) *Understanding Contemporary Ireland*, London: Pluto Press, 2007, pp. 1–26.

Kitchin, R., O'Callaghan, C., Boyle, M., Gleeson, J. and Keaveney, K., 'Placing Neoliberalism: The Rise and Fall of Ireland's Celtic Tiger', *Environment and Planning A*, 2012, vol. 44, pp. 1302–26.

Klaehn, J., 'A Critical Review and Assessment of Herman and Chomsky's "Propaganda Model"', *European Journal of Communication*, 2002, vol. 17, no. 2, pp. 147–82.

——'Behind the Invisible Curtain of Scholarly Criticism: Revisiting the Propaganda Model', *Journalism Studies*, 2003, vol. 4, no. 3, pp. 359–69.

Krugman, P., *End this Depression Now!* New York: W.W. Norton, 2012.

Kuhling, C. and Keohane, K., *Cosmopolitan Ireland: Globalisation and Quality of Life*, London: Pluto, 2007.

Kuttner, R., *Debtors' Prison: The Politics of Austerity versus Possibility*, New York: Alfred Knopf, 2013.

Labour Party, 'Strategic Investment Bank: Financing Ireland's Investment Economy', 2010, www.labour.ie/download/pdf/investinginfuture.pdf (accessed 12 September 2013).

Labour Relations Commission, 'Draft Public Service Agreement 2013–16', 2013, per. gov.ie/wp-content/uploads/LRC-Proposals-printed.pdf (accessed 3 July 2013).

Laeven, L. and Valencia, F., 'The Use of Blanket Guarantees in Banking Crises', IMF Working Paper WP 08/250, 2008, www.imf.org/external/pubs/ft/wp/2008/wp08250. pdf (accessed 20 February 2013).

——'Systemic Banking Crises Database: An Update', International Monetary Fund Working Paper, WP/12/163, 2012, www.imf.org/external/pubs/ft/wp/2012/wp12163. pdf (accessed 4 December 2013).

Lapavitsas, C., 'Default and Exit from the Eurozone: A Radical Left Strategy', *Socialist Register*, 2012, vol. 48, pp. 288–97.

——'The Eurozone Crisis through the Prism of World Money', in Martin H. Wolfson and Gerald A. Epstein (eds) *The Handbook of the Political Economy of Financial Crises*, Oxford: Oxford University Press, 2013, pp. 378–94.

Lapavitsas, C. *et al. Crisis in the Eurozone*, London: Verso, 2012.

Laski, K. and Podkaminer, L., 'The Basic Paradigms of EU Economic Policy-making Need to be Changed', *Cambridge Journal of Economics*, 2012, vol. 36, no. 1, pp. 253–70.

Lehndorff, S. (ed.), *A Triumph of Failed Ideas: European Models of Capitalism in the Crisis*, Brussels: European Trade Union Institute, 2012a, www.etui.org/Publica tions2/Books/A-triumph-of-failed-ideas-European-models-of-capitalism-in-the-crisis (accessed 8 December 2013).

——'German Capitalism and the European Crisis: Part of the Solution or Part of the Problem?', in S. Lehndorff (ed.) *A Triumph of Failed Ideas: European Models of Capitalism in the Crisis*, Brussels: European Trade Union Institute, 2012b, pp. 79– 102, www.etui.org/Publications2/Books/A-triumph-of-failed-ideas-European-models-of-capitalism-in-the-crisis (accessed 8 December 2013).

Levitsky, S. and Murillo, M.V., 'Argentina: From Kirchner to Kirchner', *Journal of Democracy*, 2008, vol. 19, no. 2, pp. 16–30.

Levy Yeyati, E. and Panizza, U., 'The Elusive Costs of Sovereign Defaults', Working Paper #581, Washington, DC: Inter-American Development Bank, 2011, www.iadb. org/res/publications/pubfiles/pubWP-581.pdf (accessed 5 December 2013).

——'The Elusive Costs of Sovereign Defaults', *Journal of Development Economics*, 2011, vol. 94, pp. 95–105.

López, A.M.R. and Llopis, M.A.O., 'Metaphorical Pattern Analysis in Financial Texts: Framing the Crisis in Positive or Negative Metaphorical Terms', *Journal of Pragmatics*, 2010, vol. 42, pp. 3300–13.

López, I. and Rodríguez, E., 'The Spanish Model', *New Left Review*, 2011, vol. 69, May/June, pp. 5–29.

Lyons, T. and Carey, B., *The FitzPatrick Tapes: The Rise and Fall of One Man, One Bank, and One Country*, London: Penguin, 2011.

Macartney, H., 'Variegated Neo-liberalism: Transnationally Oriented Fractions of Capital in EU Financial Market Integration', *Review of International Studies*, 2009, vol. 35, no. 2, pp. 451–80.

McCabe, C., *Sins of the Father: Tracing the Decisions that Shaped the Irish Economy*, Dublin: The History Press, 2011.

McCarthy, C., 'Fiscal Consolidation in Ireland: Lessons from the First Time', in S. Kinsella and A. Leddin (eds) *Understanding Ireland's Economic Crisis: Prospects for Recovery*, Blackrock: Blackhall Publishing, 2010, chapter 5.

McCarthy, K.J. and Dolfsma, W., 'What's in a Name? Understanding the Language of the Credit Crunch', *Journal of Economic Issues*, 2009, vol. XLIII, no. 2, pp. 531–48.

McChesney, R., *Rich Media, Poor Democracy: Communication Politics in Dubious Times*, New York: New Press, 2000.

——*The Problem of the Media: U.S. Communication Politics in the 21st Century*, New York: Monthly Review, 2004.

——*The Political Economy of Media: Enduring Issues, Emerging Dilemmas*, New York: Monthly Review, 2008.

McDonald, F. and Sheridan, K., *The Builders: How a Small Group of Property Developers Fuelled the Building Boom and Transformed Ireland*, London: Penguin, 2008.

McDonnell, T., 'The Debt and Banking Crisis: Progressive Approaches for Europe and Ireland', TASC Discussion Paper, May 2011, pp. 2, 6–8, www.tascnet.ie/upload/file/DebtBanking190511.pdf (accessed 25 February 2013).

——'Wealth Tax: Options for its Implementation in the Republic of Ireland', NERI Working Paper 2013/No. 6, September 2013, www.nerinstitute.net/download/pdf/neri_wp_no_6_2013_mcdonnell_wealth_tax.pdf (accessed 20 October 2013).

McWilliams, D., *Follow the Money: The Tale of the Merchant of Ennis*, Dublin: Gill and Macmillan, 2009.

——*The Good Room: Why We Ended Up in a Debtors' Prison – and How We Can Break Free*, Dublin: Penguin, 2012.

Mansell, W. and Openshaw, K., 'Suturing the Open Veins of Ecuador: Debt, Default and Democracy', *The Law and Development Review*, 2009, vol. 2, no. 1, pp. 151–91.

Marron, M.B., 'British/Irish Media Excel in Episodic Coverage, Fail in Probing', *Journalism Studies*, 2010, vol. 11, no. 2, pp. 270–74.

MediaBite, 'The Media and the Banking Bailout', MediaBite, 2009, www.mediabite.org/article_The-Media-and-the-Banking-Bailout_679566551.html (accessed 10 July 2013).

Mercille, J., 'European Media Coverage of Argentina's Debt Default and Recovery: Distorting the Lessons for Europe', *Third World Quarterly*, 2013, vol. 34, no. 8, pp. 1377–91.

——'The Role of the Media in Sustaining Ireland's Housing Bubble', *New Political Economy*, 2014a, vol. 19, no. 2, pp. 282–301.

——'The Role of the Media in Fiscal Consolidation Programmes: The Case of Ireland', *Cambridge Journal of Economics*, 2014b, vol. 38, no. 2, pp. 281–300.

Morley, S., 'On the Effect of Devaluation During Stabilization Programs in LDC's', *The Review of Economics and Statistics*, 1992, vol. 74, no. 1, pp. 21–27.

Mullen, A., 'The Propaganda Model after 20 Years: Interview with Edward S. Herman and Noam Chomsky', *Westminster Papers in Communication and Culture*, 2009, vol. 6, no. 2, pp. 12–22.

Mullen, A. and Klaehn, J., 'The Herman-Chomsky Propaganda Model: A Critical Approach to Analysing Mass Media Behaviour', *Sociology Compass*, 2010, vol. 4, no. 4, pp. 215–29.

NERI (Nevin Economic Research Institute), *Quarterly Economic Observer*, Dublin: Nevin Economic Research Institute, Spring 2012, www.nerinstitute.net/download/pdf/qeo_spring_2012.pdf (accessed 8 December 2013).

Nolan, B., Maître, B., Voitchovsky, S. and Whelan, C.T., 'Inequality and Poverty in Boom and Bust: Ireland as a Case Study', Gini discussion paper 70, Amsterdam Institute for Advanced labour Studies, 2012, www.uva-aias.net/uploaded_files/publications/DP70-Nolan_Maitre_Voitchovsky_Whelan.pdf (accessed 8 December 2013).

Nyberg, P., 'Misjudging Risk: Causes of the Systemic Banking Crisis in Ireland: Report of the Commission of Investigation into the Banking Sector in Ireland', 2011, www.bankinginquiry.gov.ie (accessed 22 February 2013).

OECD (Organisation for Economic Co-operation and Development) *Growing Unequal? Income Distribution and Poverty in OECD Countries*, OECD Publishing, 2008, www.keepeek.com/Digital-Asset-Management/oecd/social-issues-migration-health/growing-unequal_9789264044197-en#page1 (accessed 11 December 2013).

——'Economic Surveys: Ireland 2009', November 2009, Paris: OECD Publishing.

——*Divided We Stand: Why Inequality Keeps Rising*, OECD Publishing, 2011, dx.doi.org/10.1787/9789264119536-en (accessed 12 November 2013).

Ó Gráda, C. and O'Rourke, K.H., 'Irish Economic Growth Since 1945', in N.F.R. Crafts and G. Toniolo (eds) *European Economic Growth*, Cambridge: Cambridge University Press, 1996, pp. 388–426.

O'Hearn, D., *Inside the Celtic Tiger: The Irish Economy and the Asian Model*, London: Pluto, 1998.

——'Macroeconomic Policy in the Celtic Tiger: A Critical Assessment', in C. Coulter and S. Coleman (eds) *The End of Irish History? Critical Reflections on the Celtic Tiger*, Manchester: Manchester University Press, 2003, pp. 34–55.

Ó Riain, S., *The Politics of High Tech Growth: Developmental Network States in the Global Economy*, Cambridge: Cambridge University Press, 2004.

——'Competing State Projects in the Contemporary Irish Political Economy', in M. Adshead, P. Kirby and M. Millar (eds) *Contesting the State: Lessons from the Irish Case*, Manchester: Manchester University Press, 2008, pp. 165–85.

——*The Rise and Fall of Ireland's Celtic Tiger: Liberalism, Boom and Bust*, Cambridge: Cambridge University Press, 2013.

O'Toole, F., *Ship of Fools: How Stupidity and Corruption Sank the Celtic Tiger*, London: Faber and Faber, 2009.

Palat, R.A., '"Eyes Wide Shut": Reconceptualizing the Asian Crisis', *Review of International Political Economy*, 2003, vol. 10, no. 2, pp. 169–95.

Palley, T., 'The European Monetary Union Needs a Government Banker', *Challenge*, 2011, vol. 54, no. 4, pp. 5–21.

Pedro, J., 'The Propaganda Model in the Early 21st Century, Part I and Part II', *International Journal of Communication*, 2011, vol. 5, pp. 1865–905, 1906–26.

Peet, R., 'Inequality, Crisis and Austerity in Finance Capitalism', *Cambridge Journal of Regions, Economy and Society*, 2011, vol. 4, 383–99.

Perotti, R., 'The "Austerity Myth": Gain without Pain?' BIS Working Papers No. 362, 2011, pp. 1–57, www.bis.org/publ/work362.pdf (accessed 8 December 2013).

Pettis, M., *The Great Rebalancing: Trade, Conflict, and the Perilous Road Ahead for the World Economy*, Princeton and Oxford: Princeton University Press, 2013.

Pollin, R., 'US Government Deficits and Debt Amid the Great Recession: What the Evidence Shows', *Cambridge Journal of Economics*, 2012, vol. 36, no. 1, pp. 161–87.

Posch, M., Schmitz, S.W. and Weber, B., 'EU Bank Packages: Objectives and Potential Conflicts of Objectives', Financial Stability Report 17, June 2009, 63–84, oenb.at/en/img/fsr_17_special_topics02_tcm16-140532.pdf (accessed 2 January 2013).

PwC, 'Media Research Required by the Advisory Group on Media Mergers', in Advisory Group on Media Mergers, *Report to the Tánaiste and Minister for Enterprise, Trade and Employment, Mary Coughlan TD*, June 2008, pp. 146–215, www.djei.ie/publications/commerce/2008/advisorygrouponmediamergersreport2008.pdf (accessed 10 September 2013).

Quiring, O. and Weber, M., 'Between Usefulness and Legitimacy: Media Coverage of Governmental Intervention during the Financial Crisis and Selected Effects', *The International Journal of Press/Politics*, 2012, vol. 17, pp. 294–315.

Rapetti, M., Skott, P. and Razmi, A., 'The Real Exchange Rate and Economic Growth: Are Developing Countries Different?' Working Paper 2011-07, Department of Economics, University of Massachusetts-Amherst, 2011, www.umass.edu/eco nomics/publications/2011-07.pdf (accessed 9 December 2013).

Ray, R. and Kozameh, S., 'Ecuador's Economy since 2007', Washington, DC: Centre for Economic and Policy Research, May 2012, www.cepr.net/documents/publica tions/ecuador-2012-05.pdf (accessed 31 December 2013).

Razmi, A., Rapetti, M. and Skott, P., 'The Real Exchange Rate and Economic Development', Working Paper 2011-08, Department of Economics, University of Massachusetts-Amherst, 2011, scholarworks.umass.edu/econ_workingpaper/116/ (accessed 9 December 2013).

Reinhart, C. and Rogoff, K., *This Time is Different: Eight Centuries of Financial Folly*, Princeton: Princeton University Press, 2009.

——'Growth in a Time of Debt', *American Economic Review*, 2010, vol. 100, no. 2, pp. 573–78.

——'The Forgotten History of Domestic Debt', *The Economic Journal*, 2011, vol. 121, no. 552, pp. 319–50.

Robinson, W.I., *A Theory of Global Capitalism: Production, Class, and State in a Transnational World*, Baltimore, MD: Johns Hopkins University Press, 2004.

Rodrik, D., 'The Real Exchange Rate and Economic Growth', *Brookings Papers on Economic Activity*, 2008, pp. 365–412, www.brookings.edu/~/media/projects/bpea/ fall%202008/2008b_bpea_rodrik.pdf (accessed 9 December 2013).

Rose, A.K., 'One Reason Countries Pay their Debts: Renegotiation and International Trade', *Journal of Development Economics*, 2005, vol. 77, pp. 189–206.

Ross, S., *The Bankers: How the Banks Brought Ireland to its Knees*, London: Penguin, 2009.

Ross, S. and Webb, N., *The Untouchables: The People Who Helped Wreck Ireland – and are Still Running the Show*, Dublin: Penguin Ireland, 2012.

Roubini, N. and Mihm, S., *Crisis Economics: A Crash Course in the Future of Finance*, London: Penguin, 2011.

Sandal, K., 'The Nordic Banking Crises in the Early 1990s – Resolution Methods and Fiscal Costs', in T. Moe, J.A. Solheim and B. Vale (eds) *The Norwegian Banking Crisis*, Norges Bank's Occasional Papers no. 33: Oslo, 2004, pp. 77–115.

Sawyer, M., 'The Tragedy of UK Fiscal Policy in the Aftermath of the Financial Crisis', *Cambridge Journal of Economics*, 2012, vol. 36, no. 1, pp. 205–21.

Schechter, D., 'Credit Crisis. How Did we Miss it?' *British Journalism Review*, 2009, vol. 20, pp. 19–26.

Schranz, M. and Eisenegger, M., 'The Media Construction of the Financial Crisis in a Comparative Perspective – an Analysis of Newspapers in the UK, USA and Switzerland between 2007 and 2009', *Swiss Journal of Sociology*, 2011, vol. 37, no. 2, pp. 241–58.

Sighvatsson, A. and Gunnarsson, G., 'Iceland's Financial Disaster and its Fiscal Impact', in J.R. LaBrosse, R. Olivares-Caminal and D. Singh (eds) *Managing Risk in the Financial System*, Aldershot: Edward Elgar Publishing, 2011, pp. 133–54.

Sklair, L., 'Social Movements for Global Capitalism: The Transnational Capitalist Class in Action', *Review of International Political Economy*, 1997, vol. 4, no. 3, pp. 514–38.

——*The Transnational Capitalist Class*, Malden: Blackwell, 2001.

——'The Transnational Capitalist Class and Global Politics: Deconstructing the Corporate-State Connection', *International Political Science Review*, 2002, vol. 23, no. 2, pp. 159–74.

Smith, N.J., *Showcasing Globalisation: The Political Economy of the Irish Republic*, Manchester: Manchester University Press, 2005.

Social Justice Ireland, 'Investing for Growth, Jobs & Recovery', Policy Briefing, September 2013, www.socialjustice.ie/sites/default/files/file/SJI%20Briefing%20 Docs/2013-09-02%20-%20Policy%20Briefing%20-%20Investment%20-%20jobs%20- 20growth.pdf (accessed 13 July 2013).

Sparks, C., 'Extending and Refining the Propaganda Model', *Westminster Papers in Communication and Culture*, 2007, vol. 4, no. 2, pp. 68–84.

Special Group on Public Service Numbers and Expenditure Programmes, 'Report', July 2009, www.finance.gov.ie/viewdoc.asp?DocID=5861 (accessed 31 October 2013).

Starkman, D., 'Power Problem', *Columbia Journalism Review*, 2009, May/June, pp. 24–30.

Stiglitz, J., *Globalization and its Discontents*, London: Penguin, 2002.

Sturzenegger, F., 'Toolkit for the Analysis of Debt Problems', *Journal of Restructuring Finance*, 2004, vol. 1, no. 1, pp. 201–23.

Sturzenegger, F. and Zettelmeyer, J., *Debt Defaults and Lessons from a Decade of Crises*, Cambridge, MA: MIT Press, 2006.

Taft, M., 'Fiscal Reductionism and the Disconnected Debate: Developing a New Fiscal Platform', in S. Kinsella and A. Leddin (eds) *Understanding Ireland's Economic Crisis: Prospects for Recovery*, Blackrock: Blackhall Publishing, 2010, chapter 6.

TASC (Think Tank for Action on Social Change), 'Roadmap to Greater Inequality: TASC's Response to Budget 2012', December 2011, www.tascnet.ie/upload/file/ Roadmap%20to%20Greater%20Inequality_final.pdf (accessed 23 January 2013).

——'Tax Injustice: Following the Tax Trail', September 2012a, www.tascnet.ie/upload/ file/TASC%20Tax%20Injustice.pdf (accessed 23 January 2013).

——'Lost Opportunities: TASC's Independent Equality and Economic Analysis of Budget 2013', December 2012b, www.tascnet.ie/upload/file/TASC%20Response% 20to%20Budget%202013.pdf (accessed 23 January 2013).

——'Budget 2014: Choosing and Equitable Route to Recovery', September 2013, www. tascnet.ie/upload/file/TASC_Budget2014%281%29.pdf (accessed 8 December 2013).

Taylor, L., Proaño, C.R., de Carvalho, L. and Barbosa, N., 'Fiscal Deficits, Economic Growth and Government Debt in the USA', *Cambridge Journal of Economics*, 2012, vol. 36, no. 1, pp. 189–204.

Theodoropoulou, S. and Watt, A., 'Withdrawal Symptoms: An Assessment of the Austerity Packages in Europe', working paper 2011.02, Brussels: European Trade Union Institute, 2011, www.etui.org/Publications2/Working-Papers/Withdrawal- symptoms-an-assessment-of-the-austerity-packages-in-Europe (accessed 8 December 2013).

Thorgeirsson, T. and van den Noord, P., 'The Icelandic Banking Collapse: Was the Optimal Policy Path Chosen?' Working Paper no. 62, Central Bank of Iceland, March 2013, www.sedlabanki.is/library/Skr%C3%A1arsafn-EN/Working-Papers/ WP%2062.pdf (accessed 9 December 2013).

Toussaint, E., 'Greece-Germany: Who Owes Who?' Committee for the Abolition of Third World Debt, 2012, cadtm.org/Greece-Germany-who-owes-who-1 (accessed 14 January 2013).

Tzogopoulos, G., *The Greek Crisis in the Media: Stereotyping in the International Press*, Farnham: Ashgate, 2013.

Unite, 'Beyond Austerity: Proposals for a Thriving Economy, Pre-Budget Submission 2014', September 2013, unitetheunionireland.files.wordpress.com/2013/09/beyond- austerity-final-upload2.pdf (accessed 13 October 2013).

Vale, B., 'The Norwegian Banking Crisis', in T. Moe, J.A. Solheim and B. Vale (eds) *The Norwegian Banking Crisis*, Norges Bank's Occasional Papers, 2004, no. 33, Oslo, chapter 1, pp. 1–21.

Vanags, A., 'Latvia's Exports: The Real "Success Story"', BICEPS research report, 2013, biceps.org/assets/docs/izpetes-zinojumi/Latvias_exports (accessed 13 October 2013).

van Appeldoorn, B., *Transnational Capitalism and the Struggle Over European Integration*, London: Routledge, 2002.

van der Pijl, K., 'A Theory of Global Capitalism, Feature Review', *New Political Economy*, 2005, vol. 10, no. 2, pp. 273–77.

Wade, R. and Sigurgeirsdottir, S., 'Iceland's Meltdown: The Rise and Fall of International Banking in the North Atlantic', *Brazilian Journal of Political Economy*, 2011, vol. 31, no. 5 (125), pp. 684–97.

——'Iceland's Rise, Fall, Stabilisation and Beyond', *Cambridge Journal of Economics*, 2012, vol. 36, no. 1, pp. 127–44.

Weisbrot, M., Johnston, J. and Lefebvre, S., 'Ecuador's New Deal: Reforming and Regulating the Financial Sector', Washington, DC: Centre for Economic and Policy Research, February 2013, www.cepr.net/documents/publications/ecuador-2013-02.pdf (accessed 5 December 2013).

Weisbrot, M. and Ray, R., 'Latvia's Internal Devaluation: A Success Story?' (revised and updated), Washington, DC: Centre for Economic and Policy Research, December 2011, www.cepr.net/documents/publications/latvia-2011-12.pdf (accessed 8 December 2013).

Weisbrot, M., Ray, R., Montecino, J.A. and Kozameh, S., 'The Argentine Success Story and its Implications', Washington, DC: Centre for Economic and Policy Research, October 2011, www.cepr.net/documents/publications/argentina-success-2011-10.pdf (accessed 9 December 2013).

Weisbrot, M. and Sandoval, L. 'Argentina's Economic Recovery: Policy Choices and Implications', Washington, DC: Centre for Economic and Policy Research, October 2007, www.cepr.net/documents/publications/argentina_recovery_2007_10.pdf (accessed 9 December 2013).

Whelan, K. 'ELA, Promissory Notes and All That: The Fiscal Costs of Anglo Irish Bank', September 2012, www.karlwhelan.com/IrishEconomy/Whelan-PNotes-September2012.pdf (accessed 16 February 2013).

——'Ireland's Promissory Notes Deal', *Forbes*, 11 February 2013, www.forbes.com/sites/karlwhelan/2013/02/11/irelands-promissory-note-deal/ (accessed 16 February 2013).

World Bank, 'Country Assistance Strategy for the Argentine Republic 2006–8', Report No. 34015-AR, May 2006, siteresources.worldbank.org/INTARGENTINA/Resources/1CASAr.pdf (accessed 9 December 2013).

Wylde, C., 'State, Society and Markets in Argentina: The Political Economy of *Neo-desarrollismo* under Néstor Kirchner, 2003–7', *Bulletin of Latin American Research*, 2011, vol. 30, no. 4, pp. 436–52.

Zettelmeyer, J., Trebesch, C. and Gulati, M., 'The Greek Debt Exchange: An Autopsy', 11 September 2012, draft, p. 3, av.r.ftdata.co.uk/files/2012/09/The-Greek-Debt-Exchange-An-Autopsy.pdf (accessed 1 December 2013).

——'The Greek Debt Exchange: An Autopsy', July 2013, draft, p. 2, scholarship.law.duke.edu/cgi/viewcontent.cgi?article=5343&context=faculty_scholarship (accessed 1 December 2013).

Index